MUSEUM BUILDERS

MUSEUM BUILDERS

EDITED BY JAMES STEELE

A.D. ACADEMY EDITIONS • Ernst & Sohn

ACKNOWLEDGMENTS

The idea for this book was first suggested to me by Andreas Papadakis, who also contributed several thoughts on its content. I am indebted to Academy Group Ltd, particularly John Stoddart, Maggie Toy, Andrea Bettella, Jan Richter and Rachel Bean for their continual support, diligence and patience in finally bringing the project about. I would like to recognise the assistance of all of the architects represented here, but most especially the following: Richard Meier and Lisa Green of his staff; Moore, Ruble, Yudell and James O'Connor; Robert Venturi and Denise Scott Brown; Frank Gehry and Josh White; Thom Mayne; Gae Aulenti and Milena Archetti; Rafael Moneo; Renzo Piano; Kisho Kurokawa and Yoshiko Takanawa; Fumihiko Maki; Sir Norman Foster and Sarah Conrado; Ian Ritchie; Aldo Rossi and Jan Greben of his New York Studio; Antoine Predock and Lisa Sharp; Eldred Evans and David Shalev; Rasem Badran and Abdul-Halim Ibrahim; Ricardo Legorreta; Janet Adams Strong at Pei, Cobb, Freed & Partners; Hans Ibelings at the Netherlands Architecture Institute; Thomas Muirhead at Stirling Wilford; Erica Stoller; David Jenkins; Penny Padovani and Janet Glasgow.

Editorial Offices
42 Leinster Gardens London W2 3AN

Art Editor: Andrea Bettella
Chief Designer: Mario Bettella
Designers: Jan Richter, Meret Gabra
House Editor: Maggie Toy
Editors: Rachel Bean, Lucy Coventry

COVER: The Tate Gallery at St Ives, Evans and Shalev
(John Edward Linden Photography)
PAGE 2: Museum for the Decorative Arts, Richard Meier
(Scott Frances, Esto Photographics)

Photographic Credits
All photographs courtesy of the architects except the following: Tom Bonner pp158, 160, 161, 162, 164 (ABOVE), 165 (ABOVE), 166 (ABOVE), 167; Richard Bryant, Arcaid pp216, 218, 220, 222, 226 (ABOVE), 227 (ABOVE), 234, 238, 239; S Couturier p180; Scott Frances p142 (BELOW); Jeff Goldberg, Esto Photographics pp48, 52-53, 90, 92-93; Peter Mauss, Esto Photographics pp78, 80-81; Jock Pottle, Esto Photographics pp134, 135, 144 (ABOVE and BELOW); Ezra Stoller, Esto Photographics pp136, 138 (ABOVE), 139 (ABOVE), 140 (ABOVE and BELOW), 149 (ABOVE and BELOW); Esto Photographics p142 (ABOVE); Alastair Hunter pp188, 190; Timothy Hursley pp156, 158, 160 (ABOVE and BELOW), 176, 194, 196; John Edward Linden Photography pp54, 56; Pascal Maréchaux/The Aga Khan Award for Architecture pp168, 169, 170, 171; Ned Matura p215; Tomio Ohashi pp110, 116, 118, 119, 120; Paul Peck 129 (CENTRE and BELOW), 128 (BELOW); Tim Street-Porter pp98-103; Paschall/Taylor pp84, 85; William Taylor p82; Joshua White pp74, 76

First published in Great Britain in 1994 by
ACADEMY EDITIONS
An imprint of the Academy Group Ltd

ACADEMY GROUP LTD
42 Leinster Gardens London W2 3AN

ERNST & SOHN
Hohenzollerndamm 170, 1000 Berlin 31
Members of the VCH Publishing Group

ISBN 1 85490 191 5

Distributed to the trade in the United States of America by
ST MARTIN'S PRESS
175 Fifth Avenue, New York, NY 10010

Printed and bound in Singapore

Contents

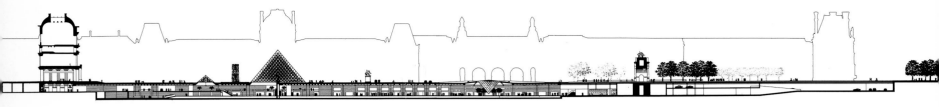

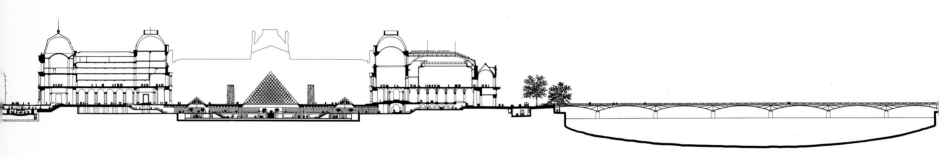

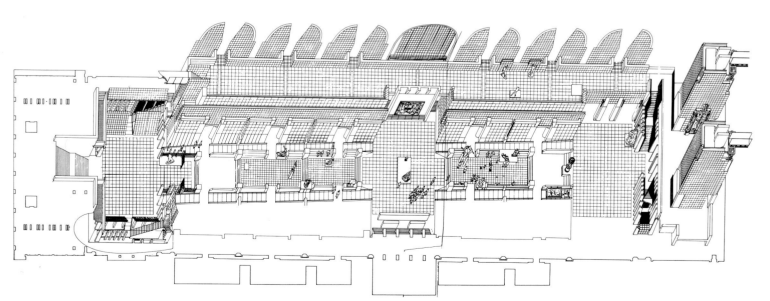

ABOVE AND CENTRE: Pei, Cobb, Freed and Partners, extension of the Louvre, sections; BELOW: Gae Aulenti, Gare d' Orsay, down-view cutaway axonometric

James Steele

A New Inclusive Architecture

The advent of the museum as a recognisable public institution is usually associated with the French theorist JNL Durand who published his concept of an ideal museum in 1805. The plan was based on long galleries surrounding four courtyards and a central rotunda. This image of the ideal museum was to have enormous influence in the following century, and was the culmination – or standardisation – of a typology, rather than the beginning of a search to find one.

The bison drawings in the Lascaux caves and the vulture paintings in the Neolithic dwellings of Catal Huyuk are two of the most spectacular examples of the basic human need to collect and present images and objects, and to protect them inside a pre-existing or constructed precinct. One of the most sophisticated repositories in the ancient world was the open air pantheon of Hittite deities carved into the rock walls of a crevasse at Yazilikaya, the mouth of which was blocked by a compartmentalised temple structure, intended for the purification of the select few who were privileged enough to pass through it to the canyon beyond. In the same way, Egyptian and Greek temples held votive statues of the deity they were dedicated to, restricted to the view of priests and social personages. Eventually small buildings called *pinakotheke*, after the paintings on planks placed inside them, were made accessible to the citizens of the Greek polis, as the small room adjoining the propylaeum of the acropolis was to those who joined in the Panathenaea procession. It is significant that in the Hellenistic age the motive behind such structures changed, due to the eclipse of the polis as a social construct and the expanding horizons that characterised the time. The Attalid dynasty of Pergamum were, along with Alexander the Great, among the first rulers to understand the value of public relations, as evidenced by the statuary around the base of the altar of Zeus which is a thinly veiled metaphor of their own struggles with the Gallic tribes that surrounded them, representing their attempt to placate them. Such attempts continued in the open space adjacent to the library of Pergamum, where the statues of duelling Gauls, immortalised in Roman copies, also reminded the citizens of the city that they had to remain unified in the midst of a common enemy. The subtle shift from a sacred to a political purpose is an important one, reinforced thereafter by many similar examples. Alexandria, which was the rival of Pergamum in its collection of books – to such an extent that Ptolemy boycotted shipments of Egyptian papyrus to Asia Minor, forcing the invention of parchment by the Pergamenes – also had a famous museum, founded in the third century BC. This well known building, called the Mouseion, included statues of philosophers along with a botanical and zoological park, and was associated with an academy where Euclid, Archimedes, Erastothenes and other scholars taught. Consistent with Alexander's promotion of Greek culture, the rulers who divided the empire he left behind also used similar means to establish their own legitimacy. The Roman library of Celsus, in Ephesus, which is directly influenced by Hellenistic values, shows the degree to which they carried over into the following era, during which the collection and display of artefacts from throughout the empire was used to consolidate and perpetuate power.

Some historians, such as Göran Schildt, are extremely careful to distinguish between this shift from the sacred to the secular (claiming that Yazilikaya, or the *pinakotheke* on the Acropolis are not museums as such) and other historical examples such as Hadrian's Villa, where the emperor, who was an avid traveller, recreated his favourite places including the Vale of Tempe, the Academy of Athens and the Egyptian Temple of Serapis at Canopus, which begins to enter the realm occupied by the institution as we know it today. In Schildt's view, the idea of the museum arose when the connection with sympathetic magic and religion was broken, and an artificial premise was substituted for a material one. What Attalid Pergamum, Alexandria and Tivoli have in common is substitution, isolation and detachment and 'the crystallisation of a humanistic cultural programme'.

Following the religiosity of the Middle Ages this motive was rekindled, surfacing again during the Renaissance to assert cultural legitimacy and nascent nationalism, as well as proscriptive humanism cloaked in a Classical model, with wealthy collectors, led by the Medici, taking the initiative in providing galleries, such as the Uffizi, for public use. However, Schildt stresses that this fell into the realm of revival, rather than real aesthetic appreciation. He believes that during this time the purpose of collecting and exhibition was not to express 'the timelessness of art, but the fascination with classical culture and the desire to illustrate a humanistic conception of the world'.

While Renaissance artists such as Leonardo, Michelangelo and Raphael dealt primarily with religious themes and sought to glorify the Church, the work exhibited at the Uffizi and the Capitoline Museum in Rome dealt primarily with a resurrection of an entirely different sort, putting forward vestiges of a dimly remembered cultural heritage.

The third critical stage in the presentation of art – taking the sacred precinct as the first, and its use as a means of establishing cultural legitimacy as the second – was to heighten the sense of aesthetic pleasure in a way that has been thoroughly analysed by Kant and Hegel. Such pleasure, which was treated with distrust by the ancient Greeks who felt that the purpose of its source must be related to utility, became an autonomous subject of desire by the beginning of the seventeenth century when Charles I commissioned a portrait of himself by Velasquez and purchased the entire Gonzaga collection as well as works by Leonardo, Raphael, Tintoretto, Titian, Rubens and Van Dyke. His collection of more than 1,387 and drawings and 399 sculptures, put together with the help of his friends Thomas Howard the Earl of Arundel and George Francis Villas the Duke of Buckingham, was dispensed with after his execution, but served as the impetus for royal collections to follow, establishing a tradition that had also been given a firm grounding by Marie de Medici in Paris. By the eighteenth century, London and Paris were the most lucrative art markets in the world, with the majority of the pieces sold going into private collections in great homes and large estates.

The evolution of such private collections into public museums of the kind first seen at the Uffizi and the Capitoline Museum continued in the Hermitage in St Petersburg, expanded by the acquisitions of Catherine the Great in 1767; in the Pio-Clementine Museum, established to house the Vatican collection in 1773; in the National Museum in Naples in 1735; and in the eventful decision by Louis XV to allow the public to view his private collection in the Luxembourg Palace twice a week, announced in 1750. During the Enlightenment, with its emphasis on scientific enquiry and the importance of categorisation – which led to the biological studies of Limné, the *Essai sur l'Architecture* by Abbé Laugier and the *Encyclopédie* of Diderot – it is understandable that there was also an equal amount of interest in the classification and exhibition of art, and, as has been noted, the palace of the Louvre in Paris, opened to the public during the French Revolution, may be regarded as the first great national art museum organised along this premise. Under Napoleon and his hand-picked director Baron Dominique Vivant-Denon, who had direct experience of contemporary activities at the Hermitage and the National Museum of Naples through the diplomatic posts he held in each city, the Louvre burgeoned, due mainly to military requisitions, and formed the centre of a network of museums that penetrated into the furthest reaches of French influence at that time.

Thus the significant shift from art appreciated privately in palaces to exhibitions in public museums as 'palaces of art', took place in a relatively short time, greatly assisted by democratic initiatives that took place on both sides of the Atlantic, and the somewhat spurious techniques of collection that took place as a result, instigated by the intellectual liberation that was characteristic of the Enlightenment. This new concept of the museum as a repository of aesthetic experience, in the same way that a concert hall is intended for the appreciation of music, or the theatre for performance and dance is still with us. In its initial two hundred years of existence, the museum began to fulfil its nominal etymological function as a secular 'temple of the Muses', those deities associated in the Classical world with music, poetry, drama, dance and oratory, an exalted hall insulated from the mundane cares of the outside world. In the course of those two centuries the relentless bequest of the Industrial Revolution, a phenomenon also born of the same rationalistic world view that spawned the museum, eventually also changed the museum's character from a 'reliquary of curiosities' to an environment for which artefacts were specifically created for exhibition. In this time it has not only become a repository for the artefacts of the dying cultures of the world – a time capsule of sorts – where in anthropological museums, the progressive deterioration of traditional society is now recorded, but also reflects in inverse proportion the dearth of culture in the outside world from which many are still divorced.

The pedagogical function of the first public museums – which was slowly transmuted into one of secular chapels set aside for an aesthetic purpose in which the work of art, as Malraux has noted, is separated from its context and divested of its intrinsic meaning – was felt to make them forbidding to many who were unschooled in their rituals and unable to appreciate the subtleties involved. The classic example of this sense of alienation as well as a gauge of the barrier that had been erected by what the public sensed to be an impenetrable inner sanctum, is the bequest of the Byker housing estate for the purchase of art, and the television series hosted by presenter Muriel Gray, which recorded the progress of the Committee's choice. The decisions they made were based on disarmingly candid opinions and although exaggerated for effect, helped to contribute to the current populist mood of debunking the establishment now being catered for by museums themselves.

The fourth stage in the evolution of the museum, which may now be said to be in full swing today, is its transition from a 'palace of art' to a 'palace of fun', with architecture commissioned to match. Denise Scott Brown has said in reference to the many related projects being designed by Venturi Scott Brown:

I think something else is happening in museums now. In the museums we designed we had to provide a great deal of non-museum space. Today's museum is part restaurant, part shop and part education department; it is full of lecture halls, conference rooms and computer spaces, where visitors can find information away from the paintings. Museums want to offer people different ways of knowing art.

Part of that 'different way of knowing' is inclusive rather than exclusive architecture that invites people in and puts them at ease. The work presented here is extremely varied, and yet shares the common denominator of responding in some way to this basic premise, since the trend towards accessibility is too overwhelming to allow artists and the clients that commission them to remain neutral. The museum park, which is the latest and largest manifestation of this move towards extroversion has now become a ubiquitous urban phenomenon, and Rotterdam is one of the latest European cities to build one following the Museumplein in Amsterdam, the *Museumsufer* in Frankfurt and the Kunstberg in Brussels. While other initiatives, most notably the Frankfurt programme, have been approached as a way to unify the city as cultural focal points experienced peripatetically, Rotterdam's Museumpark has been designed as a single environment, rather than a name linking scattered institutions through an initiative for improvement. With the new Architecture Institute by Jo Coenen as one of its biggest attractions, along with the Kunsthal by OMA, the Natuurmuseum's Mecanoo extensions and the Boymans museum among others, the park exemplifies this new inclusive attitude writ large; a cultural Disneyland that recognises the new social realities also informing the design of individual museums elsewhere. For directors and curators it can no longer be business as usual, and Durand's prototype, as the following projects illustrate, is no longer operational.

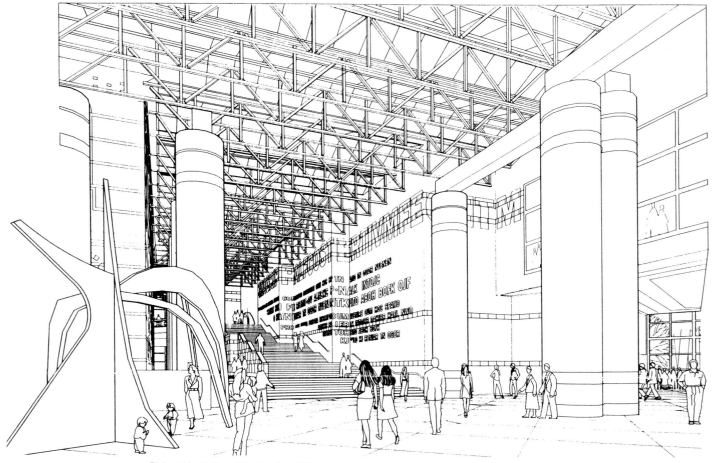

Robert Venturi and Denise Scott Brown, Amsterdam Museum, perspective of entrance hall

Ian Ritchie

The Museum as Public Architecture

The last two decades, architecturally speaking, will, I am sure, be looked back upon as one of the great eras in museum building. There can be no denying the recent impact of these typologies on post-industrial society. Many architectural masterpieces have been realised, whether renovations, recycled buildings, extensions or entirely new ones. These museums are the kings, queens and sometimes aces in each city's hand as they vie with each other across the Western world for attention. Museums have become barometers of an urban, and in some cases, of a national cultural virility.

Museums have unique characteristics: they have a natural and recognisable hierarchy of perception and most are object based whether they be art, anthropological, ethnological, technological or archaeological, giving them an intimate scale with personal and private contact. All are, or should be, more than mere containers for these objects. They should offer an internal spatial experience to be shared with others, something which some people consider a more important aspect of museum design than individual display, since one can very quickly become intellectually and emotionally saturated after studying only a few artefacts.

Museums are also important as public architecture. As such they can be perceived singularly as the art and science of building for a specific human purpose, for the storage and exhibition of objects and artefacts. They exist publicly in their own right.

Museums have been revolutionised by the desire, indeed the perceived need, to attract as many visitors as possible. The days when they were frequented by the researcher, the odd school party and the Sunday family are very distant indeed. Today clean shoes become trainers, the walking stick, the rucksack. This revolution has had a dramatic impact on the spatial programmes of museums, on the very nature of their organisation and indeed, in many instances, on the very role for which they were created. Most dramatic, perhaps, is the ability of these buildings to simply accommodate the flow of visitors, and from a marketing view, hold them long enough without boring them so that they spend at the book store and shops, but short enough to allow more visitors in. For existing museums increased accommodation needs have meant extensions, remodelling, renovation and refurbishment. Entrance lobbies have become *Accueils* – welcome halls – to collect and distribute the visitor; cloakrooms have become hangers preceded by security check lines; the ticket desk, information centres and toilet facilities the size normally associated with stadia. And all 'serious' museums boast their restaurant, cafeteria, temporary exhibition galleries, lecture auditoria and conference facilities. And these in turn, dancing to the market clock, are available out of hours for private use and city functions.

Temporary exhibition space and marketing leads to more transportation needs within the building: wider corridors, packaging and unpacking areas, transitory storerooms, increased media space and publications libraries. Truck parking, increased public access and transitory artefacts lead to increased security arrangements and security accommodations. Security leads to more sophisticated technical installations which leads to increased staff and maintenance costs. The upward spiral of complexity, of skilled management resources and, ultimately, revenue to compete nationally and internationally, demands very serious reappraisal. If the revolution of the last twenty or so years continues it must lead to a certain level of saturation, and of cultural institutions becoming bankrupt or becoming plcs quoted on the stock exchanges of the world, and subject to the vagaries of such markets. Museums have become such big business that some of the larger ones are inevitably going to lose all sense of direction and of their intrinsic value. The age of the interactive painting has arrived: the time when you scratch a Turner and smell the sulphur, ozone and steam can't be far away.

An overview of several of the most important European museums of the past two decades, focusing on those with which I am most familiar, may help to clarify the extent of this revolution.

There can be little doubt that the Centre Pompidou in Paris (1972-77) represented a dramatic shift in museum design and the image of museums in contemporary cultural life. Conceived as a technically and spatially flexible container for art, books, research and exploration, it provided, on an enormous scale, the opportunity for virtually any cultural contents to be housed, from small objects, paintings and sculptures to site happenings and music. This approach produced very large floor plates, whose intrinsic spatial characteristics were uniform, although far from neutral, with the presence of the large span beams and colour-coded servicing elements dominating the spaces.

However, this internal architecture was not necessarily the most significant aspect of the Centre Pompidou. The very nature of its entrance and its celebratory escalators took away the 'front steps' to high culture. It was, in its very essence, populist and freely accessible, and the strength of the public piazza in front of the building gave additional emphasis to the informality of the concept. There was no longer any notion of having to be 'educated' to participate in culture. The polemic created by the Centre Pompidou was not only architectural, but political. It represented the beginning of a renaissance in French government policy towards expressing its belief in its own time and culture. This renaissance is still active today – having enjoyed the support of three French presidents, opposing political parties in government, and the introduction of a certain autonomy for Paris through the re-establishment of the City Council and role of the Mayor – and is significant in that Paris was already, along with London and New York, a traditional centre of museum culture.

In 1978 Frankfurt embarked on a programme to redefine its image as something more than a financial centre, and in the ensuing decade thirteen cultural institutions were conceived, many designed by internationally renowned architects. This city of five hundred thousand people succeeded in transforming and enhancing its urban fabric by spending 11.5 per cent of its budget on culture. Through political will, Frankfurt, more than any other European city not previously a cultural centre, has influenced other non-capital European cities to invest in culture, in particular in museums.

But it is France, largely through its museums, which has been in the vanguard in implementing a cultural industry, first and foremost in Paris, but also in the provinces. The duality arising from the need for cultural facilities responding to our own age, its desires and quest for public awareness of recent cultural developments, and from the need for a national and capital identity in a rapidly shrinking world, has created an industry in both an economic and social sense. France, recognising the tendency of a leisure-orientated society in the 1960s (for example, Dumazedier's *Vers une Société de Loisir*), constructed a coherent strategy which has resulted in Paris remaining at the top of the world's cultural capitals; its major provincial cities emerging strengthened in the wider European context and its smaller towns sharing the cultural facilities boom of the 1980s.

But the actual typology of the museum is undergoing change, and their historical role as storehouses is being challenged by contents becoming events, and container becoming catalyst, which in turn is leading the contemporary museum to become the place, not of study, but of provocation and debate.

This can be restated as a decision on the part of museum directors for the museums to be part of today's real world and to be an active educational ingredient in our thought about the future. This is true for many museums of art, natural history, science and technology.

The design and building of the Museum of Modern Art (1987-1991) in Frankfurt by Hans Hollein continued the architect's challenge of the museum typology:

Since sculpture has broken away from its pedestal, the picture has dispensed with its isolating frame and the installation (environment) has come to represent a spatial totality which goes beyond an additive series of works and exists in a specific dialogue with the space containing it.

This necessitates a new museum presentation which goes beyond linear or chronological enfilades, 'no artists, no museum'. (One is reminded of artist Robert Filliou walking the streets of Paris in 1962 with his 'museum in a hat', in order to show that the art museum, the nineteenth-century version, has become completely unnecessary). The architecture of Hollein's building has its origins in his desire to create spaces within which contemporary artists feel that it is their art which is on display, and where they can, if motivated, interact with the container. As regards the image, Hollein appears to have responded to the triangular site and its position as an entrance to the historical part of the city, nearby the old town wall and cathedral, through the use of materials evoking *gravitas* – red sandstone and render. This museum, as a triangular urban block, is expressive of modernity as process – researching and redefining gallery space, while at the same time responding in a distinctive, yet compositional way, to the urban texture of this part of Frankfurt.

By contrast, Meier's Museum for the Decorative Arts engages the urban context by means of a two-dimensional grid, while not seeking *gravitas* through colour and material. Here the collection is domesticated within rooms and precious items placed in intimate niches.

In recalling Frankfurt's intense programme of museum building, one is drawn to the conclusion that this new collection of museums is the new image of Frankfurt, and not any of the individual buildings. This new image is unquestionably one of expressive modernity and has revitalised the heart of Frankfurt, bringing people back to the city at weekends, along the River Main, the commercial district and old town.

In Karlsruhe the project for the Centre for Art and Media Technology by ZKM can be seen to crystallise a view of modernity as process and creative connectivity between two contemporary social facts, art and technology. In this centre, the element of debate, rather than the study of collections, is paramount. By its very nature it will be experimental as a place fostering research in the collaboration of art and science. Visitors' current opinions and views on the place of art and science in the modern world will be challenged, though they will not necessarily find defined views as to what this contemporary world is or should be. The visitor will become part of the process of gaining insights and helping to anticipate the needs of the next century. In this project, the media content is both undefined in terms of scale and composition, is ephemeral and yet requires spaces that allow the contemporary expression of 'connected art and science'.

As the projects in Frankfurt showed, MOCA's architect Rem Koolhaas will be involved in the process of modernity, but with the knowledge that as an experiment in itself the centre's container and image may well be dynamic and as such offer the possibility of being a 1990s witness to the evolution of a cultural architecture of change so powerfully stated by Piano & Rogers at the Centre Pompidou in the 1970s. As Koolhaas has said:

> If the museum becomes the place where, without commercial pressure, one can obtain information about the worldwide developments of our own time, then the museum realises its most valuable function. I can say that culture consists of three pillars: art, science and spirituality. Bring all three into the museum and show the similarities of development within the different fields. Only then can the museum remain the temple of culture that we expect it to be.

In Italy, just north of Florence, there is the Contemporary Art Museum at Prato, not state directed, but developed on the initiative of an industrialist, Enrico Pecci, very much in the Prato tradition of private collectors donating to the city. This project, designed by Italo Gamberini, addresses the spatial questions of contemporary art, initially through the three key components of the brief: the museum/gallery, the CID (Centre of Information and Documentation on the visual arts, architecture and industrial design) and studios for artists to work at the museum. The museum/gallery container is conceived as a static structural grid of 12 by 12 metres, resulting in an interior space which is akin to an eighteenth-century enfilade, or suite of rooms. The intention at one level is the well serviced industrial container, with regular top lighting capable of a degree of modification.

The three components appear physically separated, arguably as a response to the site where an intersection of two important avenues occurs, and result in the creation of landscape spaces which subtly influence the rationalism of the structural grid design of the museum.

To the northeast, at Faenz, a delightful Museum of Natural Science to house the Domenico Malmerendi natural history collection has been realised in the solitude of one of the town's parks. It is a compact, geometrically well-defined object, with no attempt at camouflage or historical pastiche. It sits calmly as a pavilion. However, the internal spaces are surprising in their interesting rhythms, originating from the winding ramp which gives access to the open central gallery, and from here to the side rooms. This image is modern, reminiscent of early modernist designs, with simple geometric volumes, an understated formal composition and refined details. The inside of the apparently neutral container is by contrast dominated by primary coloured vertical elements – showcases and screens – and is a rare example of exhibition space with no provision of zenithal light.

Carlo Scarpa's sensitive handling of the Castelvecchio Museum and Gae Aulenti and Piero Castiglioni's more modest refurbishment of the Palazzo Grassi both demonstrate a belief in the notion that old buildings are palimpsests upon which the contemporary architect makes his or her mark, in differing degrees of sympathy with the original, but undeniably contemporary and showing some change from what was there, thus distinguishing those moments in history when social or economic need demanded architectural intervention.

New museums in Spain have largely been renovations and/or additions to historical containers, the diversity of design approaches reflecting the prevalence of architectural pluralism, and the questioning of the functional and social role of museums. Spain has not yet undertaken the realisation of new museums on a scale comparable with that of France or Germany, however, the investment programme has not been modest. Totally new museum buildings have been rare, such as Valencia's Museum of Modern Art and the Madrid City Museum, although several more are being advanced, such as the Museum of Contemporary Art in Barcelona and the provincial museum of Leon.

The Centro de Arte Reina Sofia (CARS), restructured from an eighteenth-century classically Baroque general hospital in Madrid, compares in scale and cultural intent to that of the Pompidou Centre. Regarding the creation of a new image, the problem was to publicly overcome the immense solidity and history of the existing building. This was very successfully achieved by placing the main public vertical circulation outside the main facade in two transparent, yet structurally audacious glass towers.

Internally, the challenge was to create spacious exhibition areas, sufficient natural lighting and climate control within the rigid, yet sometimes elegantly proportioned structure of the building. The architects José-Luis Iniguez de Onzoño and Antonio Vázquez de Castro achieved major structural and environmental improvements which are virtually invisible, in fact their whole internal architectural approach was minimalist, leaving vast white containers free for art and installations. One regret, however, is the very limited public access to the generously proportioned landscaped courtyard, containing a magnificent Calder mobile.

A few hundred metres from CARS, and opposite the Prado, the industrialist Baron Thyssen and his wife have selected an early nineteenth-century classical palace, once a bank, to house their enormous art collection of some seven hundred paintings. They chose the Spanish architect Rafael Moneo to remodel the palace for 1992, Madrid's year as European City of Culture. The choice of site is significant, in that it may cast light on the nature of Baron Thyssen. From initial thoughts of a new building in Lugano by Stirling, to England (a Manchester ship canal site!), to the site in Madrid's museum mile that not only benefits from a city population of four million (estimated to be six million by the year 2000), with a tourist influx of forty million, but also from the fact that paintings in the proposed collection significantly 'compete' with the weaker areas of one of the world's great collections at the Prado – seventeenth-century Dutch and twentieth-century. Though according to Thyssen, at the end of ten years the paintings will become part of the national patrimony under current Spanish law.

Moneo's architecture is a stately modernism, also to be seen in the remodelled Atocha Station at the end of the Castellana, opposite CARS, and his Roman Museum at Mérida. And in contrast to the neutrality of most national and private galleries, Thyssen has made a significant and personal impact on the colour scheme of the containers – there is green (old masters), burnt sienna (modern) and red (for the eighteenth and nineteenth centuries) – and this with his extraordinary collection and museum location suggests that it will prove hugely popular.

Barcelona is a 'city of Olympian projects' with architects of international stature designing them. Behind this resurgence of the Catalan capital is the city council and its dynamic mayor, who is quoted as saying 'the public facades of buildings and external spaces they create are the property of the citizen'. In this context, on a site adjacent to the University and the Ramblas, Richard Meier is creating the Museum of Contemporary Art, but there will also be libraries, symposium centres, exhibition venues, and other cultural institutions knitted into the existing fabric of the old quarter. True to form, Meier has produced a signature image for the MOCA. It is organised on three main levels and a basement: on ground level, sculpture and industrial design – revealing the evolution of Catalan forms; on the first level, later twentieth-century avant-garde art; and on the naturally lit upper level, temporary exhibitions for works of living artists in more generously proportioned containers. The spatial architecture – white, shadows on white, solid and void – is Meier's oft repeated formula for museums, whether in America or Germany, although there is a rigour to the rectilinear geometry of the medium sized galleries at all levels, as opposed to the rooms in his Frankfurt museum, and its success will be as much to do with its location, the flow of the public spaces created through the museum and the concentrated richness of the neighbouring cultural activities.

There are many more provincial museum projects completed and proposed in Spain for art, archaeology, science and technology – Cataluña's Generalitats' museum network dedicated to science, technology, industry and labour and the Caixa de Pensions's Museum of Science in Barcelona, for example – which are very popular with children through their technological gadgetry.

However, there is a lingering feeling that in Spain the museum phenomenon, particularly in the world of art, is possibly over-ambitious, leaving the question of the contents, their acquisition, display and management to be more fully resolved.

In England, three London museums – the Sainsbury Wing at the National Gallery by Robert Venturi and Denise Scott Brown, the Sackler Galleries at the Royal Academy by Norman Foster and the temporary Ecology Gallery at The Natural History Museum by Ian Ritchie – have made differing architectural and museological statements, all financed privately. There is no major government commitment to new museology in Britain.

Venturi has said of his architecture 'that it would be hard to take for both classicists and modernists', and it has received enormous press exposure, being published in all the major national, architectural and art magazines. The internal arrangement is of an enfilade of rooms, painted in neutral grey according to the Gallery Director's wishes, and lit with token daylight – inspired by Soane's Dulwich Picture Gallery –

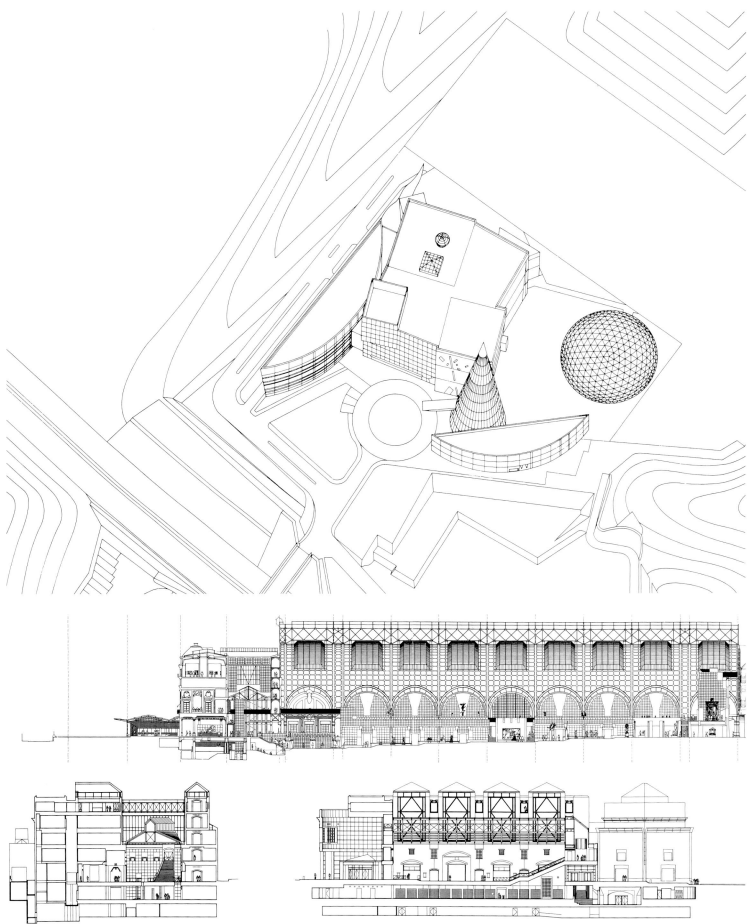

FROM ABOVE: Kisho Kurokawa, Ehime Museum of Science; Gae Aulenti, Gare d'Orsay; Pei, Cobb, Freed & Partners, Holocaust Museum

supplemented with artificial lighting to provide containers for the viewing of a superb collection of early Renaissance paintings.

The architecture of the containers is so subtle as to be almost invisible to the average visitor – in Venturi's words: 'their symbolism refers to the kind of spaces the painters were painting for Tuscan fifteenth-century palaces.' The result is a marked dissociation of the container from the contents, as if the container is attempting to camouflage itself. This is not the case with Soane's Dulwich Gallery, where the spatial pleasure is in harmony with the contents. The external image of the Sainsbury Wing has been much criticised at many levels, not least for the imposition of a philosophical programme based on a personal re-interpretation of classicism, and an imposition of an intellectual symbolism. There is a strange banality and inelegance to the extension when seen against the National Gallery, and for me the architecture provides no enjoyment, internally or externally, but a lot of pleasure in seeing the qualities of the paintings.

At the Sackler Galleries, Norman Foster has achieved the renovation of the old top-floor studios of Burlington House by an astute exploitation of the vertical space of a small, naturally ventilated void between the back of Burlington House and the later main Royal Academy galleries. The success of the project lies in the route, the vertical ride in the lift from the low light levels at ground floor to the generous diffusion of natural light at the new gallery level. This offers a short but welcome moment of contemplation of space and time. The modest sized, barrel vaulted galleries are almost neutral, the plastered white walls and pale wood flooring suggesting that the contents of most traditional art collections would be at home here. (Though the zenithal light coming through the generous rooflights is not as calm as one would wish, due to the continuously adjusting and somewhat noisy light-control louvres, which with the narrow linear air-conditioning slots disturb the initial impression of serenity.)

Finally, the Ecology Gallery at the Natural History Museum has, through its aim of challenging ecological preconceptions and knowledge, both attempted to give a factual base to the essence of ecology and provided an exhibition to encourage debate. The controversial design of this exhibition container is daringly contemporary, and creates another image within the magnificent Gothic building. This image – a spectacular asymmetric glass chasm, crossed by four bridges, is also a symbolic element of the exhibition content. The glass enclosure, as exhibition route, attempts to cross the conventional boundaries of image, container and contents, whilst permitting the more programmatic contents the 'privacy' and individuality to convey the detailed messages of ecology in a sequential manner.

With this short architectural review I hope that I have illustrated the plurality of proposals prevalent in European museum design during the last few years, which are indicative of changes happening internationally. In the sixties artists left the museums, denouncing them as art graveyards. This has been followed by a museum resurgence through the heightened commercialisation of art in the eighties, which has challenged architects to redefine, for their own time, the character of the container, between specific and generic space, or expressive and neutral galleries. When the content is known, the design of the container has a starting point, and architects can vary their bias towards or away from the content's influence as a means of not only creating the container's relationship to the content, but also in creating the museum's character. When the content is unknown, or there is no collection as such, the tendency is towards the notion of the 'workshop', whether within a repainted factory space such as the Saatchi Gallery, or a new container for experimentation such as ZKM's Centre for Art and Media Technology.

Each generation of designers must determine their own solutions to the architectural space, both externally and internally, which is ideal for the presentation of the art, science and technology and issues of their own time. This is the spirit of modernity which is at the very core of Western civilisation, the research without preconceived formulae or stylistic prejudices; the creation of the most appropriate solutions to improve our understanding of ourselves and our environment.

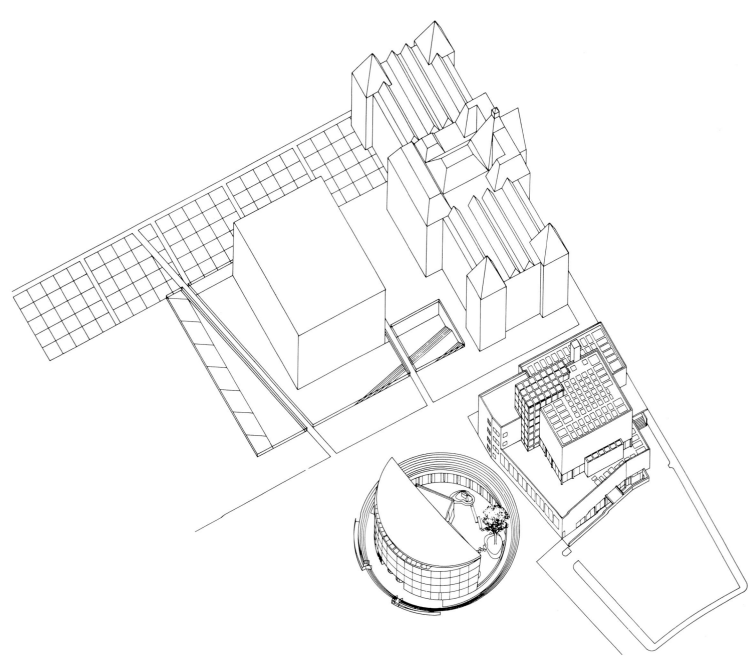

ABOVE: Kisho Kurokawa, New Wing of the Vincent Van Gogh Museum; PAGE 10: Ian Ritchie, The Ecology Gallery at the Natural History Museum

Gae Aulenti

Museum of Catalan Art, Barcelona

As in her involvement with the refurbishment of the Gare d'Orsay, the focus of Gae Aulenti's work in Barcelona, carried out from 1985 to 1991, has been on the restoration and re-articulation of a much loved historical monument. In this instance it was the Palau Nacional, the main building of the 1929 Universal Exposition on Montjuic, designed by Pedro Cendap and Enric Catá. The rapidity with which it was built in order to open in time, and the lack of flexibility of its interior, as well as lack of maintenance, had made action to save the building absolutely necessary. The Library of Art Museums Plan, drawn up by Lluis Domènech in 1984, gave first priority to this task, and of establishing in the Palau a Museum of Catalan Art, in which an existing collection of Gothic and Romanesque art, which is the most extensive and valuable in Spain except for that of the Prado, be complemented with the collection at the Museo d'Art Modern at Cintadella Park.

The problem facing the architect, along with her local associate, Enrique Steegmann, was twofold: to restore and upgrade the gallery to enable it to exhibit its own collection better and to allow for the accommodation of other collections as well. Her first move was to reinforce the crumbling foundations of the Palau, and to create expansion joints to prevent further unwanted separation. Shoring up of the structural slabs, to accept heavier dead and live loads in the future, was accompanied by patching of the perimeter walls and the roof, prior to any plans for the interior being considered. Once the envelope and structural system were repaired and secure, Aulenti tackled the problem of renewing the galleries with the same thoroughness and precision that has come to characterise her efforts elsewhere. She took her cue from the curators of the Palau, organising a layout according to three possible options, as she has described them:

the chronological, which is usual in all museums, the typological, which singles out works which exemplify the integration of figurative and spatial relationships, and the symbolic, drawing attention to the transformation through time of universal figurative references. The analysis of these continually intersecting itineraries in terms of an all encompassing, active dialectic, the analysis of the works of art, their grouping and the logic of their rhythms, has effectively determined a system of articulation at variance with the Palau Nacional itself. The degree of this variance, which has also been determined by a careful study of both natural and artificial lighting patterns at acceptable levels, is evident in both of the square galleries, flanking the newly liberated entrance hall, as well as in the elliptical Gran Saló with its glass roof, which terminates the formal, processional axis, with an asymmetrical assortment of interlocking elements within. The result is a masterful blending of past and future, of old and new, tradition and national modernity, executed with singular authority and grace.

BELOW FROM ABOVE: Longitudinal section through main gallery space; longitudinal section through entrance

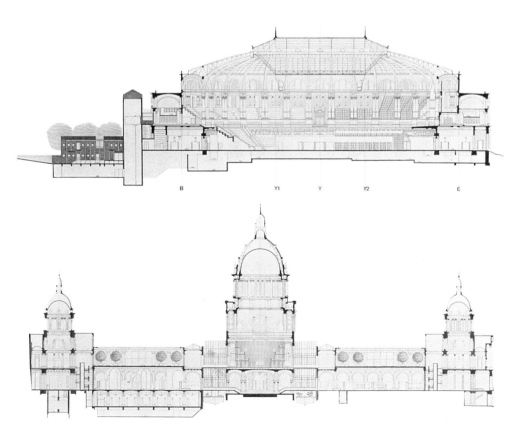

Gae Aulenti

Gare d'Orsay, Paris

Victor Laloux's station, which was built by the Paris-Orleans Company in 1900, closed in 1969 because of a slow obsolescence that began with its inability to accept the longer electric trains introduced in 1939. After an abortive attempt to convert it into a luxury hotel through a much publicised competition, it was saved by the uproar following the decimation of Les Halles Centrales and the construction of the Pompidou Centre shortly afterwards. In 1971, the demolition order was lifted, and the Gare d'Orsay was added to the list of Monuments Historiques two years later. Its possible new purpose, however, remained a mystery until 1977, when the directors of the Musées de France convinced then-President Valéry Giscard d'Estaing that it should become a museum dedicated to the art of the nineteenth century, to which France had contributed so much.

ACT Architecture was successful in a limited competition, with their proposal for a central 'promenade' flanked by individual 'buildings' that contained exhibition spaces, and supported another gallery level above them, but there were reservations about certain aspects of the design. A second competition, to find an architect to sort out these inconsistencies, was won by Gae Aulenti, and an inevitable struggle for design autonomy began. Aulenti found that the basic flaw with the ACT proposal, which she could not alter at the time of her commission, was how to encourage people to move from the central 'street' to the galleries inside the 'buildings' that flank it, without resorting to obvious and excessive tactics like signs; and how to make these 'buildings' stand up against the scale and level of detailing of Laloux's breathtaking central nave. The solution that was finally implemented was to set up an ordered system of stairways and landings keyed in with the openings into the side-galleries, which tie both together in linear progression through the grand space, along a concourse that rises in level as it reaches its termination. While this decision may seem to have been based on abstract considerations, it is extremely perceptive because it shows an awareness of the way that people move. Being faced with the

choice between a flight of five steps and lateral doorways made more mysterious by their pylon-like jambs, the popular tendency has been to turn to the side, explore these chambers, rest, and then move on to the next landing. In order that the facades of these 'buildings' might hold their own inside the vast hall around them, they have been treated as massive objects with the parapet of the second gallery level above forming their cornices. Two towers complete the ascent along the concourse, and these are designed as small, freestanding, ingeniously detailed cabinets, full of objects that are presented in niches on each level.

A second space, running parallel to the main hall along the Quai Anatole France, is covered with a mansard roof that connects to the semicircular trusses over the concourse. This wing has been subdivided with the Pavilion Aval and galleries for temporary exhibition on the ground floor, the Salon Oval on the first floor, and the Impressionist Gallery on the third, which draws a great number of visitors. This upper gallery is particularly interesting because of the position that Aulenti has taken on the importance of introducing natural light – which is such an important part of the work of these artists – into the space. Wide, vertical baffles along its ceiling have been calculated to deal with all conceivable solar angles, diffusing the sun's rays, and protecting the paintings below.

The Gare d'Orsay has come alive again, and a complex programme has been dealt with in a confident way, providing a significant prototype for similar renovations in the future. It is the attention to detail, down to the choice of a colour which brings out the elegance of Laloux's faceted glass roof, or the use of decorative bouchons on the ceiling as acoustic baffles, which finally makes this conversion such a success.

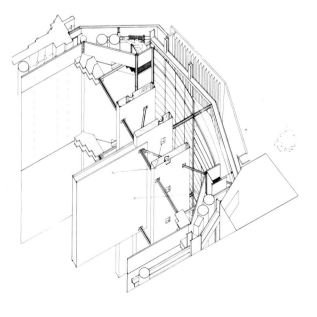

RIGHT: Cutaway axonometric of the Galerie des Hauteurs
PAGES 22-23 FROM ABOVE: Cutaway axonometric of main entrance level; longitudinal section
PAGE 23 RIGHT: Cross sections through main entrance level

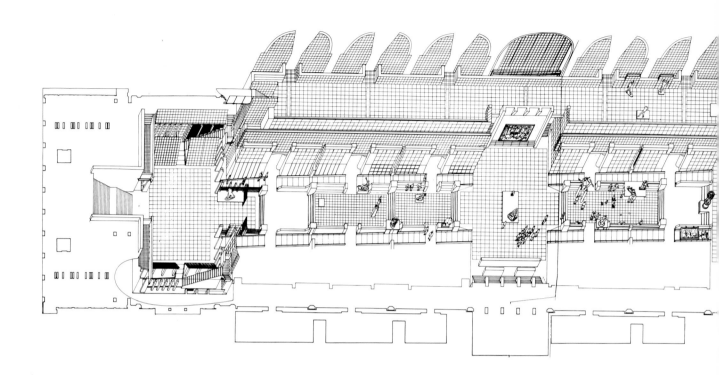

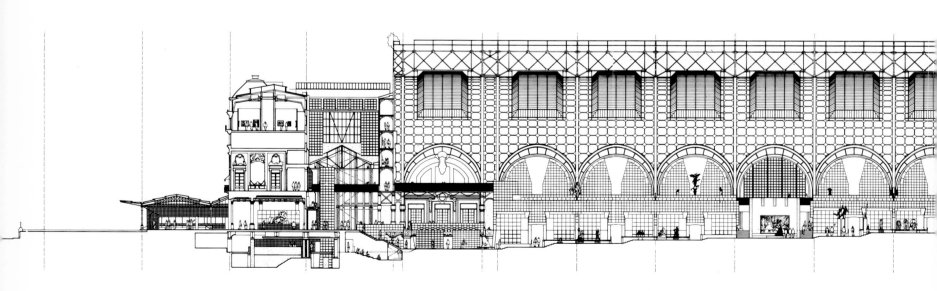

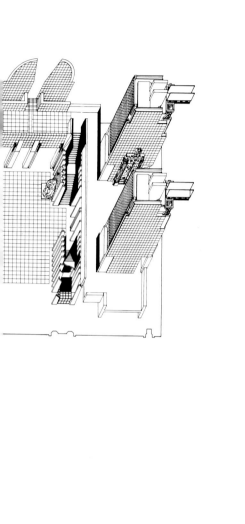

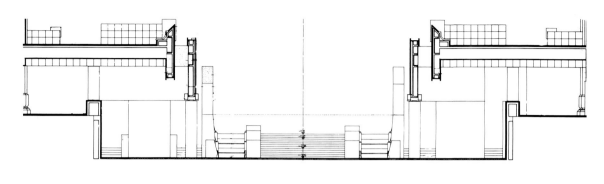

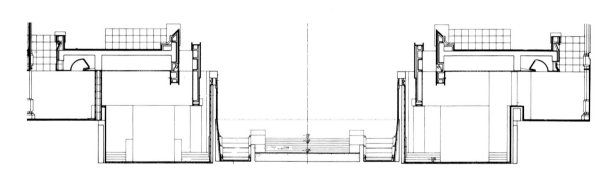

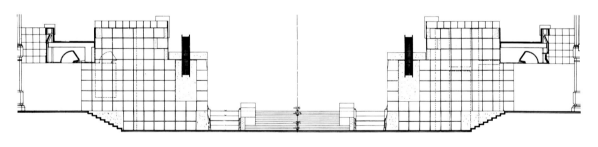

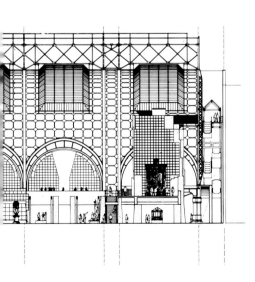

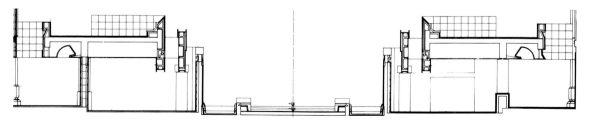

26

Rasem Badran and Abdul-Halim Ibrahim

The National Museum of Archaeology, Amman, Jordan

The study for the urban reconstruction of the centre of Amman has brought Badran's attention full circle to an urban rather than a residential scale, and has finally provided him with an opportunity to implement the principles uncovered elsewhere. In this study, which focuses on the National Museum of Archaeology and the Municipal Plaza, the architects have concentrated on image as well as structure, using the historical patterns that are layered throughout the city as a template for its future growth. They explain that those patterns:

> . . . can be traced through all of the various sites that have been preserved in various parts of Amman. Our proposal for the urban centre concentrates on evolving a spatial pattern which reflects the historical content of the city as well as enriching its complex culture. Our aim, therefore, is to arrive at a scheme that will begin a dialect about what the city should be and to provide the basis for an ongoing intellectual discourse, rather than submitting an individualistic formal proposal that is in contradiction to the cultural continuity of the city.

As the cornerstone of his strategy for regeneration, the Archaeological Museum is not a static warehouse full of artefacts, but a physical embodiment of the collective memory of the city, with the capacity to make people aware of the complexity of their heritage through the spatial experience that the architect provides. The steep hills in Amman have always necessitated the use of retaining walls, and these have become a device for expressing continuity as well as creating a closer connection with topography. By looking at the wall as an edge and a skin, as well as an engineering necessity, Badran and Ibrahim were able to expand it into a space of its own. They see it as becoming a:

> . . . place of definition between the theatre and the mountain, providing new, unexpected experiences of the entire setting. This solid wall is then extended to form a skin that also redefines the facades of the city, creating a new space in front of them. In addition, the spaces in the wall are shaped in certain instances

to cater to new functions. Grouped in relation to the historical references most appropriate to them these spaces refer to either the Roman or Islamic era, with independent elements signifying an entrance between them.

In this project and that for the Science Museum, Rasem Badran demonstrates an uncanny ability to find what Aldo Rossi has called 'persistencies' and to distinguish between the permanent and the transitory. In his exploration of a religious and cultural tradition that is recognised as having great unity and diversity, Badran has been able to find the common denominator beneath these differences. Through extensive analysis he has shown that these usually exist because of environmental and economic rather than philosophical variations. His approach is systematic rather than purely romantic, possibly as a result of his highly rationalist training. In spite of this orderly approach, Badran's architecture is a perceptive, rather than a rigid interpretation of the world he is examining. As a result he has made many others aware of the seemingly infinite possibilities for creative expression that are inherent in tradition.

PAGE 28: Aerial view of site
PAGE 29: Site plan

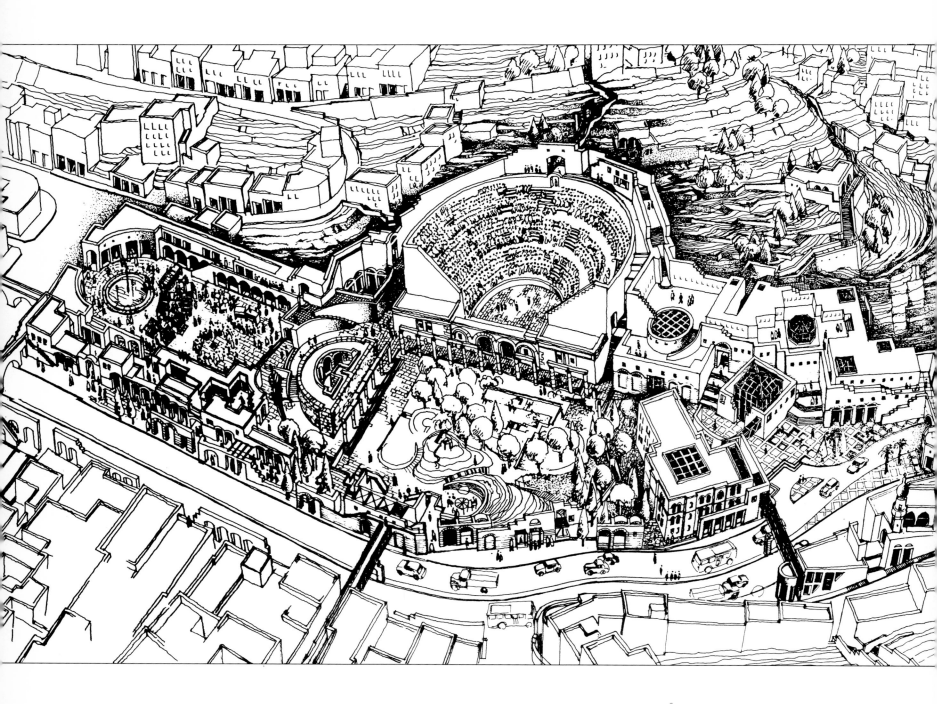

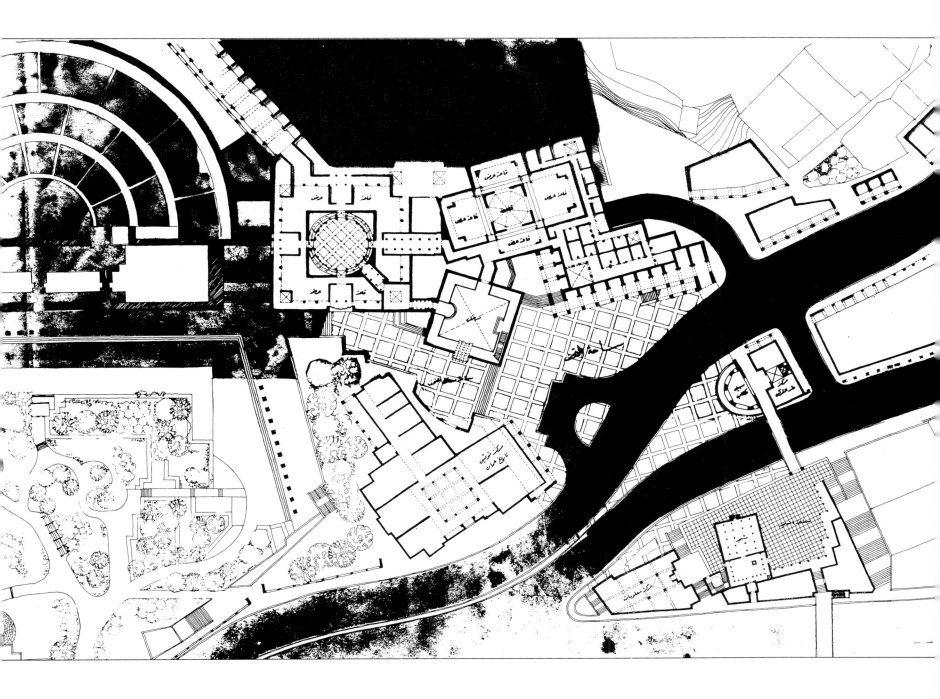

Abdul-Halim Ibrahim and Rasem Badran

The Science Oasis Museum, Riyadh, Saudi Arabia

The Science Oasis Museum addresses the place of technology in traditional architecture, in addition to looking at the meaning of technology itself. First conceived as a cosmological tracking device whose form would express a physical relationship with planetary movements, this museum is also intended to act as a vivid reminder of Muslim contributions to the science of astronomy in the past. Each of the individual galleries was initially organised in a circle around a large, elevated sphere. The sphere, in turn, was placed on a triangular pedestal reminiscent of the Mogul sundials built in India in the fifteenth and sixteenth centuries. In the first design, the galleries were shaped according to the planetary angles related to the exhibits in them, as well as the visual impact that each part of the building would have on the skyline of Riyadh, when seen in conjunction with the water tower and television headquarters that dominate it. (This question of urban 'montage' takes on an added dimension in a city which is glimpsed by many visitors solely from the raised highways.) In the interests of economy, however, the strong forms and sharp edges of this first, extremely metaphorical scheme were eroded to allow for the further definition of each part, leading the architects through a second, and finally a third phase in which many of the original ideas can still be recognised but are much subdued.

The successful collaboration between these two talented designers, and the possibility of future joint venture, is interesting because they share many of the same views on the importance of tradition. Although they may differ in the degree of literal interpretation that they favour, as well as in their methods of graphic interpretation, it is this common belief that makes such joint efforts possible. The final configuration of the Space and Science Museum, in its asymmetrical variance from the monumentality of the first scheme, and abstraction of the powerful metaphors contained in it, shows how successful this synthesis has been. The sensitivity to topography is a consistent feature of Badran's work which has remained intact

through all three stages of this project, with a sunken circular *enceinte* providing the kind of protective berm that was first used in his mosque designs. In this case, however, a round, rather than a square wall provides a line of demarcation between fantasy and reality rather than the sacred and profane. On the outer edge of that line, which is not as exclusive as first conceived, the various

parts of the museum attach themselves like the dependencies connected to the bottom of a high castle wall. The inside of the ring remains the exclusive precinct of the universal analogy the architects have created.

PAGE 31: Conceptual drawing showing relationship to planetary motions
PAGE 33: Preliminary drawings

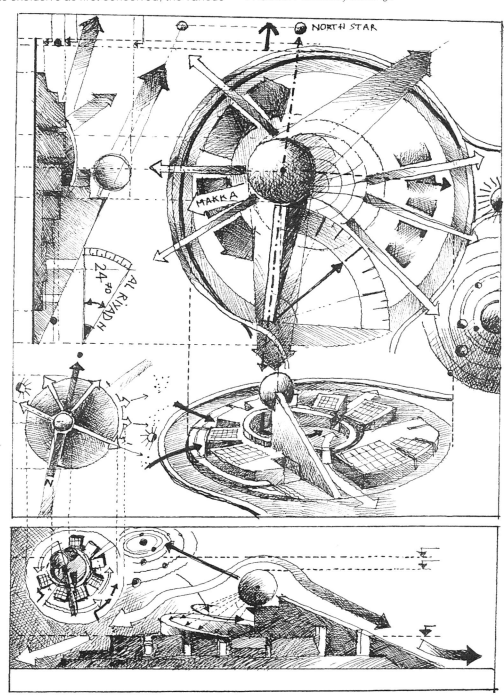

Günter Behnisch

The German Postal Museum, Frankfurt

The German Postal Museum by Günter Behnisch is the third of its kind in Frankfurt, preceded by the Imperial and Federal Museums in the past, and constitutes part of the city council's *Museumsufer* or riverside promenade of museums along the Schaumainkai. Günter Behnisch and Partners won the competition for the new headquarters of the collection, which was to be brought together and updated for the first time since its dispersal to different storage locations during the Second World War.

The decision to locate this facility on the same site as the villa that had served as the Federal Postal Museum had the advantage of providing both symbolic and physical continuity, but the restricted size of the plot made planning of an annex very difficult. Provision for any future expansion, which experience has shown to be a necessary requirement in museum design, was also a potential problem, due to lack of space. In addition, the old mansion was in great need of restoration if it was to retain any active role in the new institution. As Thomas Werner, the Director of the new museum has said, the architect's idea of placing a portion of the exhibition area underground has meant that:

> . . . the plant-covered roof of the main exhibition floor takes up the character of the old garden, and the clear division of the old and new building parts towards the outside avoided the problems usually arising when old and new buildings are linked directly with one another. A truncated glass cone at the back of the garden connects the different storeys of the new building and provides the interior with a unique transparency, at the same time allowing daylight to fall into the underground exhibition floor. The motif of the semicircle is also repeated elsewhere such as where the foundation avoids the roots of the existing trees. These semicircular elements are intended to form a contrast to the otherwise linear new building.

The German Postal Museum has five floors, of which two are underground. The first of these is used as the main exhibition floor, and the architect has established a connection between it and a corresponding level in the existing villa, which has not only expanded the available exhibition space, but has also ensured that the older building will continue to be utilised. The second underground level is used as a car park, once again to maximise space usage, as well as providing much needed storage. The entire ground floor, which has been liberated by this design strategy, has been turned over to entrance requirements, including an information desk, museum shop, cafeteria and auditorium. Two upper levels are reserved for permanent and temporary exhibitions respectively, with security of the temporary displays of postage stamps being an important factor in the location and design of that area. An amateur radio station has been installed on the roof, continuing the Museum's commitment to technological implementation and display.

As Thomas Werner noted, Behnisch has intentionally set out to contrast the new building with the old, in terms of materials and space planning, believing that this has allowed much more design freedom and is more in keeping with the forward-looking, technologically-based image that the Deutsche Bundespost seeks to convey. Such contrast has also allowed a more decentralised organisation of exhibitions, using the open, three-dimensional spaces to their best advantage.

Great care was taken to save as many trees as possible on the site to provide a park-like setting for the museum. Achieving this was not easy, because construction of underground parking and exhibition areas required special replanting techniques. Fortunately, this task was made more straightforward as many of the largest trees were located near the edge of the property. Rather than responding to fixed exhibition requirements, Günter Behnisch has provided an architectural solution that encourages flexibility and change. As he has said,

> It is our experience that achievement in art is greater and ultimately better and more varied if relatively difficult problems have had to be overcome . . . and the creation of an exhibition is probably no different.

Mario Botta

Watari-Um, Tokyo

Having received the commission for this museum and art gallery in March 1985, Mario Botta began to familiarise himself with the complex building codes involved, and produced a schematic design in eight months. A difficult site indicated a plan in the shape of an isosceles triangle, with circulation relegated to the corners, and a main entrance in the centre of one of the sides.

In the initial scheme, the chronic problem of how to deal with natural light was handled by using glass block, but this detail was finally eliminated due to budget considerations. The location of the stair towers within the triangular envelope proved to be the endgame of the design process, eventually forcing Botta to abandon his typically symmetrical solutions for a more articulated and expressive approach, in which the articulation of the main vertical tower allows it to seem detached, and to signify the entrance. A round tower, inside, used for the elevator, balances the knife-edge of this form. Banding on the exterior walls allows the entire composition to be assertive in the surrounding urban chaos, giving the museum a presence that its relatively small scale would otherwise have prohibited. The use of balconies on the second and third floors, as well as the raw exposed structure, carry this enhanced sense of scale into the interiors, making them seem more spacious than their 627 square metres would indicate.

In a letter to the client, Mrs Watari, dated 5 August 1990, Mario Botta reveals his ideas and the nature of their relationship:

. . . After years of discussions, projects and disputes, I can confirm the impact that this new building has on the city. The extent of this confrontation, the dialogue with the riches and contradiction of this enormous city, are the reasons why I embraced the challenge and the discomforts of this project.

. . . the confrontation with places and cultures distant from my daily progress caused me to determine and make clear the ways of seeing and of interpreting architecture. For this little museum, from the first drawing I followed a strong and precise course that had to resist the confusion and the contradiction of languages, styles and forms present in Tokyo . . . In this metropolis . . . one can catch accumulations of situations and of interests, which in their continuous interlacings characterise the riches and/or the poverty of today's city. Tokyo exacerbates the contradictions of 'modern' cities; the dimensional and spatial break with the pre-existent is visible at every street corner: next to the lacerations inflicted by new urban interventions a very thick urban context survives with a pre-industrial matrix which offers a conflicting contrast between a spatial relationship and an urban memory. In the everyday changing 'Babel' of urban languages, I wanted to create a strong and primary architectural sign and image, generated by a reason from within the building and supported by natural light and geometry. The result is a building, simple in its triangular geometric basis, which establishes its own proportions through a slight asymmetry dictated by the vertical connections (elevator and stairs). The desire for different solutions on the three sides with regard to the three different urban conditions, finally produced the different facades. The main front is axial and stretched to its maximum extension (as if it were the maximum wing span of a bird). The front on the little side road is flat and stretched to underline the corner stair as an element of urban appeal (as if it were a flag). The back prospect facing the bordering property is sober and almost opens southward in the high part. It is in such a way – with constant recall to the severity and rigour of that Roman architecture which is very dear to me – that I dealt with the complexity and the objective difficulty of this building. The hope is that Watari-Um will be able, as the Roman buildings have done, to survive and endure over the centuries . . . The aspiration to eternity is a 'weakness' of every architect!

RIGHT: Preparatory sketch
PAGES 40 & 41 FROM L TO R: Isometric; roof plan; ground floor plan; elevation of main entrance facade

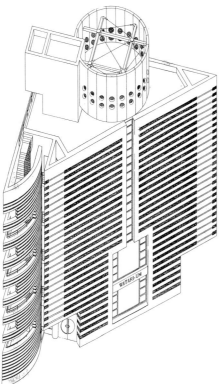

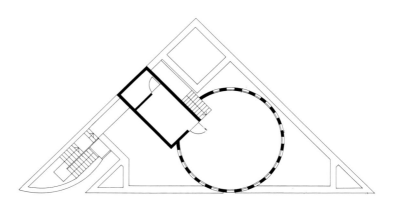

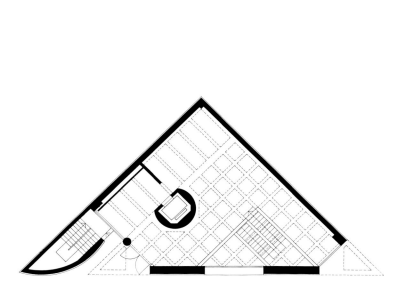

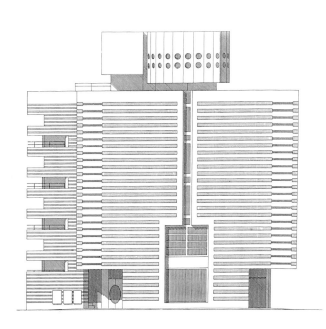

Coop Himmelblau

East Wing of the Groningen Museum of Art, the Netherlands

Originally conceived as an island in the Verbindings Kanaal, the design for the Groningen Museum began as a fragile collaboration directed by Alessandro Mendini of Milan, involving Philippe Starck, Michele De Lucchi and Frank Stella, with each of the players providing a piece of the aquatic collage. Following the withdrawal of the Stella component, Coop Himmelblau was invited to undertake a 10,000 square foot section of the complex to house art ranging from the sixteenth century to the present. Rather than continuing the self-imposed theme of a unified urban complex, connected to the land by bridges, which seemed to have governed the schemes produced before their involvement, Coop Himmelblau have opted to play their segment against the others, treating them as existing context.

Their concept is based on the idea of the unfolding of positive and negative space, and the juxtaposition of a complex roof structure against the water, and the river bank beyond.

RIGHT: Concept sketch
PAGE 45 ABOVE: First sketch, Where space ends, architecture begins

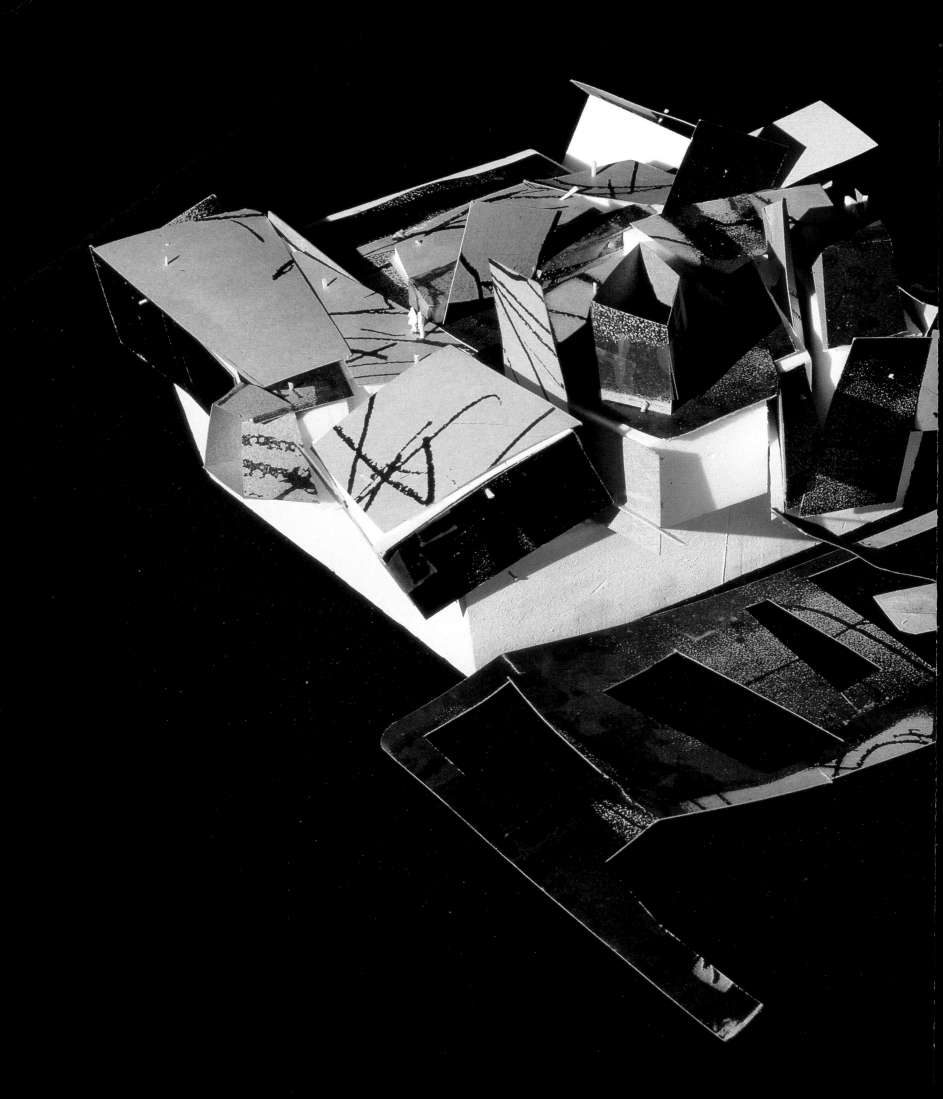

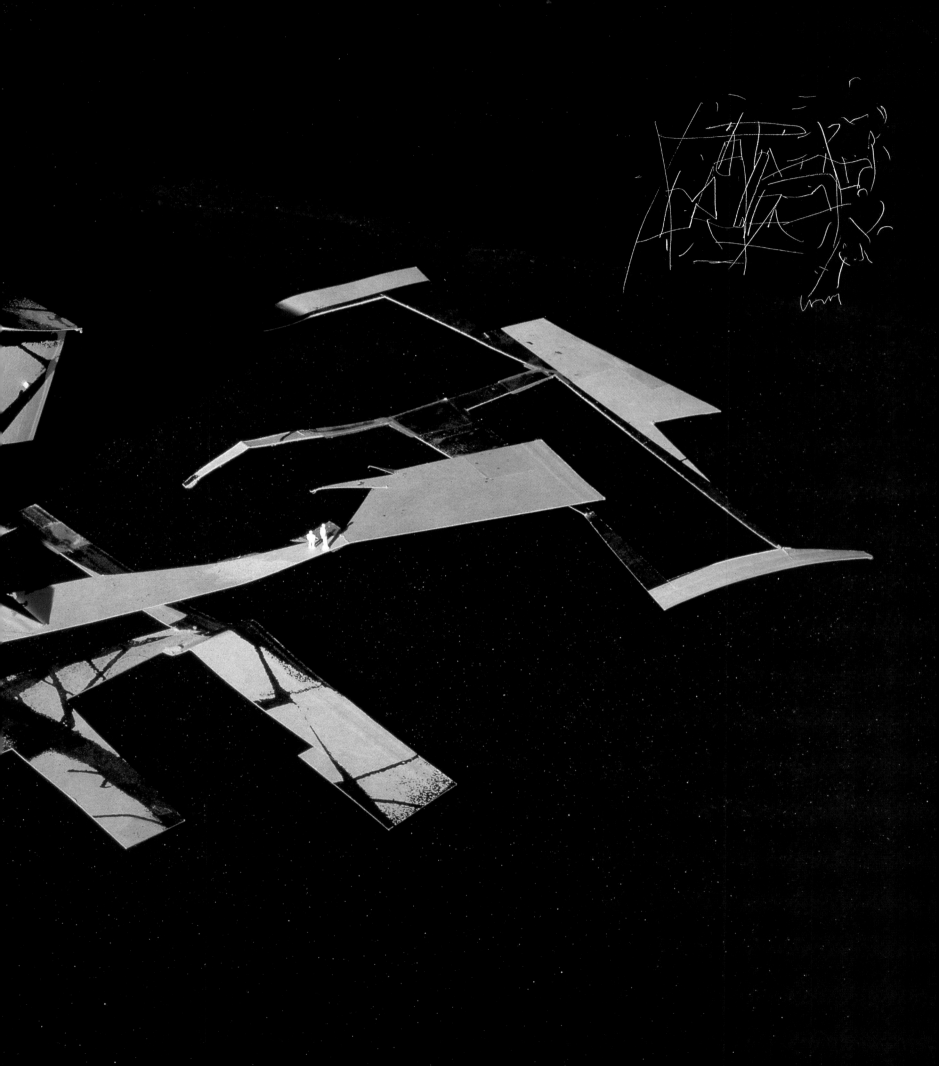

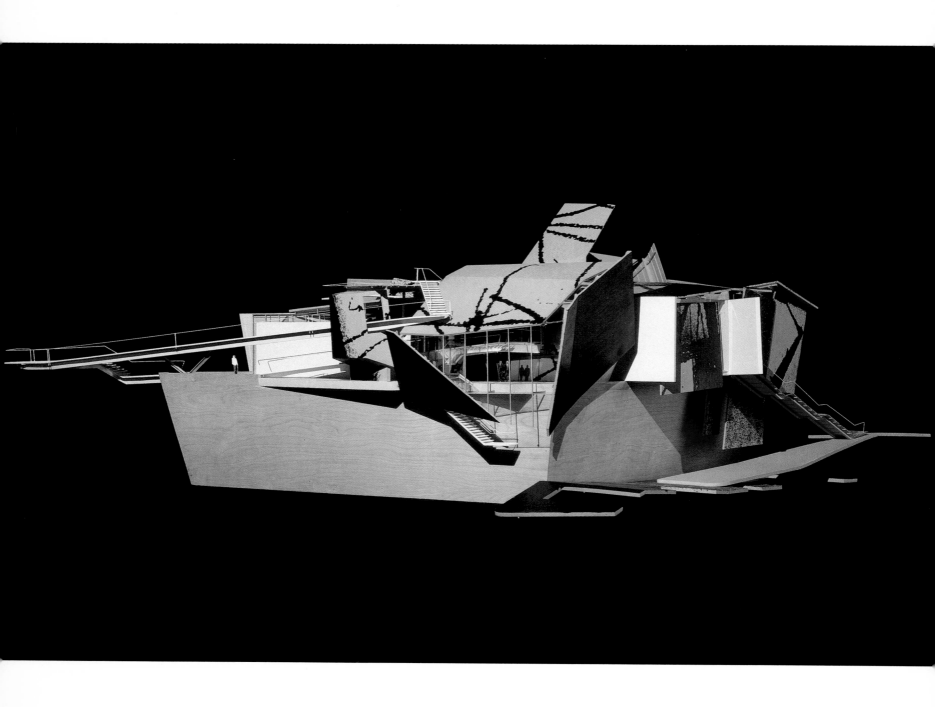

Peter Eisenman

The Wexner Center for the Visual Arts, Ohio State University, Columbus

As the first large commission by Peter Eisenman to be built since Houses I through X, the sheer size of the Wexner Center reveals more about his theories than any previous project could. His intentional intervention between Weigal Hall and the Mershon Auditorium at Ohio State University serves as an important diagonal link between far-flung parts of the campus, and is the most literal translation of 'in-betweenness' that has yet to surface. In tracking the influences on his work, critic Diane Ghirardo has noted that:

> Eisenman has long employed a compositional strategy for which he is greatly indebted to Italian architect Giuseppe Terragni, in which cubes are rotated, pulled apart, gridded, transformed, and mathematical relationships are elaborated and calibrated in highly structured, regulated ways.

At Ohio State, this technique becomes especially dominant in the structural grid that serves as a veil covering a complex series of interior spaces, successfully screening each of them from view. At ground level, sequential galleries are strung out from one end of the spine to the other, recalling a similar tactic by Philip Johnson in the Muhlenberg College Art Gallery in Pennsylvania, where triangular exhibition spaces are less successfully attached to both sides of a central, processional way. It is this level at Wexner that is most identifiable as a museum in the traditional sense, in spite of the functional compromises that are made to adjust each space to the angular axis running through it.

This series of spaces, which are consistently wedge-shaped because of their divergence with the orthogonal grid of the pre-existent buildings on either side of them, use the structures that define them as a back-wall, and typically have glass running along the opposite side, facing the spine. Because of this, these galleries frequently have very little wall space of the kind typically found elsewhere, with more natural light than usual, lending themselves to the installation of panels or the use of the floor area only. Additional gallery space in the basement, while limited in size, is much

less restricted and the remainder of the Center is made up of libraries, laboratories, classrooms, a theatre and storage.

As in Eisenman's earlier work, the structural grid tends to dominate space rather than define it, creating areas that are unprecedented in this typology, and which also require a novel approach in the design of the exhibits placed in them.

In contrast to the diaphanous and repetitive quality of the grid that is used to create the spine, the reconstruction of an Armory tower that once stood on the site stands out as a solid anchor for the white frame extending from it. In his unrealised scheme for Parc la Villette, Eisenman proposed a similar reinterpretation of the Parisian Wall, which also served as a visual foil for the overlapping grids that he proposed there. In each case, these regenerated forms are reminders of the Derridean concept of a palimpsest, in which nothing is produced *de novo*. The pivotal

purpose of the tower, which is also cleft in two in simulation of the division connected to it, becomes more evident when seen in section. From this vertical line the grid gradually slopes upwards to produce an elongated composition with fine balance. In spite of all his protestations against functionalism, the skill seen in this section, as well as the competence of the detailing throughout the museum, show Eisenman to be a consummate professional. In projects that have followed the Wexner Center, such as the Biocentrum and Carnegie Mellon, such considerations have developed further, leading to speculation that the opportunity to build larger buildings may eventually bring about a necessary compromise between theory and practice.

BELOW: Preliminary sketch of overall scheme
PAGE 50: Combination drawing showing perspective of main walkway, plan and elevation
PAGE 51: Combination drawing showing front elevation with interlocking walkway, plan and axonometric

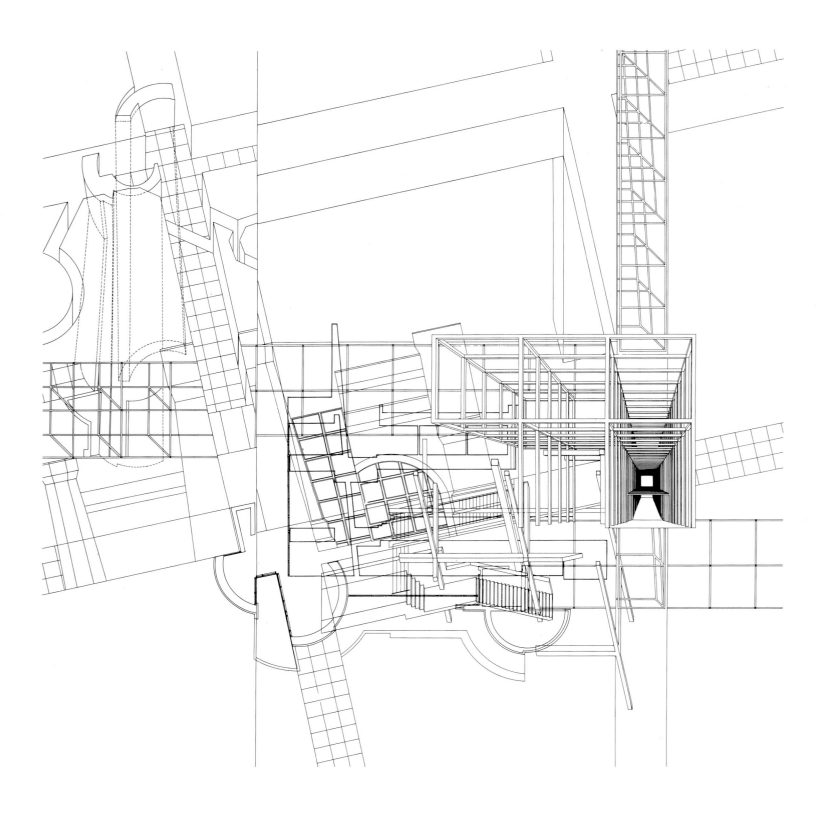

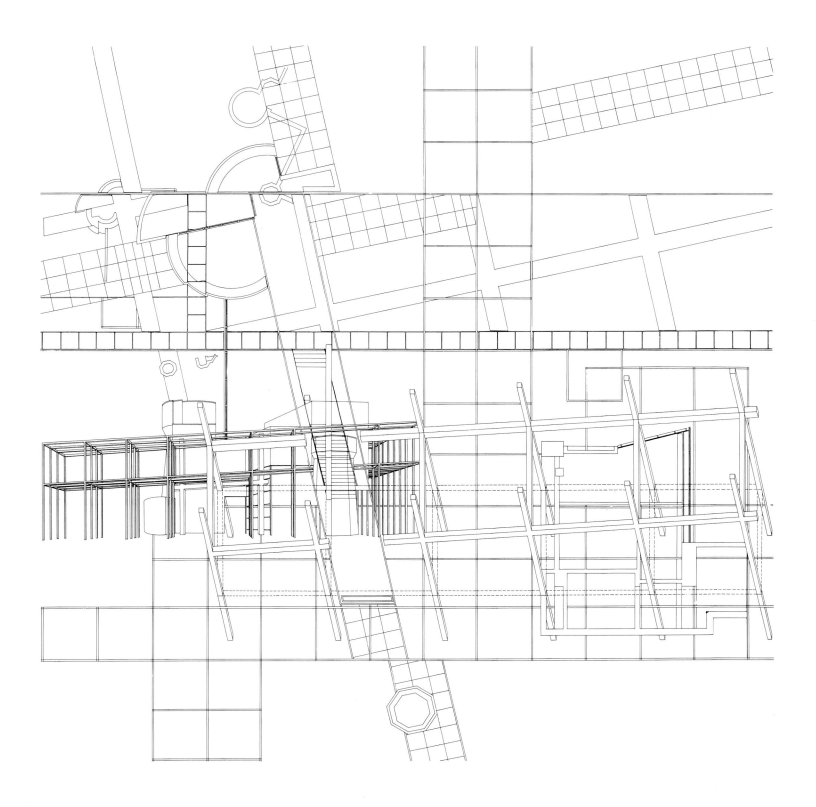

Evans and Shalev

The Tate Gallery at St Ives, Cornwall

The Tate in St Ives is decidedly aligned with that faction of international museums which have been intentionally designed to contribute to their surroundings as well as providing a suitable interior environment for display. The Gallery has a look of inevitability about it achieved through the painstaking efforts of its architects, in their belief that the works of art exhibited there, which have mainly been created locally, are best appreciated when viewed against their local context. As with many such integrally related installations, such as Stirling's Stuttgart Staatsgalerie and Meier's Museum for the Decorative Arts, the building itself becomes an exhibit, and in this particular instance the architects have perfectly balanced their awareness of functional requirements with the sculptural sensibilities necessary to make their building fit into the existing architectural texture around Porthmeor Beach, while still being distinctive enough to attract curious visitors to it. The result is a structure that seems to cascade down its steeply sloping site, effortlessly accommodating the 12 metre drop with a series of four basic levels that become progressively more private as they step from the beach up the hill. As the architects Eldred Evans and David Shalev have described the scheme:

> The gallery is designed to show works of art in the surroundings and atmosphere in which they were created. It relates to the work it exhibits in that both are inspired by St Ives. Designed on four floors and comprising a number of studio-like daylit rooms, the gallery is perched on top of a sheer wall facing the bay . . . The building is entered from below. The approach to the entrance from Beach Road is via the loggia: a small amphitheatrical space which forms, once in the building, a window onto the Atlantic Ocean. The art gallery itself is on the second floor, where it occupies the length and breadth of the site. Five toplit exhibition rooms are arranged in a simple sequence around a secret courtyard – which is discovered at the end of the journey. Once on the main gallery level, the visitor follows a route

> through rooms of differing scale, proportions and light. Sparse in detail with silent floors and softly lit, the spaces allow the exhibits to come into their own . . . Four of the rooms are for paintings, each with its own distinct character. The first low and elongated space lends itself to an introduction to the St Ives School. The second room, circular and hugging the loggia, is predominantly for sculpture and ceramics – overlooking the sea, it is the window of the building . . . The route continues through the three main painting rooms with increasing height and light . . . From the outset, we intended art, building, town and nature to form part of one experience.

The final arrangement of interior spaces in enfilade, with doors positioned off-centre to increase hanging space, is the result of this clearly articulated concept, intentionally sequential to allow the story of the St Ives School to unfold.

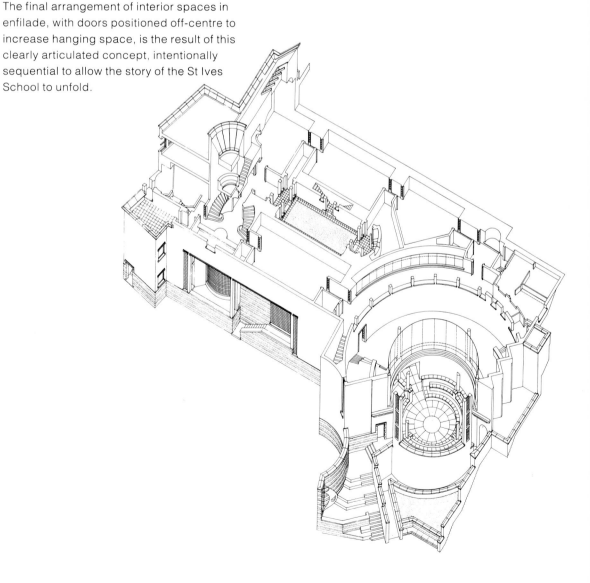

BELOW: Cutaway axonometric
PAGE 57 FROM ABOVE: Front elevation; longitudinal section showing entrance

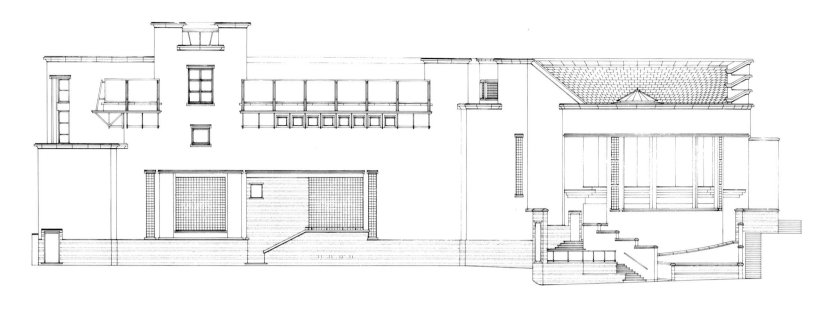

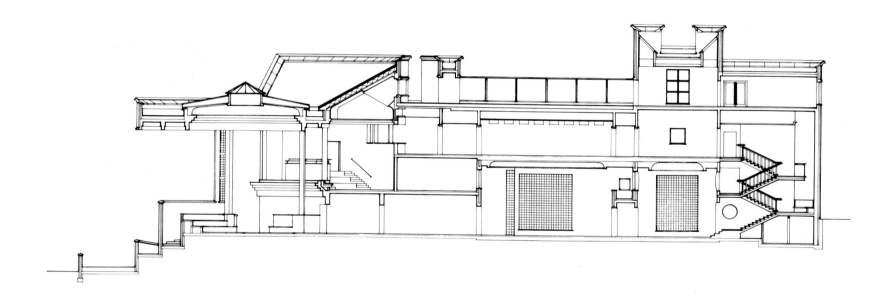

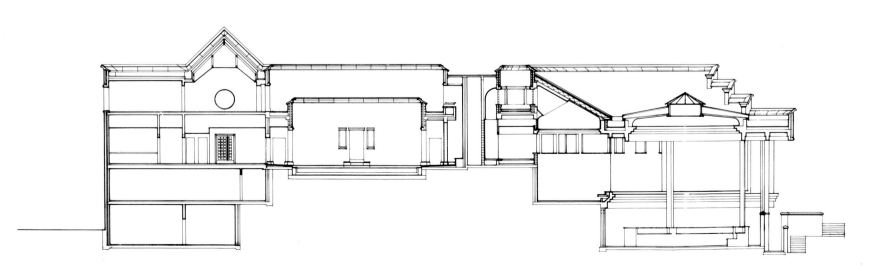

Norman Foster

Carré d'Art, Nîmes France

Located on a highly visible and historically sensitive site facing the Augustan temple known as the Maison Carrée, which dates from about 20 BC, this museum is the result of a limited international competition held in 1984, which Norman Foster won with his sensitive response to this important landmark, the traditional fabric of the city, the climatic extremes of the region and the demands of the brief.

Half of the nine-storey structure is built below ground to allow it to conform to the height of the buildings around it. The art galleries are located at the top, in order to use natural light, and the library occupies the floors immediately above and below ground level so that it is readily accessible from the street. Additional levels below ground accommodate cinema, auditorium and conference facilities, and are also used for storage. To allow light to penetrate down into the lower levels, where appropriate, a five-storey high internal courtyard has been used, which contains a glass staircase and glazed hydraulic lifts that become sculptural objects in their own right, and are reminiscent of a similar approach taken by Foster Associates in the interstitial space of the Sackler Gallery.

The basic materials used in the building are an *in-situ* concrete frame, which is left exposed, stainless steel, stone and either translucent or opaque glass, which contrast dramatically with the virtually intact Roman ruin nearby from which the museum takes its name. Characteristically, Norman Foster has chosen a design direction which is respectful to surrounding context, and so is at variance with the position typically taken by others in the hi-tech group, and yet is undeniably representative of that philosophy, to the extent that he utilises the latest technological advances available to him. This dichotomy, evident throughout his oeuvre, is what makes it personal and individual, rather than being the predictable result of predetermined rules. For this reason, against all odds, the Carré d'Art seems curiously at home in its surroundings, fulfilling the Miesian intention of classical compatibility.

*FROM ABOVE: Cross section; east elevation
PAGE 60 BELOW: Upper médiathèque plan
PAGE 61 BELOW: Entrance level plan
PAGE 63 FROM ABOVE: Sketch elevation;
longitudinal section*

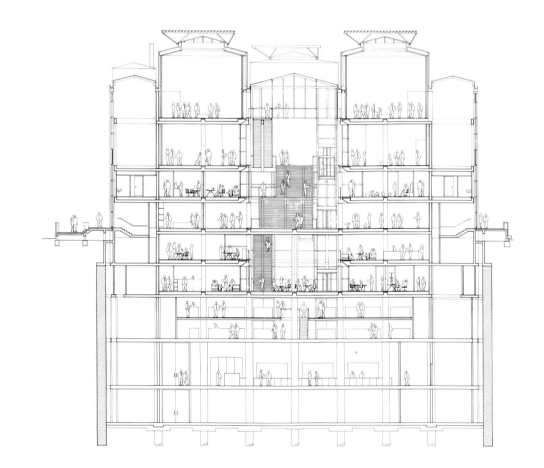

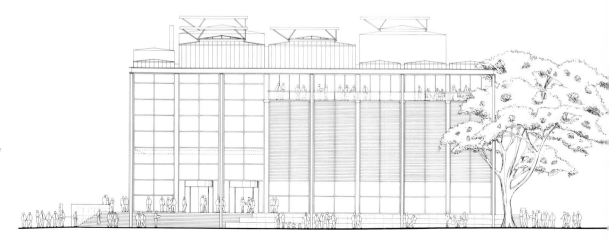

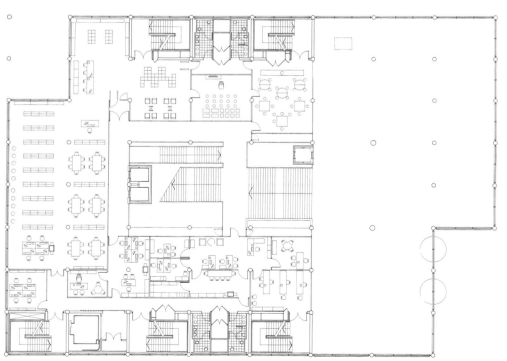

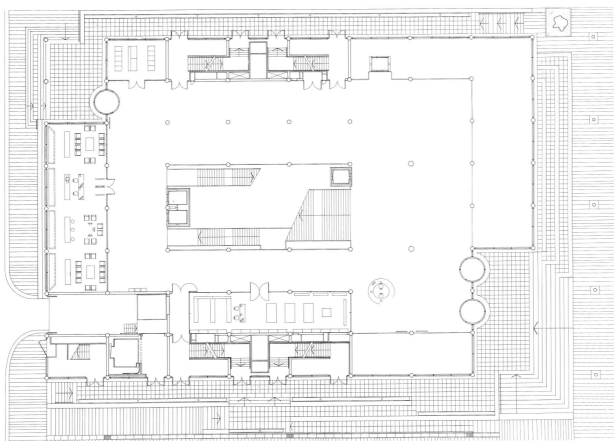

61

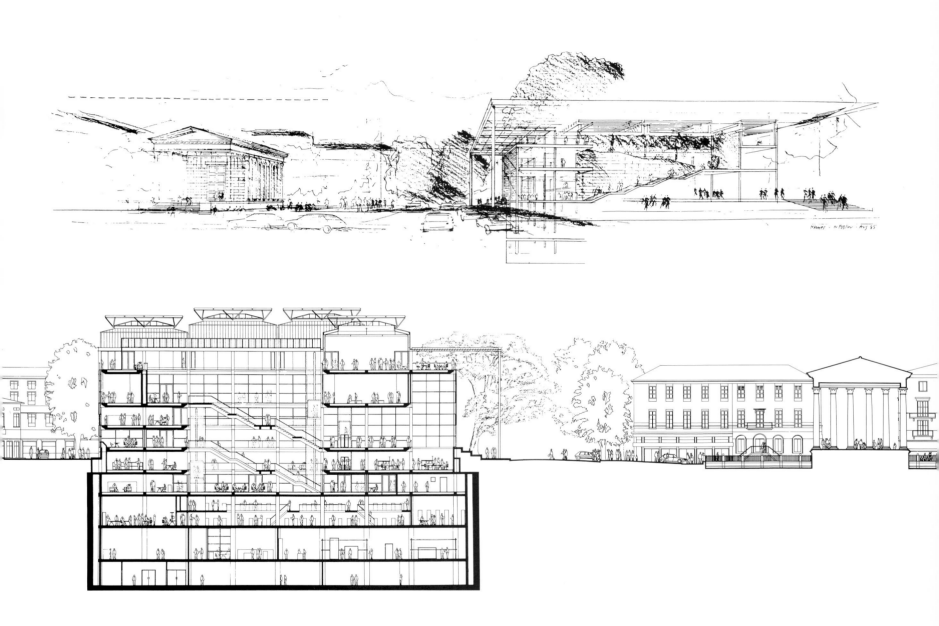

Norman Foster

The Sackler Galleries at the Royal Academy of Arts, London

With characteristic directness Sir Norman Foster has categorised the complex task of converting the Diploma Galleries at the Royal Academy as having been one of 'quantifying functions through the use of natural light'. In a masterstroke, negative space has been turned into a solution for chronic problems of inadequate servicing and poor access, and in the process, the facade of Burlington house, which was built in 1660 and redesigned by Samuel Ware in the early part of the nineteenth century, has now been revealed after having been hidden from view for over one hundred years. The ingenious scheme by Foster Associates revolves around a new circulation system, which was made urgently necessary by the growing number of visitors to major exhibitions at the Royal Academy, and began with the removal of a rather mundane Victorian staircase that had previously cut through the eighteenth-century Private Rooms. This has been replaced by a new stair, located in the space between the Diploma Galleries and Burlington House, as well as a glass lift that is an *objet d'art* in its own right. The new lift and stair which have made this transformation possible, are even more remarkable in that they are hidden from view when coming in from the main entrance hall.

In the ongoing debate that continues to occupy museum curators, on the issue of whether architecture should provide a neutral backdrop against which art itself takes precedence, or become a part of the exhibition itself, the Sackler Galleries have provided convincing evidence that the latter approach can work extremely well. Because of the close juxtaposition between the elements that Foster has added and the exhibitions in the galleries themselves, and the renewed visibility of the Burlington House facade, he has treated the lift, stair and wall with scrupulous attention to detail, playing off beige stone against shining glass and steel in a way that heightens the contrast between the old and the new. Architectural elements that have only had utilitarian connotations in the past here become the equal of the painting and sculpture around them, bringing other recent examples of this

approach, such as Stirling's Staatsgalerie in Stuttgart, to mind. At Stuttgart Stirling has shown a similar attitude toward the design of a freestanding lift that is located in the reception area of the Museum, which is obviously meant to be read as a sculptural object defined by the skylight above it. Elaborate sketches of this lift and canopies for all of the doorways have shown it to be part of a family of assemblages, rendered in De Stijl colours, that are used to glorify circulation in the same way that Foster does in the Sackler Galleries.

The analogy continues in that Stirling intentionally juxtaposes old and new, and presents the past as an artefact in much the same way that the walls and windows of Burlington House are put on display by Foster, as if, in each case, an architect who is best known for his skill in the use of the products of the technological age, has increasingly recognised the need to relate to history. The high-tech quotes that Stirling makes at Stuttgart, however, have been shown to be self-referential, while the surgically precise detailing of the Sackler is deadly serious, avoiding such subtlety. This gives it a grandeur and gravity that is absent in its German counterpart. By balancing such rational attention to detail with subjective intuition, Foster Associates, in conjunction with the Royal Academy and patrons Arthur and Jill Sackler, have managed to breathe new life into one of London's most important public buildings, and have done so in a way that has discreetly put architecture on display as well.

PAGE 66 BELOW: Cutaway axonometric
PAGE 67 BELOW: Longitudinal section

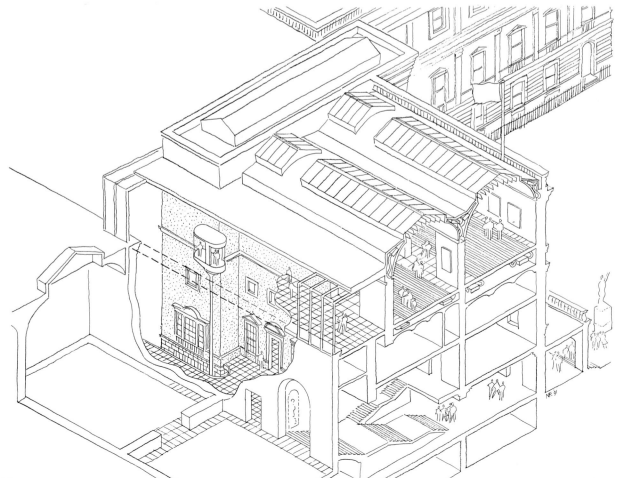

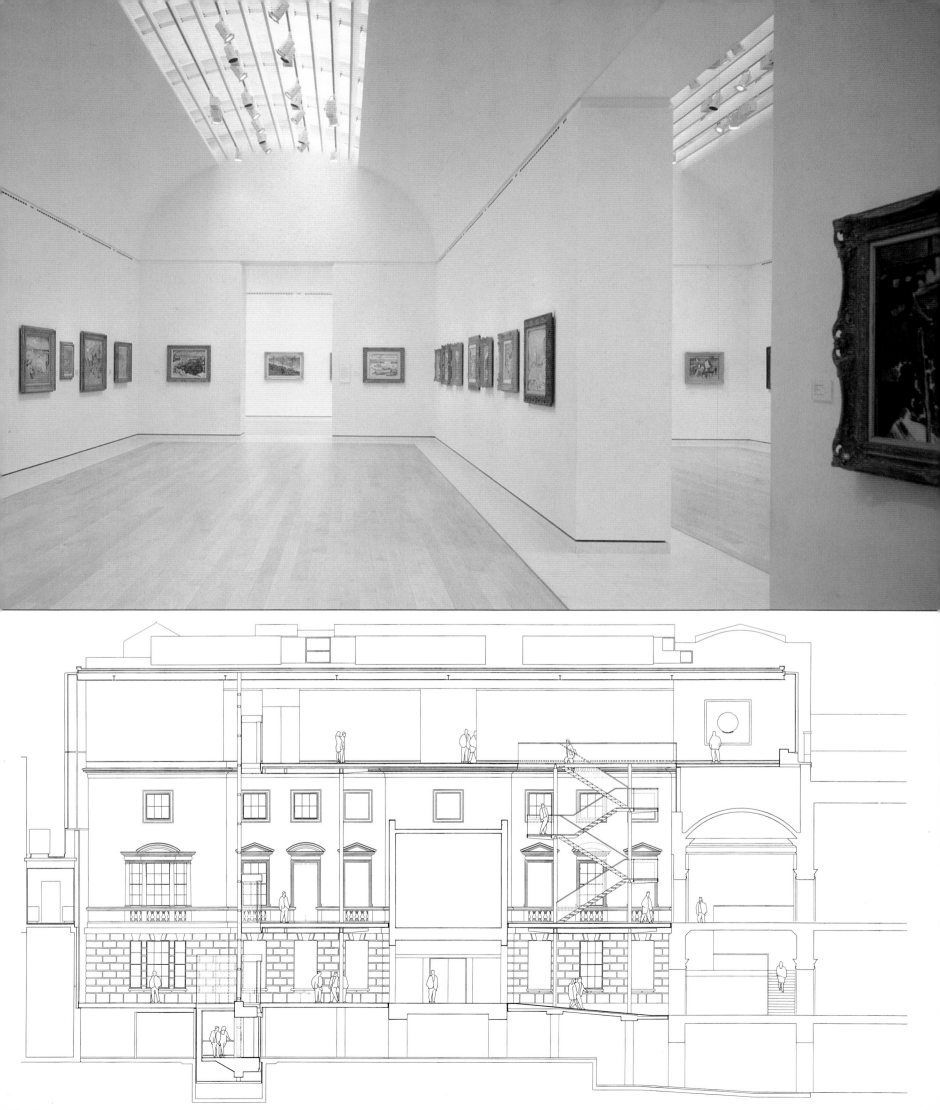

Norman Foster

The Crescent Wing of the Sainsbury Centre, Norwich

It is difficult to think of Foster's revolutionary Sainsbury Centre as a listed building, but such is the nature of our fast-paced, pluralistic world that this breakthrough in museum design is now a historical landmark. The innovative, strategic decisions made in this instance – for a flexible, mechanically climate-controlled and structurally unimpaired space, made possible by clear span trusses and secure underground storage – have now passed into legend, making this a model for many new museums.

The Crescent Wing, recently added to it, indicates the extent to which that model has become institutionalised, since the philosophy behind the two is radically divergent. The Crescent Wing gives definitive proof that Norman Foster is an anomaly within the hi-tech tradition because of his consistent awareness of context. The Sainsbury Centre, which opened in 1977, was conceived to be the ultimately flexible building, with open ends that imply unrestricted extension along its north-south axis. In the design of this extension which is nearly 75 per cent as large as its parent, Foster has indicated that the view from the Sainsbury Centre to a lake nearby is a connection which should remain 'sacred and unchanged' leading him to take a different direction in this addition. By taking advantage of a natural change in level between the Centre and the lake, he has inserted the extension into a sweeping embankment, making it an unobtrusive and yet elegant solution to the expanding needs of the museum. In addition to exhibition space, the Crescent Wing also has a range of specialised areas, which are connected to the Centre by a ramp leading from the main gallery entrance. The major attraction in the new wing is the Reserve Collection, which allows for the exhibition of pieces from the Robert and Lisa Sainsbury Collection which it has not been possible to display in the past due to a lack of space. Combining the latest concepts of 'dense storage', public access and lighting technology, the Reserve Collection Display is similar in many ways to the Henry R Luce Study Center at the Metropolitan Museum of Art in New York, which was designed by the same consultant. The Crescent Wing also houses the lower gallery, which functions as both an environmentally controlled exhibition space, specifically intended for graphics and sensitive works of art, as well as a conference room. A light slot running along one of its curved walls allows controlled illumination to be used, and the ceiling has a lighting system that is completely recessed and fully flexible. Other facilities in the new wing include a conservation laboratory, photographic studio, large art handling and workshop areas, offices for the staff of both the Sainsbury Centre and the Sainsbury Research Unit for the arts of Africa, Oceania and the Americas, and an art transit room.

Appearing as a shimmering scythe of glass during the day when seen from the university, the Crescent Wing changes character completely at night, when its reflection glows in the water. In this respect it is similar to the Willis Faber building as well as the Carré d'Art in Nîmes in its ability to transform itself from a self-effacing good neighbour to a transparent and structurally explicit shell after the sun goes down, and also shares their obvious response to energy related concerns.

The earth on its roof acts as a particularly effective buffer to temperature swings, adding another layer of protection to the environmentally sensitive conditions inside. The Crescent Wing has been called 'an art gallery for the 21st century', but as Norman Foster himself has observed, some aspects of human ingenuity never change, and this addition is evidence of that.

Frank Gehry

Frederick R Weisman Art and Teaching Museum, University of Minnesota

Bounded by the Washington Avenue Bridge to the north, Coffman Memorial Plaza to the east, Comstock Hall to the south and East River Road to the west, the site of the museum overlooks the Mississippi River and the Minneapolis skyline beyond. Vehicular access to the new 120-car parking ramp, as well as the loading facilities is restricted to East River Road at the lower level, while the main museum level is entered from a proposed pedestrian bridge/walkway that connects Washington Avenue Bridge with Coffman Memorial Plaza. The integration of this new pedestrian bridge into the architectural composition emphasises the museum as something inseparable from the campus experience, and it is hoped that there will be an increased awareness of the University Art and Teaching Museum's collection and resources through its welcoming architectural presence and strategic location.

The gallery spaces on the main museum level, including the Weisman Collection, are articulated as a large rectangular volume at the southeast corner. The sales shop, a rental gallery, the registrar and print study room are also located on this level, with frontage along the pedestrian bridge/walkway connection. Large picture windows provide pedestrian traffic with views into these spaces through the interior street to the galleries beyond. Also accessible from the pedestrian bridge/walkway is the main entry to the museum and an airlock with the elevator lobby that enables the main museum level to operate independently from the rest of the building. At the centre of this level is an auditorium for audio-visual presentations. Movable partitions on its west wall enable the auditorium to be open to the adjacent museum lobby for special receptions and events. Consequently, the museum lobby wraps around the auditorium to allow continuous circulation and entry to the south side of the galleries and views out over the Mississippi River.

The programme of the museum is distributed on four levels in response to the dual access to the site. On the lowest level are the freight elevator, art storage spaces,

a frame shop and the mechanical/electrical rooms. The next level is occupied by a carpentry shop and non-art storage area which are accessible from the freight and passenger elevators as well as from the intermediate parking levels. The top level of the museum houses administrative offices and the mechanical/ electrical space for the galleries.

From the west, the museum facade is articulated in a faceted manner to capture views up and down the river. A tower-like structure rises from the loading area off East River Road and anchors the undulating geometry of the elevation at the southwest corner. Inside the tower, offices for the technical director, a seminar room and the museum director's office stack on top of each other to further take advantage of the spectacular views from the site.

In response to the university context, brick with butted joints will be used as the exterior finish for the gallery volume and the parking ramp. However, the north elevation along the proposed pedestrian bridge, the projecting museum lobby and the entire west elevation will be finished in sandblasted stainless steel.

Natural light through a linear monumental skylight is introduced to reinforce the

spatial connection between the museum lobby and the galleries. Two sculptural skylights provide additional natural light at transition points between galleries. In addition, a combination of cove lighting, a monopoint grid and a floor light system are integrated into the galleries to give maximum flexibility for different lighting needs.

BELOW : Conceptual sketch
PAGE 77 FROM ABOVE : Plan of main museum level; longitudinal section; north elevation

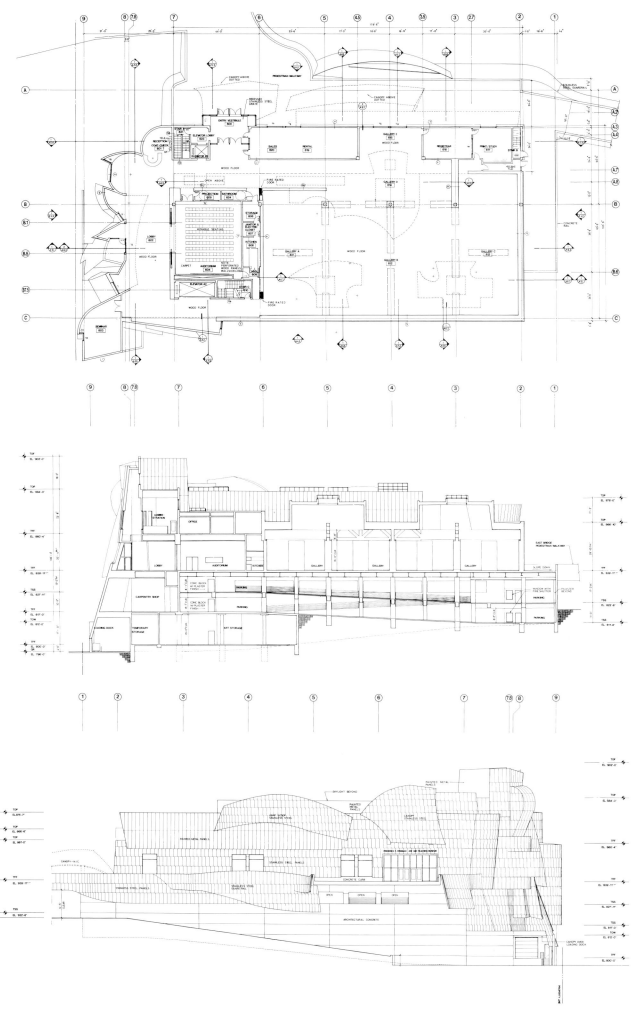

Frank Gehry

Vitra International Furniture & Design Museum, Weil am Rhein, Germany

In addition to the design museum which is its central focus, Vitra International consists of an assembly plant, which includes offices and a distribution area, on a rural site near the French and Swiss borders. The rectangular factory component of the project is placed in such a way as to provide a background for the museum, as seen from the main road which passes to the north. This awareness of the view from the road is critical to an appreciation of Gehry's intentions; the groupings are meant to read in a layered way when seen at high speed from either direction.

As in the Chiat/Day/Mojo Offices in Santa Monica, which is also a composite, car-related grouping, Claes Oldenburg and Coosje van Bruggen have contributed a sculpture which in this case is entitled *Tool Gate*. It contributes to the entire panoply and indicates Gehry's continued identification with artists in his work. Ramps and entrance canopies flank the factory facade, creating expressionistic brackets for the museum, and extending the horizontal visual field of the elevation.

The Design Museum houses the owner's collection of chairs that date from the nineteenth century to the present, as well as a library of manufacturers' catalogues. Rolf Fehlbaum, president of the Vitra Group, has a passion for industrial design, and the museum contains pieces by Charles Eames, George Nelson, Adolph Loos, Gerrit Rietveld, Marcel Breuer, Le Corbusier, Frank Lloyd Wright, Jean Prouvé, Gio Ponti, Ettore Sottsass and Gehry himself, who is equally well known for furniture design.

This is Gehry's first major European building, marking a turning point in his career as an international, rather than just a regional figure. While the collision of the forms used is familiar, there is a marked difference in his use of materials here, which has been expanded upon in other large institutional projects, such as the Disney Concert Hall in Los Angeles. The smoothly plastered masonry used on Vitra with titanium zinc roofing further accentuates the formal massing, rather than calling attention to the singularity of the materials themselves. The galleries are treated as interpenetrating, connecting volumes, with a continuity that allows exhibitions to communicate between one space and another; and yet each has a different character as far as the quality of natural light, volume, scale and surface area are concerned, with skylights positioned to bounce and diffuse natural light. In spite of this continuity, each gallery is designed to be secured separately.

The master plan includes additional galleries that will be added in the future, to the west side of the entrance road.

BELOW: Cross section
PAGE 80: Elevation
PAGE 81: End elevation

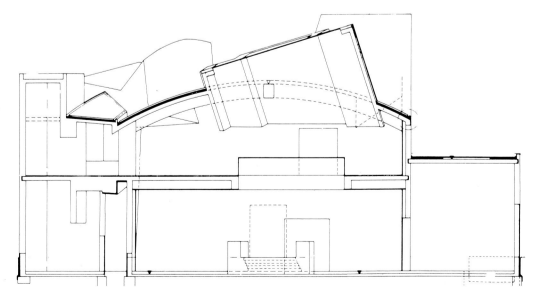

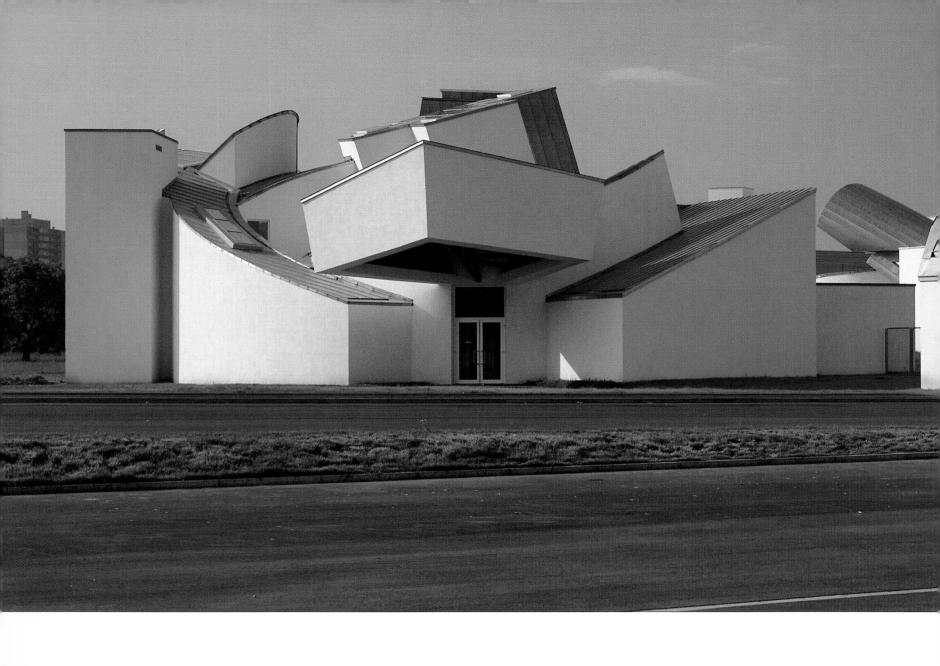

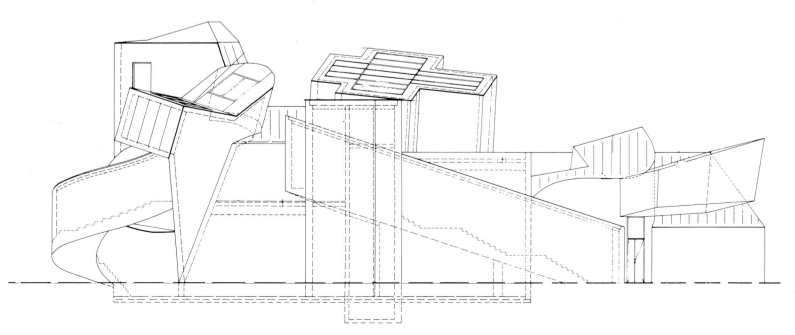

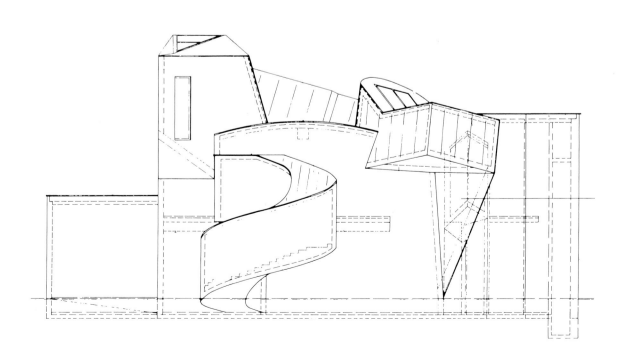

Michael Graves

Emory University Museum of Art and Archaeology, Atlanta, Georgia

In the early 1980s Michael Graves began this project by planning the renovation of one of the oldest buildings on the Emory University campus: a three-storey marble clad structure, the Michael C Carlos Hall, designed in 1916 by a famous Pittsburgh architect, Henry Hornbostel. Originally built as a law school, the building is now listed on the National Register of Historic Places. The renovation programme outlined by Graves had two main components: the Museum of Art and Archaeology, and the teaching spaces and faculty offices for the Departments of Art History and Anthropology. Due to a difference in floor levels between the two sides of the building, the museum is organised on one side and the departmental offices and class rooms on the other. Graves designed special exhibition cases and *vitrines* for the permanent collection as part of this reorganisation, and stencils of the plans of historical structures, such as the Parthenon and the Temple of Rameses II, placed on the floor near the collections they are related to, help to reinforce their themes, just as the floors of Henry Hornbostel's Architecture Building at Carnegie Mellon University are also inlaid with plans of significant historical monuments.

Following this renovation, Graves was also commissioned to design a 35,000 square foot addition to the museum, which was completed in the spring of 1993. The new building contains galleries for the archaeological collection, temporary exhibitions, the permanent collection and works on paper, as well as staff offices, museum support work spaces, and a reception hall serving the university. Located on the cross-axis of the university quadrangle, the new museum building was approached as being a primary landmark on the campus and has succeeded in becoming one.

RIGHT: Sketch view of gallery
PAGE 84 BELOW: First floor plan with the Museum of Art and Archaeology to the left of the vestibule and the Department of Anthropology to the right
PAGE 85 BELOW: Second floor plan with the Museum of Art and Archaeology to the left and the Department of Art History to the right

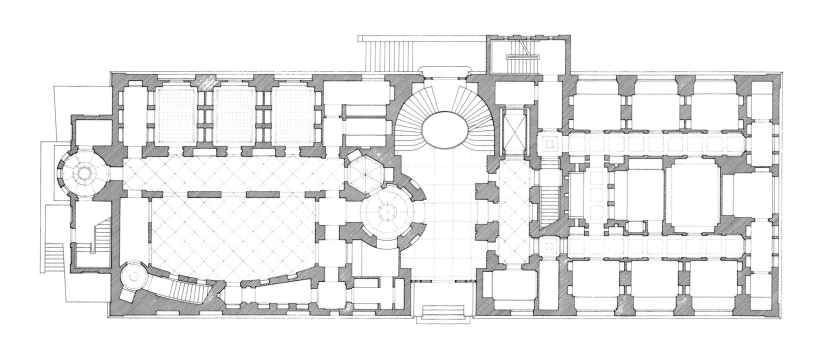

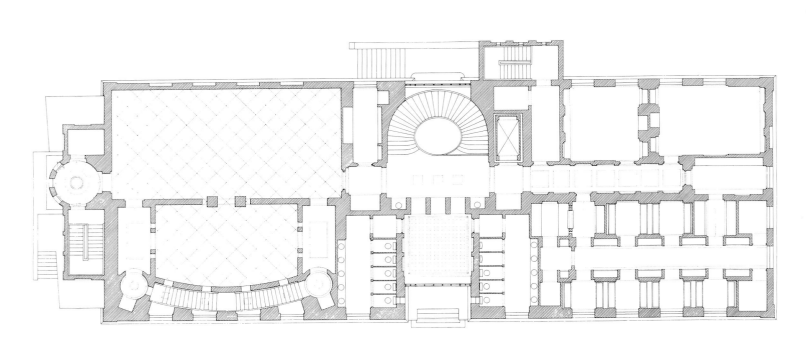

Michael Graves

Newark Museum, New Jersey

The renovation of the Newark Museum includes new public facilities and the expansion of support areas in all four of the museum's main buildings. Acquisition of an adjacent YWCA building in 1982 allowed the Museum to be enlarged and improved. The main idea of Graves' design was to reorganise the interiors to allow visitors to orient themselves more easily in the expanding complex. This is achieved by the introduction of three large skylit courts, joined together by passages which serve as galleries. The existing museum court acts as the centre of this sequence, while a new, three-storey sculpture garden connects the main museum, north wing and Ballantine House. The sculpture court also serves as the entrance to new exhibition galleries in the north wing. The old YWCA building has now been converted into the south wing of the museum, and has had a lobby and new side entry incorporated into it, as well as offices, a library, a junior museum for the education department, an arts workshop, and the lending collections as well as a 300-seat auditorium in what was previously a gymnasium. A 'mini-zoo' in this wing is also indicative of the changes taking place in museums today in which functions previously felt to be incompatible with the rarefied aesthetic experience have now been incorporated in the transition from 'temple of art' to entertaining palace of fun. The new side entry leads visitors down to the auditorium and up to the junior museum and other activities in the education department.

The north wing of the museum has been expanded to facilitate the exhibition of the permanent collection in a more appropriately scaled space. Exhibitions of American painting and sculpture are located on the first two floors, Oriental art on the third floor, and decorative arts in the connection to Ballantine House. The ethnology and science collections remain on the second and third floors of the original museum building.

RIGHT: Addition building and sculpture court
OPPOSITE: Elevation of garden entrance
PAGE 88 FROM ABOVE TO BELOW: Section showing garden entrance facade; elevation of addition building facade; basement plan; section showing entrance gallery
PAGE 89: Axonometric of site

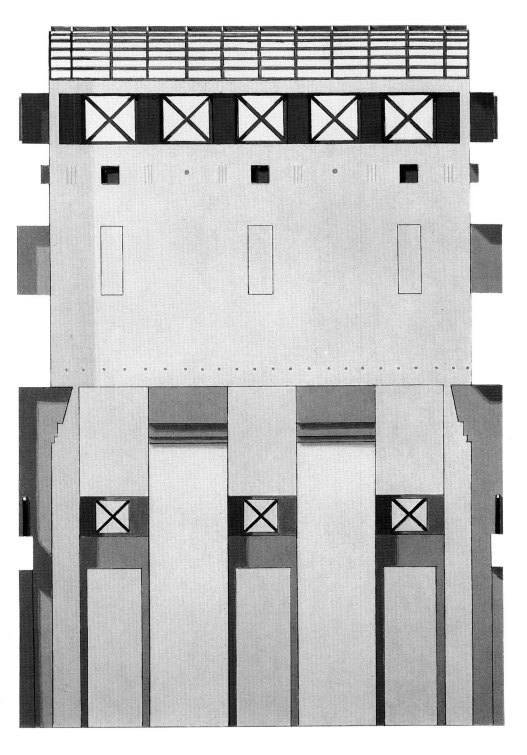

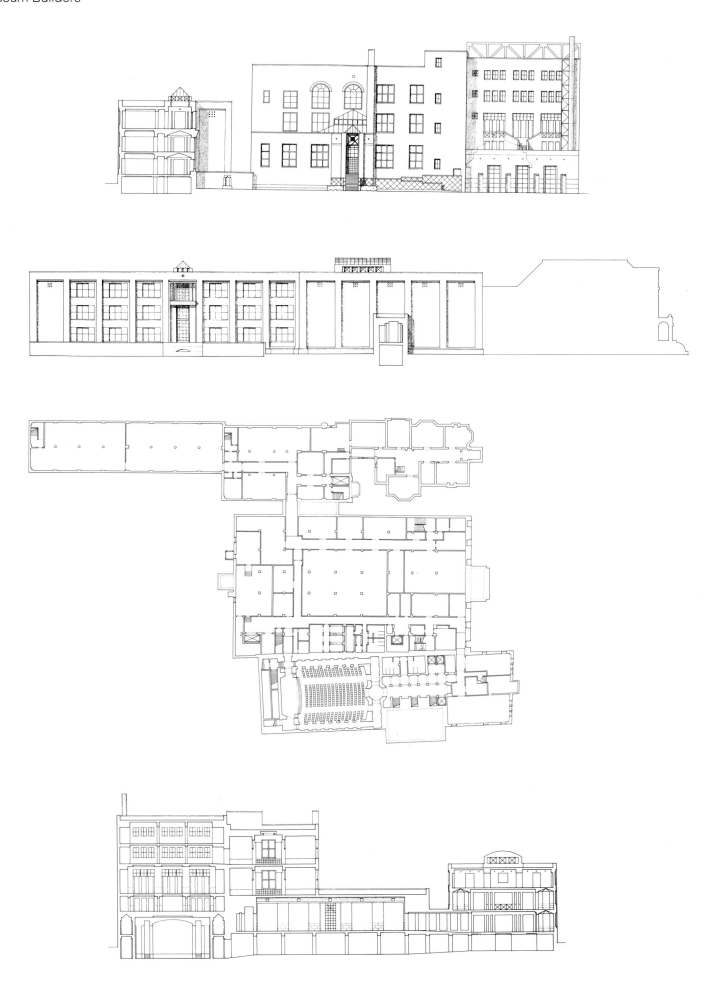

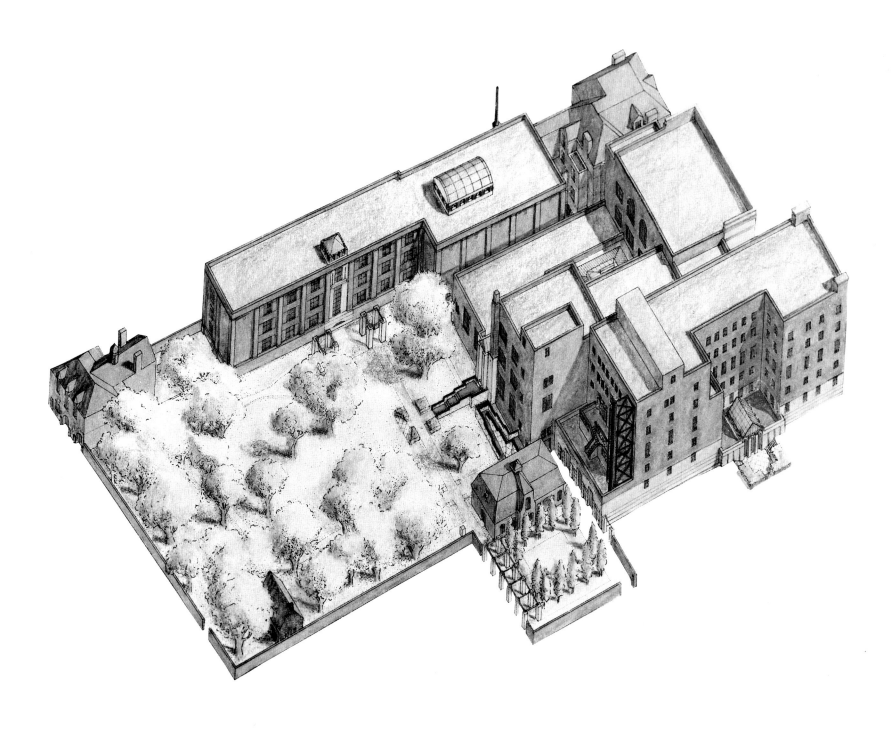

Gwathmey Siegel

Renovation and Extension of the Guggenheim Museum, New York

The addition, renovation, restoration and completion of Frank Lloyd Wright's building into a consummate 21st-century museum proved both demanding and complex. The revelation of the entire original building for the first time and the completion of Wright's exterior and interior master plan realises and fulfils the promise of his fifty-year-old vision. The transformation and variations have emerged from the seminal concepts. One now experiences Wright from 'within' as well as from 'without'.

The seventh-floor ramp, completing the ascension and fulfilling the volumetric climax, has been opened for the first time to the public as a route to and from the addition. The renovation of the third and fourth floors of the monitor building as exhibition pavilions engaging the park gives the visitor a new sense of orientation as well as a connotative reference to Frank Lloyd Wright's architecture and nature. The new fifth-floor gallery sculpture roof reveals the building anew both in relation to Central Park, and to the new addition. The architects write of their work:

> We believe the addition both enriches and engages the original building in a perceptual and spatial dialogue which is both compelling and clarifying . . . The layering, the sense of exploration, the expectation and the aspirations are all fulfilled in a way which was nonexistent. The sense of spatial variation and reinforcement, of moving in and out of the original building . . . reinforces the 'idea' as well as the phenomenon of Wright's masterpiece. The new galleries have finally 'freed' the original building and the institution, affording a flexibility which never before existed. The manifestation is neither automatic nor obvious, rather an extended elaboration and dialogue with Wright and modern architecture. The large rotunda space is now the new courtyard for the whole. Retained in its pure vision as a compelling and unique volume, awaiting creative counterpoint and intervention.

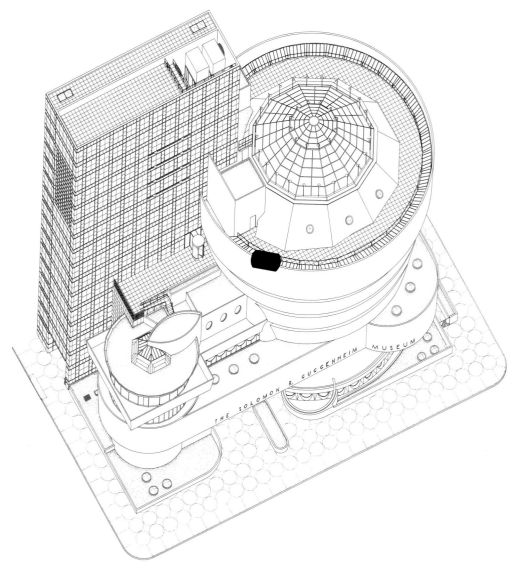

RIGHT: Axonometric

THE SOLOMON R. GUGGENHEIM MUSEUM

Hans Hollein

The Guggenheim Museum in Salzburg, Austria

The Guggenheim Museum represents one of those rare coincidences in which an architect and client are brought together through the mutual recognition of a similar vision. In 1989 the Mayor of Salzburg, on behalf of the Carolino Augusteum, commissioned an international competition in which Giancarlo de Carlo, Gerhard Garstenauer, Hans Hollein, Jean Nouvel and Paul Kleihaus were invited to submit schemes for a museum on the Mönchsberg mountain, directly related to the old town of Salzburg. Hollein's proposal, which was selected by the jury, seemed doomed by controversy and red tape because of its unconventional approach to an environmentally and contextually sensitive site, until Thomas Krens, the new director of the Guggenheim Foundation, was shown the plans and became interested in the project. Hollein's approach involves nothing less than carving away the Mönchsberg to incorporate the museum into the rock. The Gross Festspielhaus, as well as the Felsenreitschule both represent historical precedents for this approach, which has been expanded by Hollein to include a complex network of underground spaces sporadically lit by skylights reaching all the way up to the plateau which culminate in the expanding, dome covered spiral of 'the Sunk' where a natural declivity in the mountain now exists. Professor Karl Heinz Ritschel, editor-in-chief of *Salzburger Nachrichten* describes Hollein's approach:

> . . . this plan envisages an impressive entrance hall behind the Bürgerspital Building that elegantly incorporates (its) Gothic hall into the museum. He has created a structure of rooms in the rock . . . the natural depression on the Mönchsberg plateau behind the casino will be deeply excavated so that the 'Sunk' with its glass dome will be seen from the top as a fascinating rock architecture. Over a length of some 80 metres and a width of 20 metres on the Mönchsberg plateau there will be the daylight area of the museum and the dome . . .

The arrangement of spaces in the lower level plan is reminiscent of Hollein's prior designs for both the museum in Mönchengladbach and MOMA in Frankfurt, demonstrating the chequerboard compartmentalisation of the former, and the tendency to use the carefully choreographed sequences and gradually increasing scale of the latter. After entering the circular foyer with its adjoining, designer cafe and bookshop, visitors are presented with two options of procession; either through an arc of rectangular rooms to their right or a linear hallway opening up to their left, which both eventually lead to the Sunk. A labyrinth of square, interlocking galleries between these two pathways, which is accessible from each of them, continues the architect's exploration of a typological alternative to the enfilade of rooms. Skylights intelligently located mid-way along each of the two paths around this chequerboard help to alleviate their length, with one of them reflecting the curving narrow profiles of the alleys in the old city nearby.

The Sunk, which is the dramatic destination of each of these lower level routes into the museum from the old city, is also the circular, axial anchor for another grouping of galleries extending to the southeast, on the plateau above. Unlike their subterranean counterparts, these are then organised in a more conventional fashion, strung out along a sunken, glass covered spine that serves as the second entry foyer, from the top of the Mönchsberg. (The Sunk was designed before Thomas Krens became interested in the scheme).

The future of this audacious design now rests on a feasibility study, intended to answer technical concerns about geological stability, moisture problems, environmental impact analysis, economic benefits and costs to the city and client, and legal governance. When and if these questions can be answered to the satisfaction of all parties, a museum totally unlike any other may finally be built.

BELOW: Sketch of light shaft
PAGE 97 FROM ABOVE: Upper level plan showing the entrance from the top of the Mönchsberg plateau; early sketch of the project

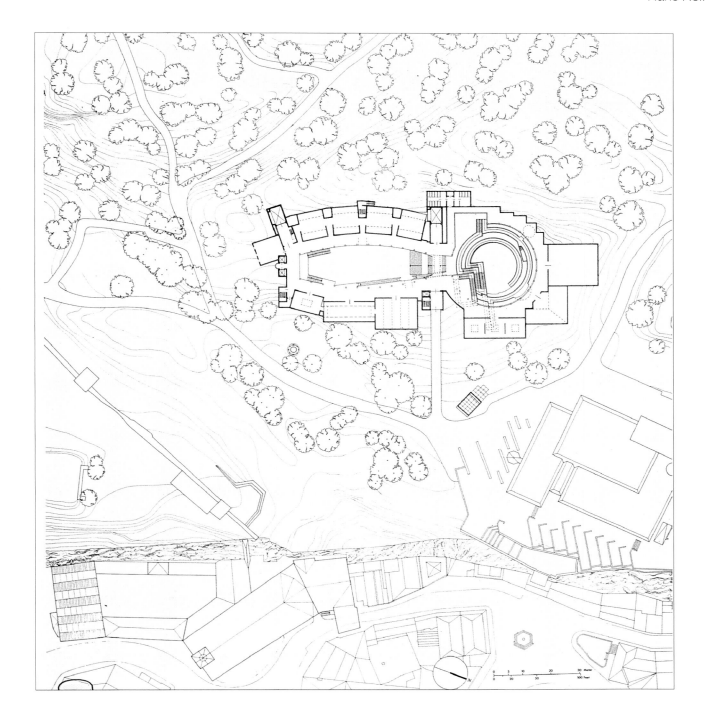

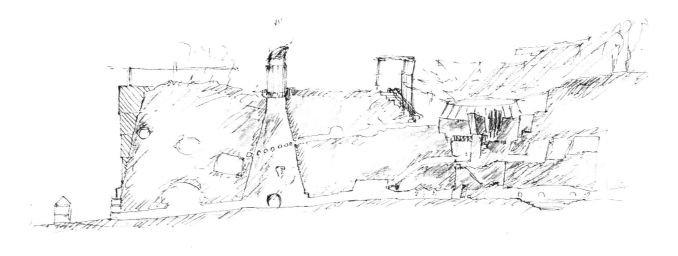

Arata Isozaki

Museum of Contemporary Art, Los Angeles

Taken in the context of previous museums designed by this architect, MOCA in Los Angeles represents a critical juncture, both as a synthesis of formal preoccupations seen elsewhere and as a determined effort to establish a new language. Isozaki's reliance on Platonic solids is still very much in evidence here, with the semicircular vaults that first surfaced in the Fujima Clubhouse and the Kitakyushu Central Library in the early seventies dominating the roof. The omnipresent cube, which can be traced in every one of his buildings from the Oita Prefectural Library of 1966 onwards, is also a major part of his formal vocabulary, as is the pyramid, which is used to light the galleries. While it would be easy to attach rationalistic motives to this choice of forms, or even to explain them away as purely aesthetic preferences which are consistently used in spite of functional prerequisites, the real reason behind their reappearance here is a bit more complex.

In an insightful analysis of the current direction that architecture is taking in his own country, Isozaki has identified three different attitudes stemming from the influence that culture should have on the building tradition. The first of these, which he equates with a revival of the Sukiya style, involves a transformation of historical forms from wood or stone to concrete, the second, which he believes was typified by his mentor Kenzo Tange, is the abstraction of such forms, which, while altered, are still recognisable, the third is an expansion of cultural concepts, such as Ma and the attempt to use them, rather than traditional typologies as the basis for a new physical expression. He has frequently said that his own tendency runs parallel to this third direction, but he constantly questions the relevance of the past as well as the validity of such concepts, which grew out of total isolation from the West, since this condition no longer applies. While working on the Gumma Prefectural Museum in the seventies he described how he suddenly realised that there was an element of architecture that had been completely absent from Japanese design throughout history, and that was design in three dimensions. As he

said, 'we have squares and circles, but no cubes and cylinders. It's very had to find such forms in Japan'. His determination to master these pure solids gradually led him to study Western architectural history, and he found a common and three-dimensional theme running through all periods.

MOCA, then, can profitably be interpreted as a significant step in Isozaki's continuous attempt to exercise what he feels to be a cultural restriction on understanding pure form. After the site for the museum was changed three times, and Isozaki's patience was stretched to breaking point, a central location in the middle of California Plaza, in the Bunker Hill section of Los Angeles, was finally selected. The museum today looks diminutive in comparison to the office towers, hotels, condominiums and housing blocks around it, but its small scale is partially due to the developer's intentional desire to maintain sight lines to the retail stores in the plaza behind it. Nearly 34,000 square feet of gallery space, as well as an auditorium, library, cafeteria and office space, along with the requisite workshop and storage areas, are all set into the vast parking levels of California Plaza, so that only the vaulted library, which acts as a gateway to the museum, and the pyramids that identify the galleries are visible from Grand Avenue. These are separated by an entry court which also provides for the outdoor exhibition of sculpture and eventually leads into the entrance lobby and galleries themselves. Computer aided studies of the most appropriate colours for the bold forms chosen for the museum originally showed a red base supporting cylinders, cubes and pyramids in green. This strong contrast, however, which would have been more effective in offsetting the diminutive scale of these forms was eventually toned down by the choice of dark red Indian sandstone for the base and copper sheathing for the vaults.

Since its completion, American architects have consistently selected MOCA as one of their top ten favourite buildings, and its forms are now in evidence in much of the new work of the Los Angeles school. In spite of its diminutive physical stature, it has

also provided a focal point of civic pride for a city that is slowly beginning to try to live up to its designation of 'cultural capital of the West Coast', and is tangible proof that Isozaki's history lessons have had a lasting civic effect.

Kisho Kurokawa

In an exhibition of Kisho Kurokawa's museums, held to coincide with his lecture at the Royal Academy of Arts in June 1993, he consistently described them in terms of three criteria: 'symbiosis with nature', 'abstract interrelationships' and 'asymmetry'. By doing so, he provided an important clue to his work, which, in spite of its highly contemporary aspect is in fact traditional to a surprising extent, considering his international reputation as an avant-garde catalyst for change. His close association with the Metabolist movement at the beginning of the sixties has done much to reinforce that general perception and yet, in his view, that initiative came about in reaction to, rather than in support of, changes then taking place in architecture. As he has described his intentions:

> In the thirty years since I first advocated metabolism, I have consistently emphasised the principle of life. The very choice of the term metabolism was an expression of this life principle. The concepts that I have presented with metabolism, such as intermediate zones, open structures and information are all also, by nature, life principles. And the principle of symbiosis is a philosophy of the life principle that encompasses everything from metabolism onwards.

To an extent not evident in any of the other architects' work presented here, each of the museums designed by Kurokawa is intended as an exploration of a certain facet of his own culture, what he refers to as 'the invisible tradition', related to the idea of renewal embodied in the Shinto Shrine at Ise. This dialogue remains regardless of location, as may be seen in the Musée de Louvain-la-Neuve, in Belgium, where the concept of free arrangement found in Japanese landscape design is used for the building forms. A forum, museum and hall are freely dispersed on the site in a way that allows each to have an individual identity, but still remain part of the grouping. The exterior wall of each space is intentionally different, being either solid concrete, transparent glass, or semi-transparent lattice, to make the variations more complex. The museum segment of the grouping has been designed to house comparative exhibitions of Eastern and Western art as well as those examining the role of technology in art. The dichotomy between East and West is most graphically expressed in the formal, arrow-like axis leading into the centre of the complex, which ends at the square form, intended to represent a Japanese Noh stage, on the artificial lake at the perimeter of the museum. This combination of landscape elements, relating interior and exterior space can also be seen in the Nagoya City Art Museum and Saitma Prefectural Museum.

The Noh performance is also the central feature of the Honjin Memorial Museum of Art, built to accommodate a collection of 170 pieces, mostly made up of Japanese paintings, which were donated to the city of Komatsu by Mr Kanichi Honjin. The site in Rojyo Park was once the site of Komatsu Castle, and the moat and bridge of the museum recall this connection. The 'kura', a store house used during the Edo period, is also quoted, just as it was in the Hiroshima City Museum of Contemporary Art where it is a prominent metaphor. In Honjin, the main entrance is placed in the cleft formed by the flanking gables of the structure, leading into a central lobby, open to the roof, surrounded by galleries. The main part of the museum is square, to allow for maximum flexibility and the exhibition of large pieces. Other historical references include the ceramic tiles, which copy traditional Japanese Kawara earthen ware, and the palette of colours chosen throughout the complex.

Similar intentions at the Museum of Modern Art in Wakayama, the Ehime Museum of Science, and the recently commissioned wing for the Vincent Van Gogh Museum underline the strength of Kurokawa's belief in what he calls 'provisionality'. In his view, this is not only something that is short lived or easily amended, but is related to the philosophical concept of change. It leads him to an architecture that is asymmetrical, lacking a core, which 'rejects consistency'. As he says, 'life is defined as a process of continuous growth, a dynamic instability'. This dual quality, of stable impermanence lends a high degree of excitement to his work.

PAGES 104-07: Ehime Museum of Science, Japan: BELOW: First floor plan; PAGE 106 BELOW: Section; PAGE 107 BELOW: Section

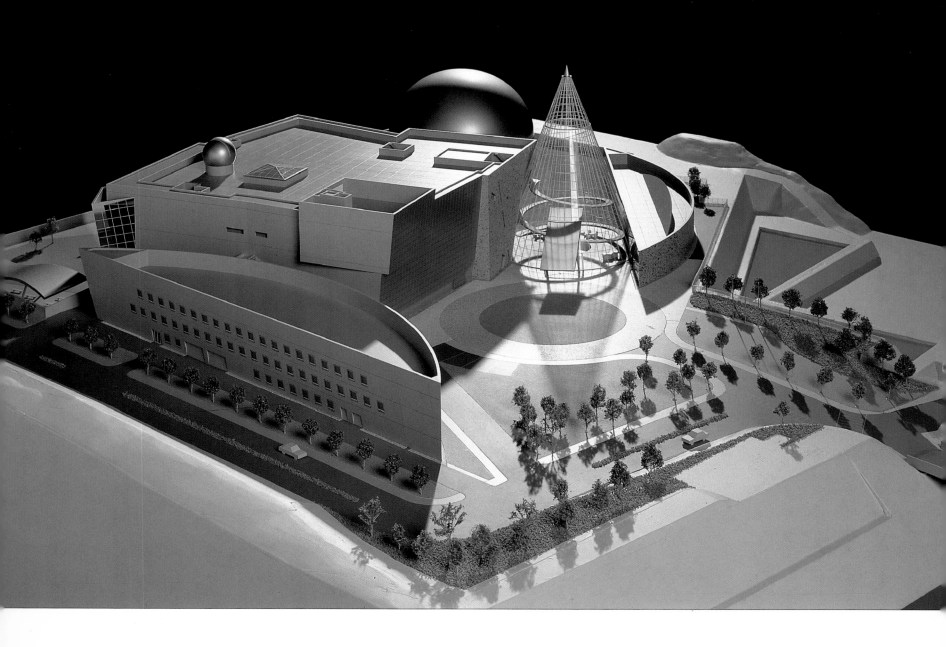

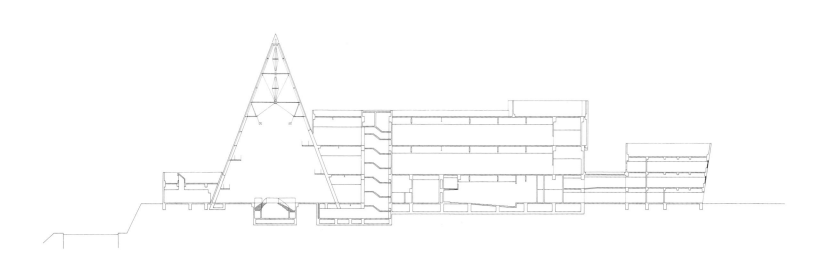

106

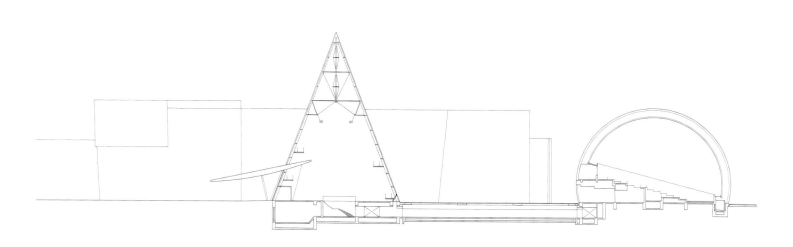

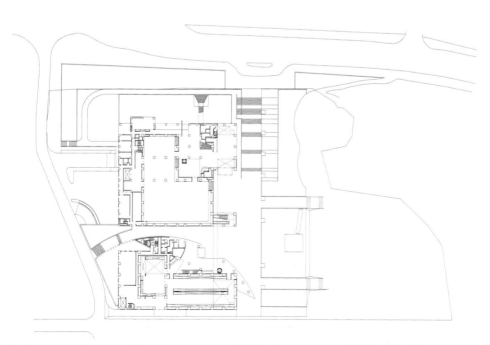

PAGES 108-09: Wakayama Museum of Modern Art, Japan: ABOVE: First floor plan; OPPOSITE BELOW: Longitudinal section

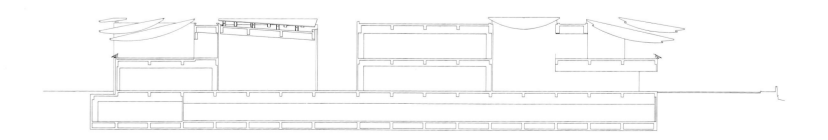

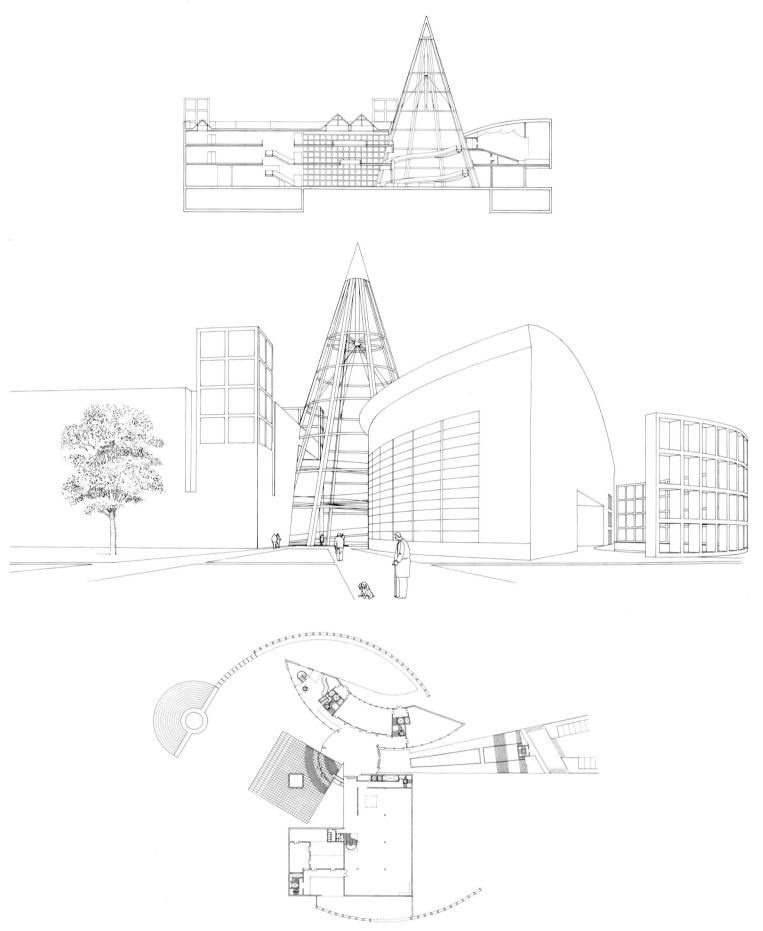

PAGES 110-11: Musée de Louvain-la-Neuve, Belgium: FROM ABOVE: Cross section; perspective; first floor plan

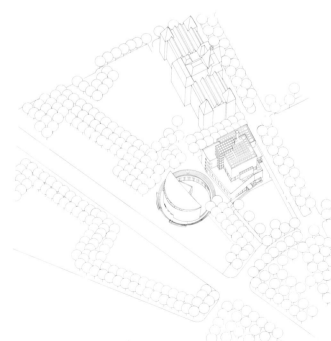

PAGES 112-13: New Wing of the Vincent Van Gogh Museum, Amsterdam: ABOVE: Axonometric of site; OPPOSITE BELOW: Ground floor plan

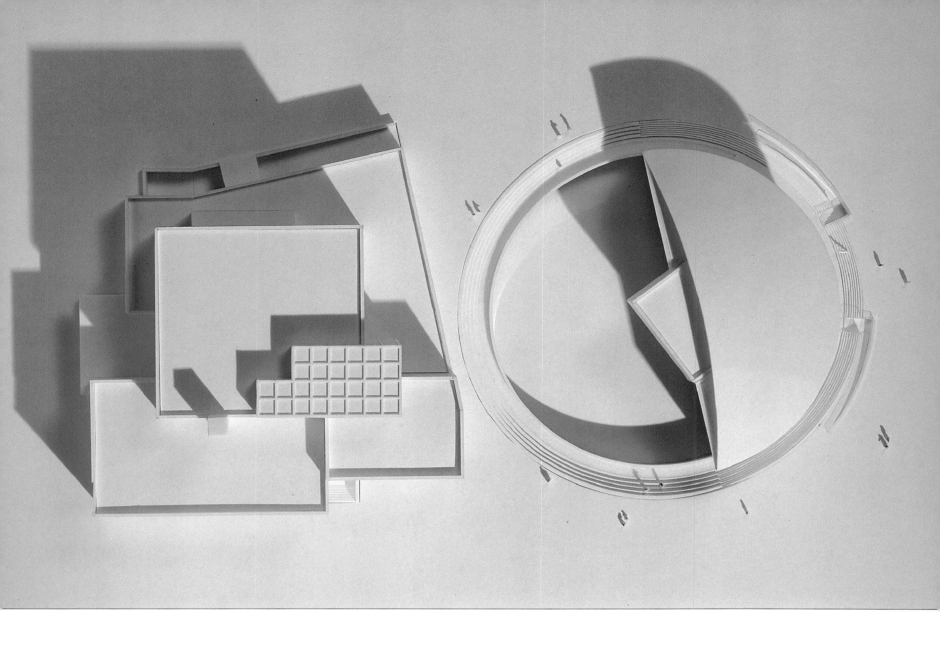

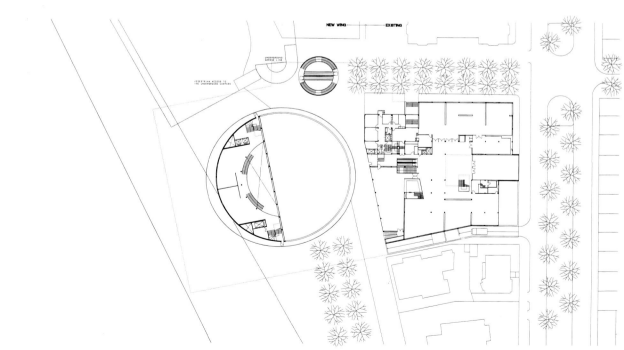

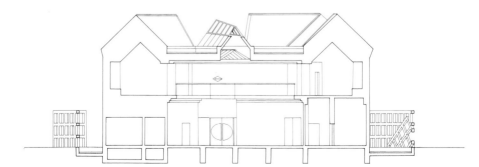

PAGES 114-15: Honjin Memorial Museum of Art, Japan: ABOVE: Longitudinal section; OPPOSITE BELOW: First floor plan

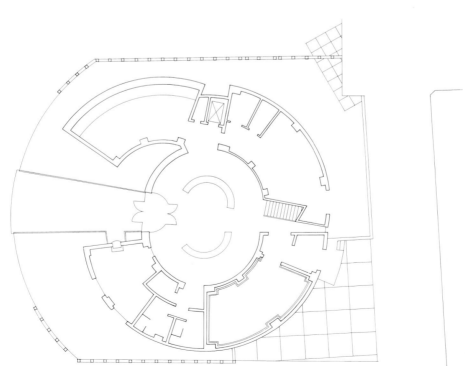

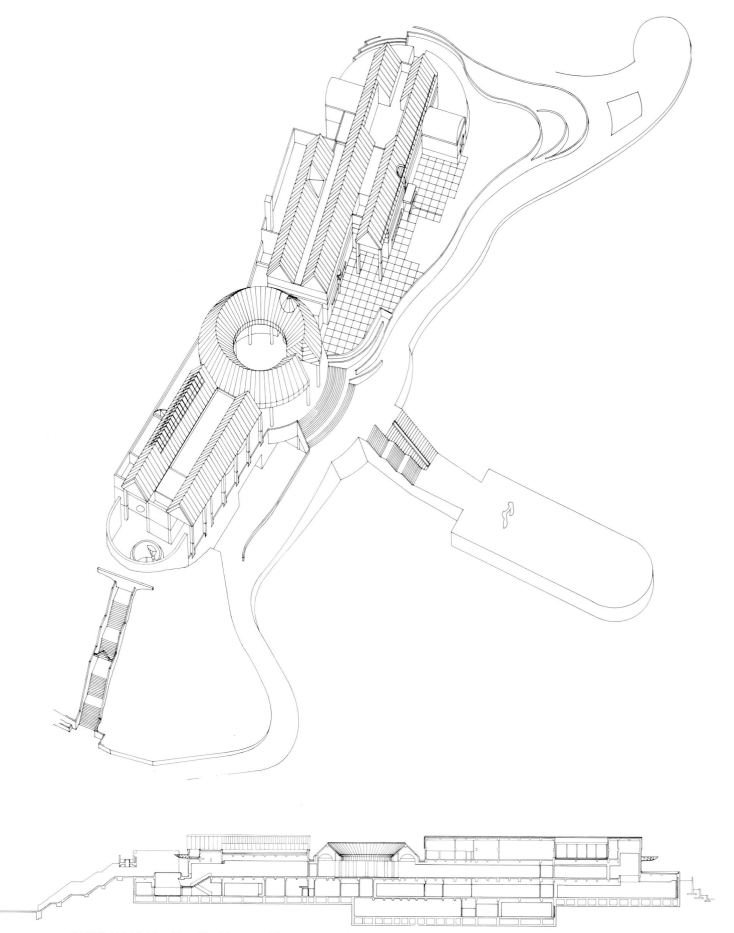

PAGES 116-17: Hiroshima City Museum of Contemporary Art, Japan: FROM ABOVE: Axonometric of site; longitudinal section

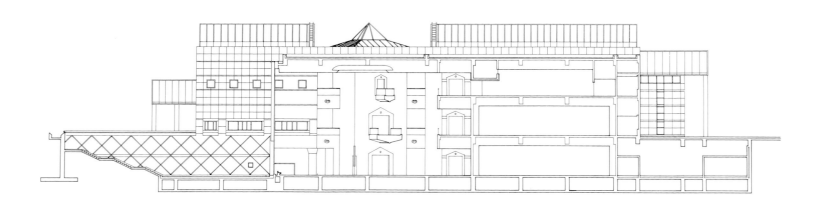

PAGES 118-19: Nagoya City Art Museum, Japan: ABOVE: Longitudinal section; OPPOSITE BELOW: First floor plan

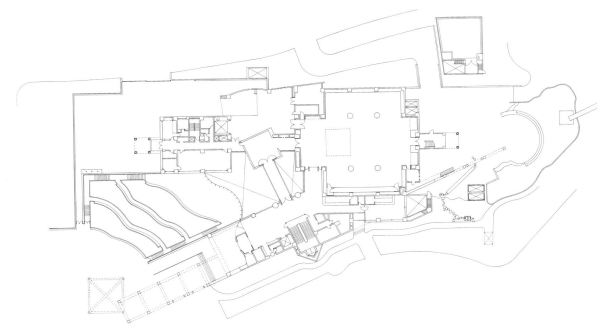

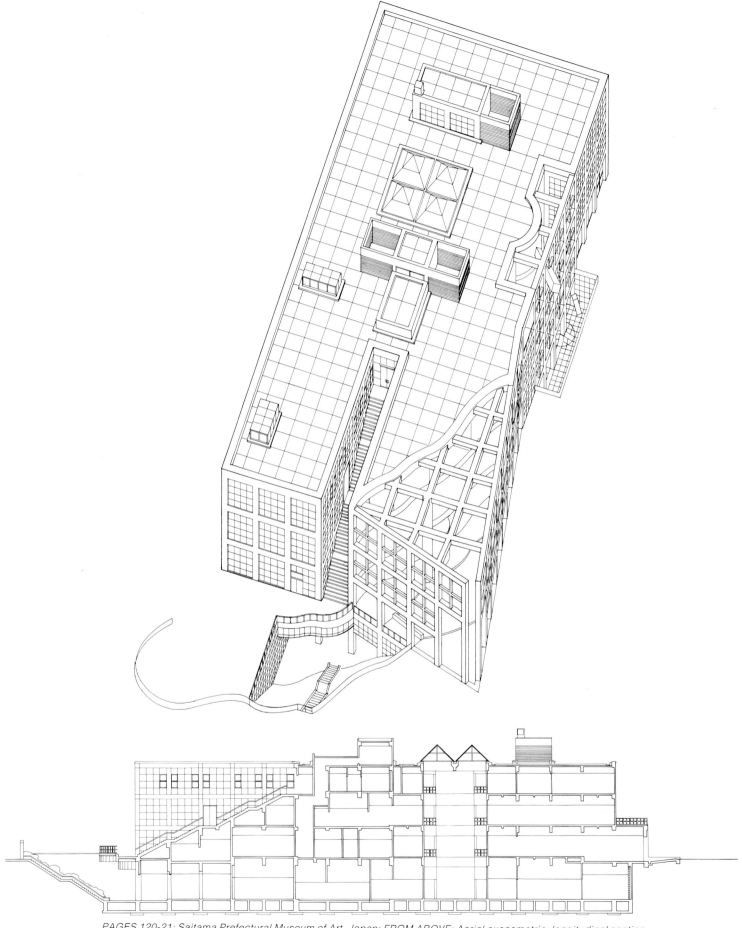

PAGES 120-21: Saitama Prefectural Museum of Art, Japan: FROM ABOVE: Aerial axonometric; longitudinal section

Ricardo Legorreta

Monterey Museum, Monterey, Mexico

As with much of Legorreta's architecture, one of the most important features of the Museo Monterey is its accessibility. Since the concept of security has always been of paramount importance in museum design in the past, the degree of openness evident here would not have been considered appropriate a decade ago. However, the popularity of approachable institutions such as Stirling's Staatsgalerie, which provides many different kinds of circulation system as well as a variety of entrances and exits on different levels, have revolutionised the administrative view of the public, who are increasingly seen as participants in an exhibition, rather than intruders in a sacred shrine to art.

While different in purpose, Legorreta's Camino Real Hotel in Ixtapalapa, Mexico, is an earlier example of the attitude taken in Monterey, where bold forms also surround an open central court. In each case the typology used is the traditional Mexican house, where life revolves around an interior patio surrounded by arcades that provide a buffer between individual rooms and a protected gathering space. At the Camino Real, the main entrance is located on a secondary street and there is never any feeling of actually passing through a doorway in the usual sense of moving from exterior to interior. Entrance into the reception area is carefully orchestrated, from the point of arrival of cars into a walled courtyard containing a fountain, past an offset opening in the external walls of the hotel, to the front of an enormous, long check-in desk.

In the Museo, which is located on an important corner of Monterey's main plaza and is flanked by both the cathedral and the city hall, visitors also enter through a gap between the massive walls that are treated as the public, civic face of the building. They then move through a small plaza, where a marble dove by sculptor Juan Soriano, dedicated to the memory of Luis Barragan, is the focal point. From this plaza, inconspicuous doors open into a high vestibule full of colour and light that serves an auditorium, cafeteria and gift shop, and finally into a latticework passageway,

leading to the main patio in the heart of the building. All galleries relate to this open space, which is also used for concerts, receptions and social events, as well as a point of orientation for each of the exhibition spaces. In addition to its functional value, the atrium has environmental advantages, since it collects the cool night air and distributes it into the surrounding spaces during the day. A thin film of water, which covers the entire surface of this court in the morning before the museum opens, naturally enhances this cooling effect.

The galleries around the patio vary in proportion and height, to allow for different kinds of exhibitions, and receive daylight that is filtered in such a way that it does not detract from the reflective quality of the exhibition spaces. The architect has consciously tried to strike a balance between isolation and urban integration. The popularity of the Museum in its inaugural year, and the willingness of people who have previously had no exposure to art to enter the building from the main plaza, and explore the galleries, testify to Legorreta's success.

BELOW: Roof plan

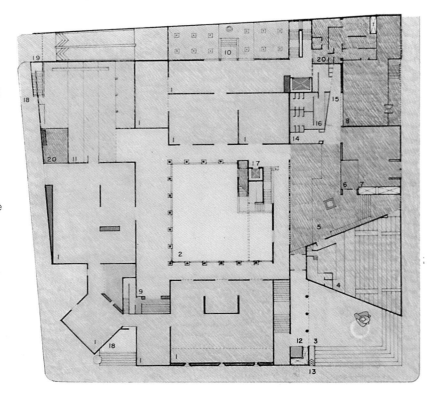

Fumihiko Maki

Yerba Buena Gardens Visual Arts Center, San Francisco

Just as the Spiral Building in Tokyo comments on the chaotic state of the contemporary city, Yerba Buena Gardens reinforces Fumihiko Maki's belief in the validity of modernism tempered by metaphorical reference which makes it specific to a particular place. He has said:

> Modernism that deals with images, as opposed to the frankly historicist architecture that introduces imagery through applied ornament, is still finding adherents . . . in our post-industrial, decentralised society, collective imagination manifests itself in unstable and diverse ways. The city today is an environment of fragmentation, vital and changing, constantly renewing itself. In [the] absence of a single dominant architectural style, the personal qualities of individual buildings come to the surface, thereby joining a sea of existing signs and icons that make up the face of the city . . .

In this new Visual Arts Center, the nautical image that has been chosen to allude to the waterfront nearby is particularly relevant to its aesthetic as first proposed in *Vers une Architecture*, complete with the prow, crowning tower and flags that Le Corbusier loved so much. Free of the dense context and the severe site restrictions that governed the form of the Spiral, this building spreads out to occupy its square site as a horizontal version of that landmark, spinning outwards from a courtyard at its core.

The benefits of such a strategy become evident after close scrutiny of the plan, since it allows a long, linear entrance loggia, with a monumental stair that contributes to the gangplank motif, facing the water, to take precedence as the primary spatial experience after entry. Because of its southeasterly exposure, this high, serene narrow hall receives sunlight during most of the day, and so has not been conceived as exhibition space (as can be deduced from the absence of continuous wall surfaces). A large gallery on the western edge of the site, on the other hand, is windowless, relying upon roof monitors to bring daylight into the space. To alleviate any lack of visual interest that such an unglazed wall might otherwise create, these monitors are treated like polished knife blades that cut into the solid, corrugated wall below providing a contrast of materials that brings life to this important entrance elevation. To continue that interest, a show-window, intended for displays related to current exhibitions, pops out of the solid gallery wall near the entry stairs to add a changing line of colour to the metallic facade greeting visitors. This gallery is lit by a window wall on its northern edge, which also serves to visually connect it to a sculpture court on a large plaza outside. Such perceptive responses to place and climate make Yerba Buena a worthy successor to previous examples of Maki's updated version of modernism, and provide a strong case for his argument that, due to the collapse of urban order, public space as it has been known in the past must now be internalised.

BELOW: Site plan
PAGE 128: Section
PAGE 129 ABOVE: First floor plan

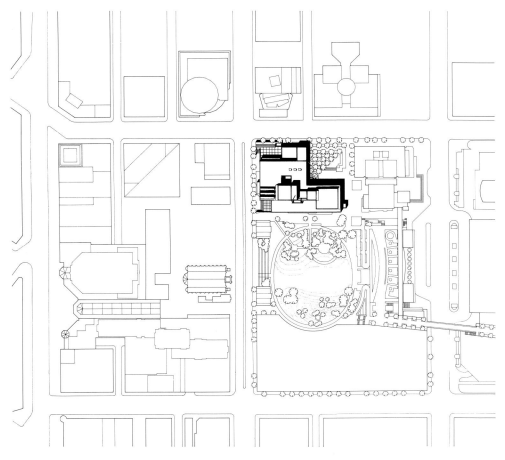

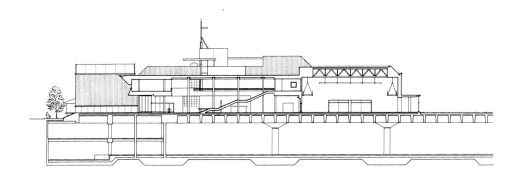

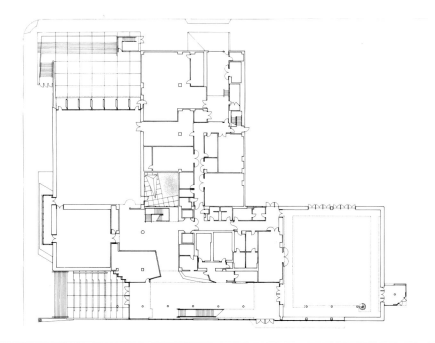

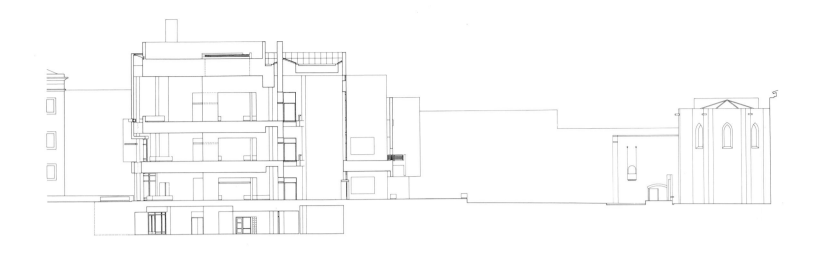

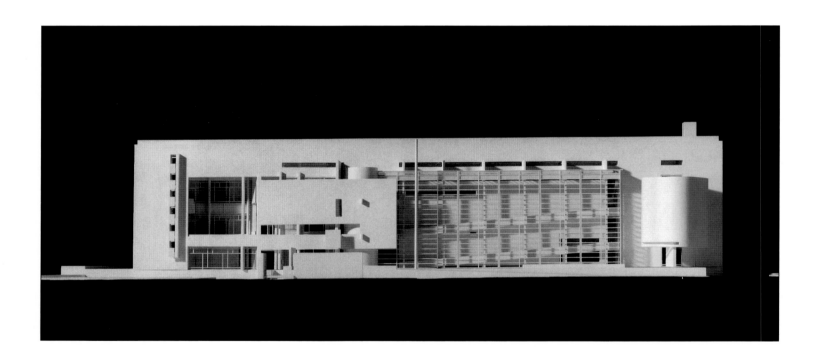

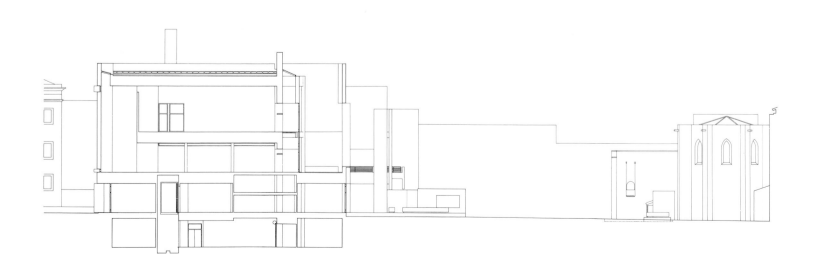

Richard Meier

Museum of Contemporary Art, Barcelona

Located in the area of the Casa de la Caritat, previously a monastic enclave, this museum creates a dialogue between the historic forms of its context and the contemporary art within. The labyrinthine nature of the surrounding urban fabric is reflected in the building's organisation. This is perhaps most evident in the main entry, which is paralleled by a passage for pedestrians between the museum's back garden and a newly created plaza to be known as the Plaça dels Angels. This *paseo* will join a pedestrian network running throughout the old city connecting various civic institutions.

A ramp leads to the main entry, which is raised 1 metre above the plaza. Once past this portico, visitors enter a cylindrical reception area where they have a view over the *paseo*. From here, a ramp in a triple height hall looks onto the galleries and the plaza, thus serving as an orientation device. The louvred hall also helps to filter natural light entering from the south.

The principal gallery spaces are close to the entry and in their bulk and placement parallel the general mass of the Casa de la Caritat behind the museum. They are large, open, loftlike spaces that can accommodate sizeable art works. Possibly the most striking feature of this exhibition sequence is the layering of space from the louvred ramp hall to the double-height gallery running the full length of the northeastern facade. Visitors must cross over full-height light 'slots', complete with glass-lensed floors, in order to enter the main galleries or to pass from these to the viewing balconies.

This sequence is complemented by a series of irregularly shaped galleries, stacked in the southwestern wing intended for the exhibition of small-scale works. Beyond these galleries to the south west lies the administrative wing containing a research library, an education centre, a museum shop and a small cafe.

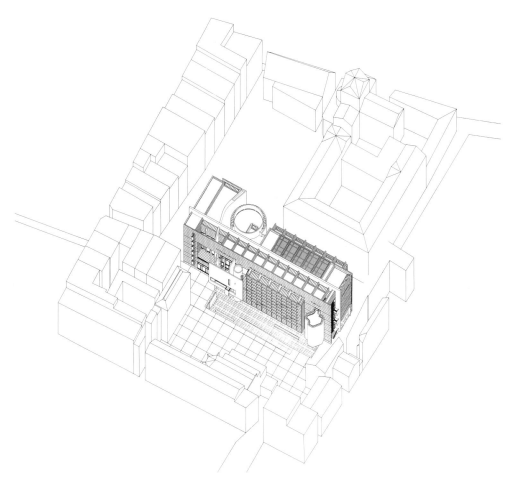

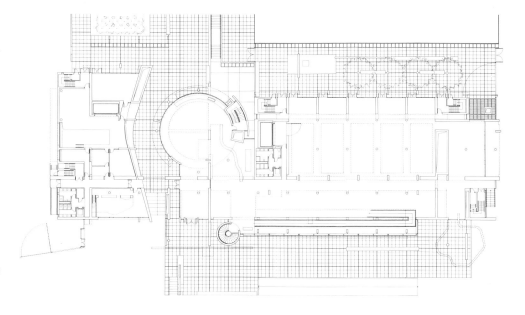

RIGHT FROM ABOVE: Axonometric of site; ground floor plan
OPPOSITE ABOVE AND BELOW: Section through lobby/special exhibition; section through west gallery

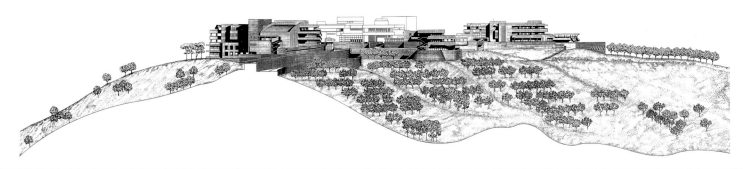

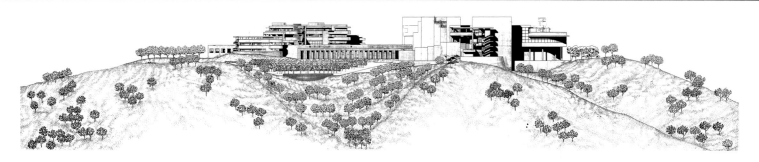

Richard Meier

The Getty Center, Santa Monica

In 1993 the trustees of the J Paul Getty Museum in Los Angeles commissioned Richard Meier to design a second, more central complex to bring together and house its expanding collections and educational initiatives on a new 110 acre site in the foothills of the Santa Monica mountains. The final design consists of six major buildings: The J Paul Getty Museum; The Getty Center for the History of Art and the Humanities; The Getty Conservation Institute/Center for Education in the Arts/ Grant Program; The Getty Art History Information Program; Trust Administrative Offices; and a restaurant and cafe. All centralised operations and service and delivery areas are located underground. The buildings are clustered along two ridges, with the museum located at the point where they intersect, dominating the eastern elevation to become the most prominent member of the group. The building housing the Conservation Institute, Grant Program and Center for Education in the Arts will be located to the north of the Museum and the Center for the History of Art and the Humanities will be on the more secluded western ridge. The cafe near the arrival plaza completes the grouping.

The Museum, which will be the principal destination for most visitors to the Center, is organised around a tall, circular lobby, providing visual orientation for the five two-storey high galleries located around a garden court. In four of these five 'pavilions' the galleries are organised around atriums which are either open to the sky or covered by glass. Enclosed and covered walkways link the lobby, the pavilions and the courtyard, allowing visitors to choose a variety of paths through the museum.

By following a clockwise route through the first four pavilions the collections can be seen in roughly chronological order. On the upper floor, European paintings will occupy twenty-two skylit galleries. Objects requiring controlled light such as drawings, illuminated manuscripts and photographs will be shown on the lower floor in thirteen galleries designed to suit the individual collections. French furniture and decorative arts will occupy a suite of fourteen galleries.

The fifth pavilion, on the west side of the courtyard, will house temporary exhibitions and a cafe with an outdoor terrace. To differentiate the function of this pavilion, it will be set at an angle to the others. Smaller facilities for temporary exhibitions within each of the other pavilions will be distinguished in the same way.

There are areas designed specifically for educational activities, ranging from lectures and demonstrations to interactive audio-visual programs. Throughout the museum there will be three information centres near the galleries, along with two orientation theatres, a 180-seat lecture hall, two multi-purpose classrooms and three seminar rooms. Conservation studios, located below the museum will more than double the space available in the Villa at Malibu.

In describing his personal vision of the project, Richard Meier has said that it:

. . . is essentially classical. With its regular rhythms and axial organisation, the Getty Center will embody that realm of the rational and the human.

BELOW: Axonometric of site
OPPOSITE ABOVE AND BELOW: North elevation; south elevation

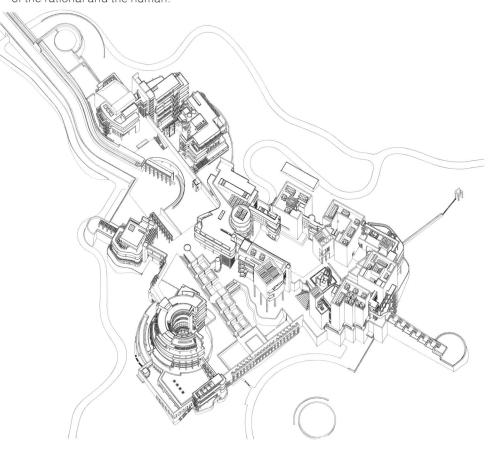

Richard Meier

Arp Museum, Rolandswerth, Germany

The Arp Museum is sited in the foothills above the Rhine, below Roland's Castle. The steepness of the slope and restrictive property boundaries limit access to the museum to pedestrians, who approach along a drive leading to an existing villa. The only exception are service vehicles and coaches that will be able to reach the forecourt for purposes of delivery and reception. The few parking spaces provided on the site are reserved for the staff.

The architects sought to preserve as much of the existing vegetation as possible and to integrate the architecture into the topography in such a way as to create a number of open-air terraces for the exhibition of Arp bronzes. A glazed conservatory at the entry serves to house Arp plaster casts, while a ramped pathway gives access to the sculpture terraces.

The museum is cradled between a podium and a screen wall that jointly serve as a visual field and foil to the drum form that is its primary mass. A cruciform gallery covered by a curved screen wall houses the bulk of the collection, which consists of the sculptural and two-dimensional works by Jean Arp and works in various media by Sophie Tauber-Arp. This area is also designed to double on occasion as an informal space for chamber concerts.

A circulation spine which also acts as an exhibition gallery is located next to the screen wall, serving to link the main exhibition space to a free standing cube situated at the northern end of the building. This foursquare prism houses a double height, temporary exhibition space on the lower floors with small apartments for visiting artists above. The whole linear complex is fed by a stepped ramp and elevator core situated close to the entry. The administration, research library and shipping and storage facilities are located one floor beneath with direct access to the entry forecourt.

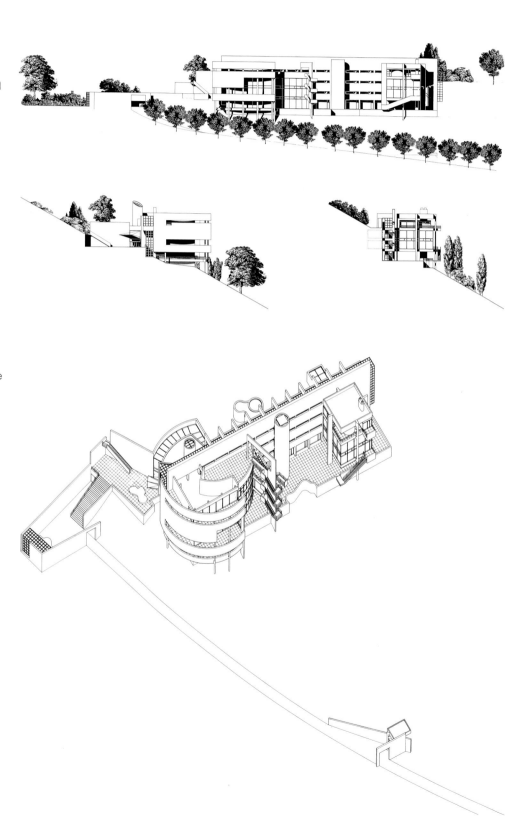

RIGHT FROM ABOVE: Elevations and sections; overall axonometric

Richard Meier

Des Moines Art Center Addition, Des Moines, Iowa

The Des Moines Art Center was designed in 1948 by Eliel Saarinen and consisted of a U-shaped single storey gallery plus a double height gallery to the west terminated by a two-storey annex. In 1965 IM Pei added a block to the south thereby closing the original U-plan in order to create an internal sculpture court. The site for the present addition is mostly to the north of this two stage complex and since the Saarinen building is visible from the downtown approach, the problem was how to design a further addition that would respect the generally horizontal profile of the Center.

It was decided to provide the new addition as a series of separate volumes that would accommodate the required expansion without producing a large mass. Thus three new additions were located around the existing complex in such a way as to reinforce the formal order of the Saarinen scheme. The east-west entry axis of the existing museum is strengthened by a new courtyard pavilion, accommodating the restaurant/meeting room which serves to activate the previously under-used court by opening it to the patio in warm weather.

A glass-enclosed link running along the north-south axis connects to the new northern addition which houses most of the additional gallery space. Volumetrically separate from the Saarinen building this larger increment is vertically condensed in such a way as to leave the preferred view of the existing museum unobstructed. The largest of its three levels is located entirely below ground and is equipped with light slots so as to admit natural light into the temporary exhibition gallery. The plan derives from a nine-square grid, in which the central square provides a four-column internal atrium, lit by clerestory windows and perimeter skylights. This cubic volume is sheathed in granite and covered by a flattened pyramid that serves as a foil to the butterfly-section roof employed by Pei. A third smaller addition accommodating services and additional gallery space above is attached to the west wing of the Saarinen building. In this way the Saarinen/Pei complex was discretely amplified by three separate additions of different sizes.

BELOW FROM ABOVE: Axonometric of site; ground floor plan
PAGE 138 CENTRE AND BELOW: South elevation; east elevation
PAGE 139 CENTRE AND BELOW: North elevation; west elevation

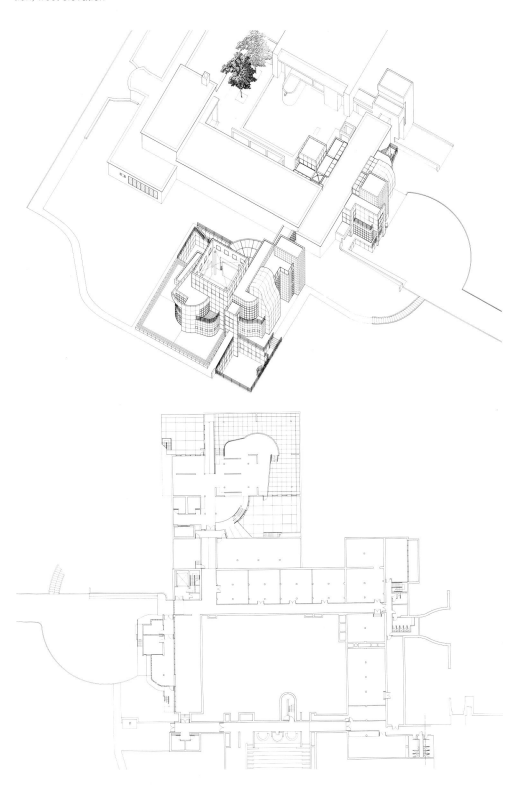

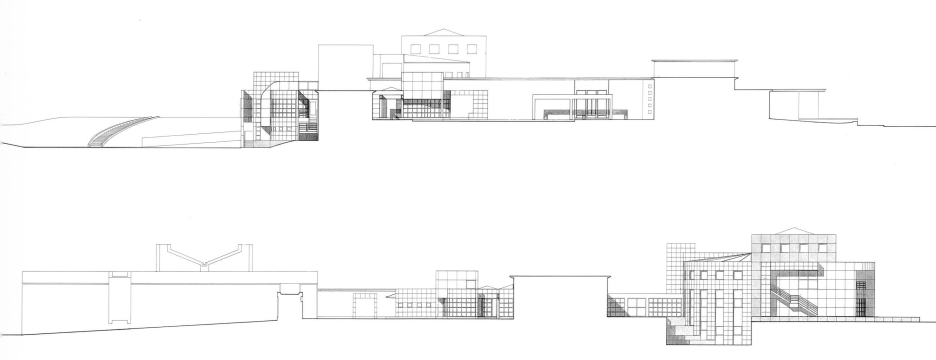

138

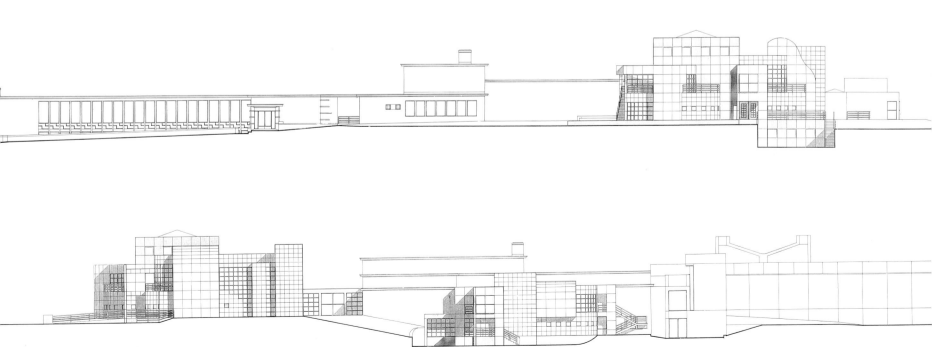

Richard Meier

The High Museum of Art, Atlanta, Georgia

The popularity of Frank Lloyd Wright's Guggenheim Museum, despite the problems it presents in organising installations (for which it is a perennial symbol of some architects' tendency to place individual expression before function) has spawned several reverential models but none has been as cleverly interpretive and analytical as the High Museum by Richard Meier. While following the prototype of a ramped curvilinear central space, the High Museum departs from its predecessor in its deliberate accommodation of the utilitarian aspects that make the formal ceremonial space possible. As in the Guggenheim, the ramp system mediates between the central space and the art itself, which is seen from various levels and vantage points while moving along it. In the Guggenheim, however, the ramp is also used as a gallery in an inappropriate attempt to make an element intended for circulation also serve as a space for contemplative viewing. As Meier's past work has demonstrated, he really understands the architectonic potential of a ramp, whereas Wright rarely used them. Having taken his cue from Le Corbusier, Meier only utilises such long angled passages, which consume a great deal of area, as well as a larger chunk of the building budget than stairs, when he is assured of an uninterrupted sensation of progression, or when it helps explicate interior space and orient visitors to internal organisation.

The design consists of four quadrants with one being given over to a monumental glazed atrium which acts as the lobby of the museum. Only 30 per cent of these sections are given over to gallery space, with the remainder being allocated to public and administrative functions, and storage.

In the ongoing debate between those who believe that the architecture of a museum, as a creative art, should predominate, and those who feel it should serve as a background to the art it presents, the High Museum unmistakeably stands out, just as the Guggenheim before, as a supreme example of the architectural prerogative, albeit on a much more functional level.

RIGHT FROM ABOVE: Main floor plan; axonometric of site

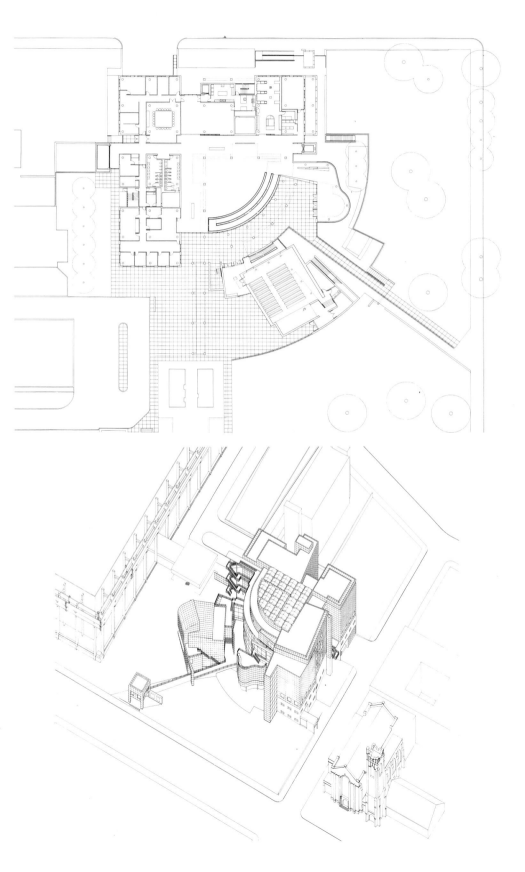

Richard Meier

Museum for the Decorative Arts, Frankfurt

The cubic form of the Villa Metzler provided Richard Meier with the starting point for an exponential abstraction based on its key dimension of 58 feet. With the Villa acting as one corner, a square grid is rotated 3.5 degrees to line up with the Schaumainkai – a busy commuter street – staking out the three remaining corners with pristine, flat-roofed clones of the existing building, and connecting each part with bridges and ramps. The inner court that results opens up to the River Main on the north and the historic city centre on its opposite side presenting a welcoming gateway. This gateway is literally marked by a freestanding threshold that delimits the Schaumainkai from the inner court of the museum. Once inside this 'gate', the main entrance projects out to welcome people inside and a ramp running along the north-south axis becomes visible, effort-lessly connecting all levels of the museum.

In the original competition drawings an east-west axis was also established to counterbalance the importance of this central spine, as well as the pedestrian way between the Schaumainkai and the Sachsenhousen running parallel to it. A small replica of the museum complex anchored this cross axis into the park, helping to tie this peripheral part of the site back to the project.

The domestic language, which began with proportional references to the Villa Metzler, is continued in each of its surro-gates through the use of screen walls that divide the display spaces into 'rooms'.

The general organisation of the museum space gives the work a specifically didactic character, with the visitor proceeding counter-clockwise through a prescribed series of spaces, outlining the history of European decorative art. Specific openings in the sequence are framed in various ways so as to sustain a sense of discovery and surprise through different apertures. The overall delicacy of the white fabric, both inside and out, and the varying quality of the reflected light recalls the German Baroque, a primary source of inspiration in all of Richard Meier's architecture.

RIGHT FROM ABOVE: Overall axonometric;
cutaway axonometric showing first exhibition floor

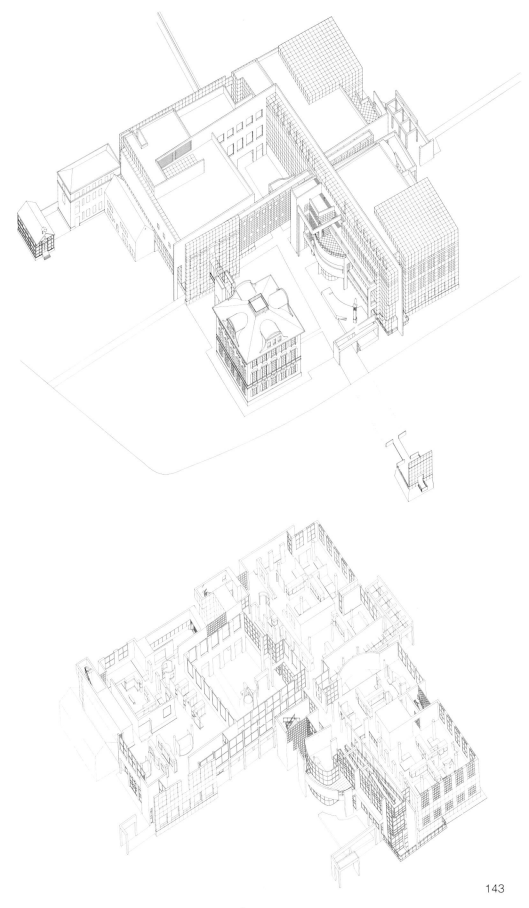

144

Richard Meier

Museum of Ethnology, Frankfurt

Beginning with the original east-west axis of the Museum for the Decorative Arts which runs through the park along the Schaumainkai, Richard Meier has established a centre of gravity for this new entity, which is almost a scaled down version of its predecessor. By their very nature, the exhibits in the Ethnology Museum required larger scale galleries than the adjunct to the Villa Metzler, and some of them have even been custom-designed to fit specific pieces. The architect also had to accommodate research and teaching facilities, which made it necessary to integrate intimate spaces with large halls. The plan twists into an 'S' to create two small courts, and positions the large galleries against the park, so that is seen as a backdrop. Those activities requiring smaller spaces are grouped around the more protected inner courts, creating a cloistered environment. Siting tight up against the edge of the Metzlerstrasse, as well as the use of a pedestrian bridge to join up with a wing on its opposite side are strategies employed to disturb the park as little as possible. The museum is also broken down into recognisable units which perpetuate the residential pattern already established along the street, and withdraw from the pavement when such a scale becomes difficult to maintain for functional reasons.

The chance to expand on themes first introduced along the Schaumainkai have provided Meier with the unprecedented possibility of continuing the New Modern commentary on urbanism, since these two buildings, when taken together, represent nothing less than a system that implies expansion. It is evident that if allowed to grow further, this system would revolve around autonomous clusters, axis and bridges in formal juxtapositions that are reminiscent of the Candilis and Woods schemes of the 1960s. In spite of proportional gestures toward the existing residential fabric, along the Metzlerstrasse on the south and the Villa Metzler on the north, this new order is supra-urban, self-contained and abstract.

RIGHT FROM ABOVE: Park elevation; longitudinal section; cross section; cross section

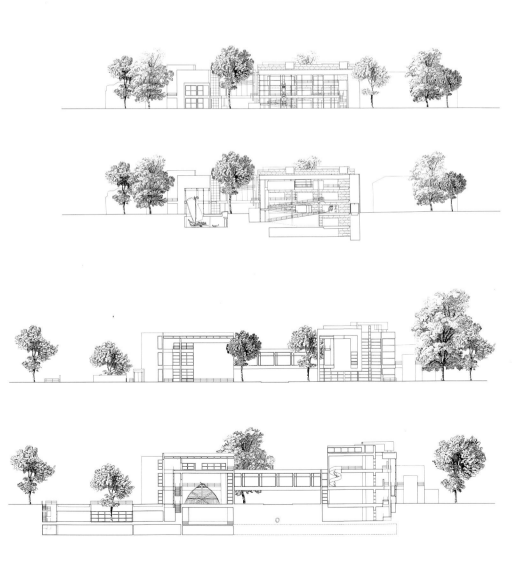

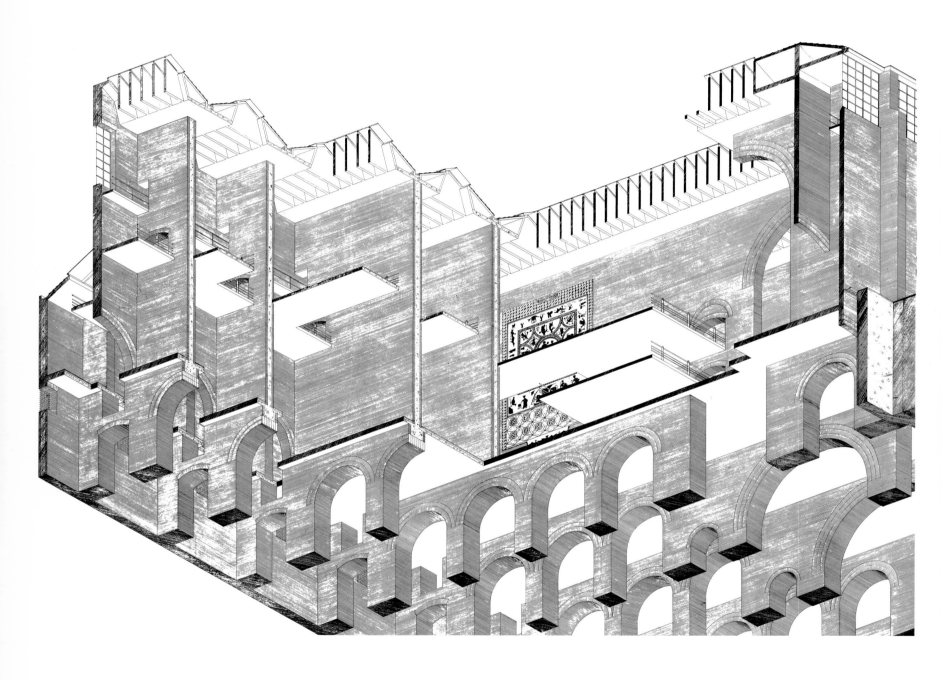

146

Rafael Moneo

The Museum of Roman Art, Mérida, Spain

The site chosen for this museum, which was known as Solar de les Torres because of the wall towers on it, lies directly behind the ruins of a theatre built by Agrippa in 18 BC, and an amphitheatre that is one of the largest existing examples of its kind in an archaeological park to the south. The large rectangle of 4,000 square metres contains the foundations of part of the old Roman city, with the characteristic accretion of courtyard houses added during the subsequent period of occupation. The difficult task Moneo faced was how to incorporate these ruins into a new structure in a way that would enhance rather than destroy them. His solution goes to the heart of the relationship between monuments from the past and urban development in the present (expressed so clearly in Aldo Rossi's *Architettura della Città*), as well as addressing the need to exhibit artifacts over two thousand years old; and is carried out through the calculated use of order and materials. By imposing the grid of the new, surrounding housing blocks over the random Roman pattern, he heightens the difference between them and makes it more evident to even the most blasé viewer. His use of thin Roman brick, and arch and vault construction, however, is more evocative of what once stood there than a more literal reconstruction of it would have been; in much the same way that Venturi's outlining of Benjamin Franklin's House in steel frame brings it to life in the imagination more vividly than an uninformed restoration could have done. Moneo has characterised the pragmatic, architectural problem here as being one of retaining walls and construction technique, so as not to unnecessarily disrupt the existing remains, and to bridge over them with the linear walls holding up the three floors and skylighted roof above. These upper floors are treated as bridges from which to look down at the past, as well as the bases of a series of rooms within the parallel walls resulting from his grid. The juxtaposition of the old and the new in this way – in which dimensions relevant to the present are rendered in the language of the past, and the evidence of the past is presented against this new background – is

startling, effective and timeless, with a sense of substance that is so often missing elsewhere today. The solidity of the bearing walls and lack of openings in them contribute to the sense of the museum as time capsule, in which each layer is interwoven like the levels still buried beneath it. Modesty of means and a strong conceptual direction have yielded an unforgettable experience.

OPPOSITE: Up-view part axonometric showing all gallery spaces
PAGE 148 FROM ABOVE: Cutaway axonometric of central circulation zone; sectional elevation
PAGE 149 FROM ABOVE: roof plan; second floor plan
PAGE 150 FROM ABOVE: First floor plan; library level plan
PAGE 151 FROM ABOVE: Plan of central nave; plan of ruins

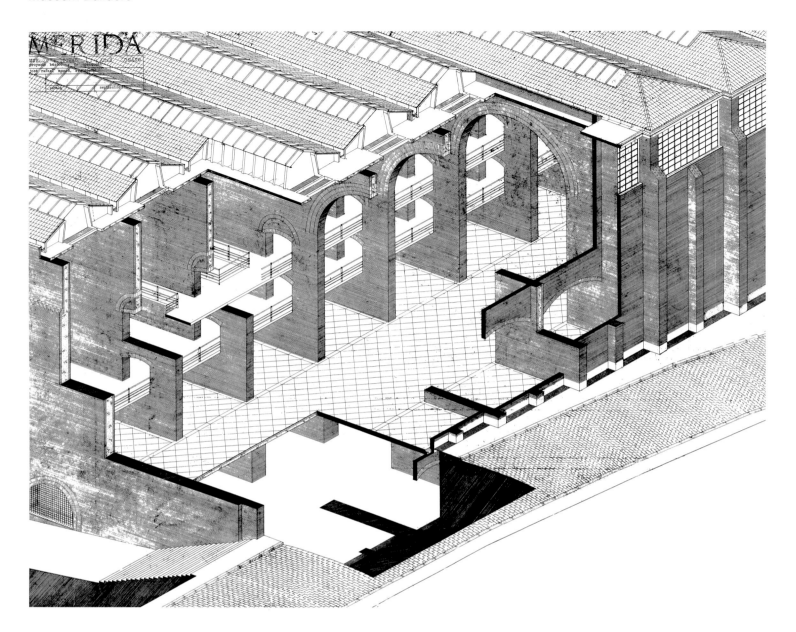

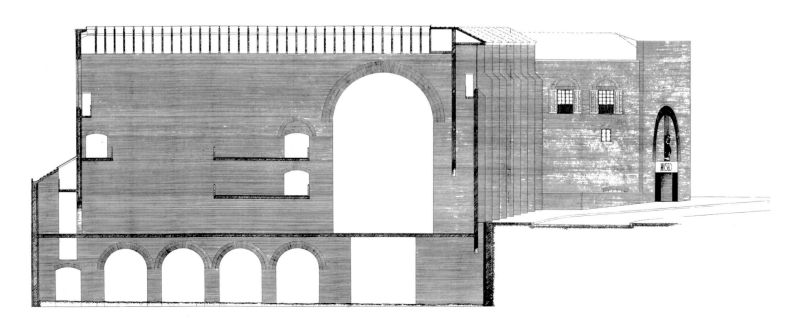

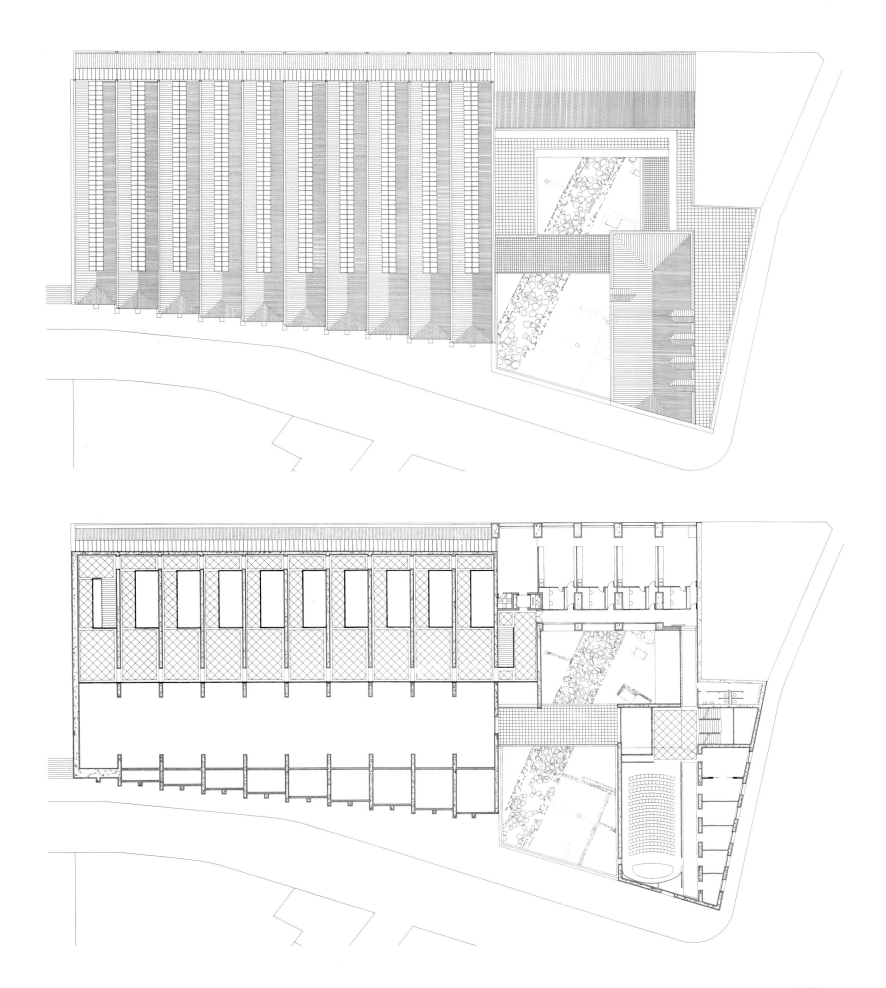

Moore, Ruble, Yudell

Hollywood Museum, Los Angeles

Entertainment is big business in Los Angeles, not only because of the income generated by the movies and television shows that are produced but also because of the tourists that the 'industry' attracts. Thousands of visitors come to Hollywood each year in search of some vestige of the glamour that the public has come to associate with it, only to find that there is not a great deal to see. Universal Studios has found a way to capitalise on its back lot, which is given over to tours when not in use, and a new City Walk project promises to expand on this market. Other than this movie-land theme park, visitors must be satisfied with an open-topped bus tour down Hollywood Boulevard, or with following a map to the homes of the stars if they want to begin to satisfy their curiosity about the Hollywood legacy, and this vacuum is the reason behind the move to establish an Entertainment Museum.

After a five-year stint at Paramount, consultants associated with this project recommended a move to the historic Hollywood Pacific Theatre at 6425 Hollywood Boulevard just west of Hollywood and Vine, the site of the original Warner Theatre which opened in 1928. Following initiatives to restore the El Capitan Theatre, and the adaptive reuse of the old Bank of America as the new Guinness Book of World Records Museum, which are both part of the regeneration of the recently designated Hollywood Cinema District, the new Entertainment Museum will occupy a landmark originally designed by G Albert Lansburgh, who also designed the Wiltern Theatre on Wilshire Boulevard, the El Capitan and the Orpheum. The Hollywood Pacific Museum which was the largest live stage and movie palace when it opened in 1927, and later housed the first radio station in the area, will serve as the entry and focal point for the museum tour. Circulation will pass through the loft space to a new three-storey structure that will house the main exhibits. The new building will evoke the spirit of the original sound stages – large industrial-like spaces that provide the backdrop and support for the various sets and exhibits. Besides providing a key element in the revitalisation of Hollywood Boulevard, the

project will contain a 'backlot' experience on the site to recreate the activity of a movie set as well as provide a place for special gatherings, openings and other events. Planning is in the preliminary stages and the design will continue to evolve along with interpretative exhibits and other project elements.

BELOW: Site plan
PAGE 154: Sketch view; sketch view from Hollywood Boulevard; section through museum and existing theatre; Cahuenga Boulevard elevation
PAGE 155: Sketch view; sketch view of tower viewing platform; Wilcox Avenue elevation; north elevation

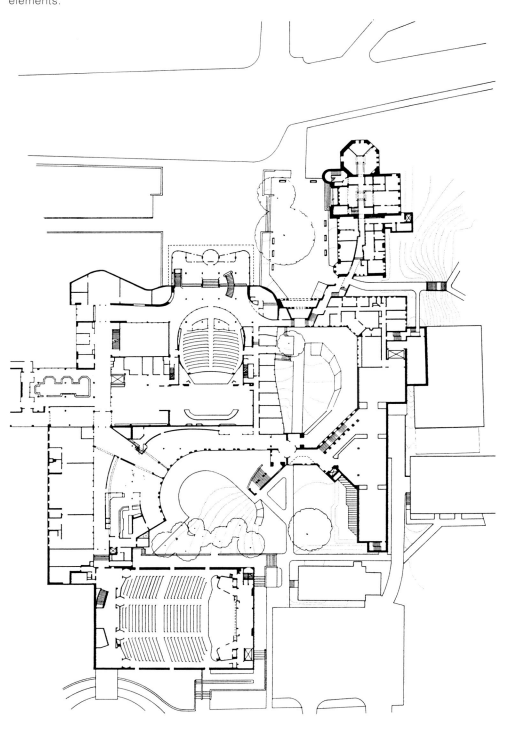

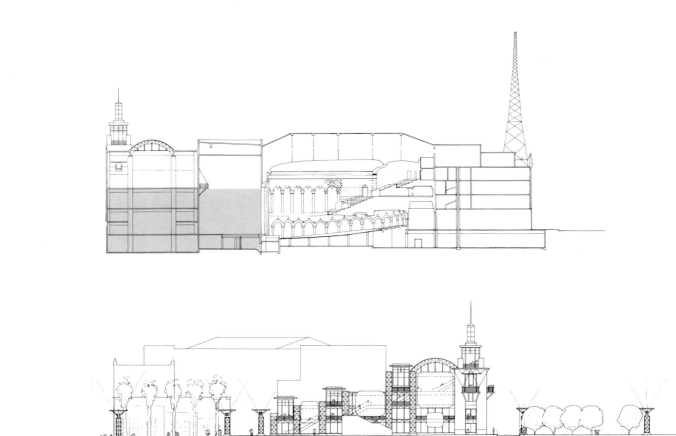

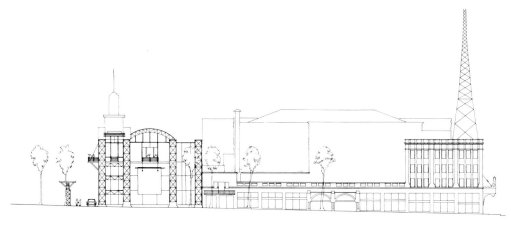
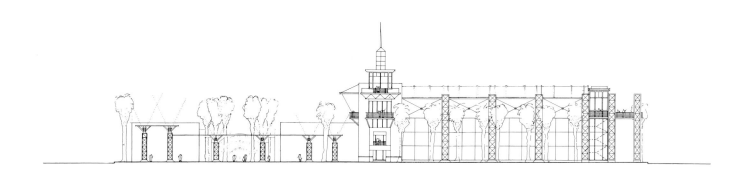

Moore, Ruble, Yudell

Renovations to the West Wing of St Louis Art Museum, Missouri

In contrast to the rather confrontational posture taken by Robert Venturi and Denise Scott Brown in their approach to the Allen Memorial Art Gallery at Oberlin College, in which a 'dumb box' is butted up against Cass Gilbert's finely detailed neo-Renaissance gem, Charles Moore has chosen a more reverential approach in this museum. It was originally completed as part of the 1904 World Fair, but piecemeal alterations made in the following century had all but obliterated Gilbert's intentions and restoring them became the first goal in the renovation process, along with the installation of state of the art support systems for museum personnel. This effort, as the architects explain, has included a variety of tactics:

In the existing West Wing galleries, our re-planning effort sought to restore the original 'plaid' of the plan; the Beaux-Arts order of cross-axes which create a matrix of linked rooms. The principal task was restorative, including the design of display cases and mouldings that reinterpret the ornate woodwork of the original galleries.

An unused mechanical shaft in the museum provided an opportunity to create a grand stair linking the restored West Wing galleries with the completely new decorative arts galleries at basement level. The stair connects the new basement galleries to all levels. The new order created by the basement level recalls the Beaux-Arts plaid of the upper levels. Exhibition areas are organised by geography and period. Connections between objects of different places and times are encouraged through the use of axial views.

The inevitable parallel with this solution is Foster's miraculous 'finding' of a space between the Diploma Galleries and Burlington House at the Royal Academy of Arts. As in that example, the results of Moore's ingenuity have been spectacular.

Once encumbered by a confusing network of circulatory options, amassed over the years, Cass Gilbert's elegant spaces have now been allowed to breathe, and his flawless sense of proportion and detail can now be fully appreciated.

The biggest beneficiaries of the renovation, however, have been the exhibits, which now take centre stage, and can be viewed effortlessly and without interruption because of the simplification of circulatory patterns.

BELOW: Floor plan of the Decorative Arts level PAGE 159 FROM ABOVE: Reflected ceiling plan; section and north elevation

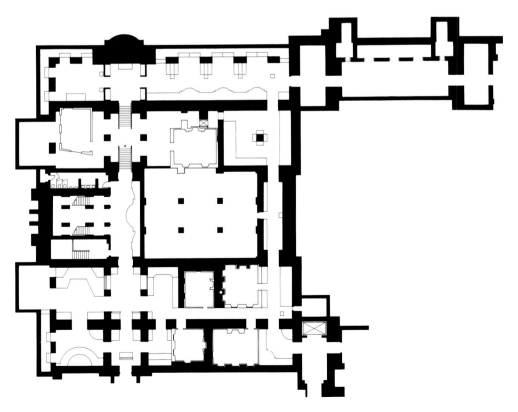

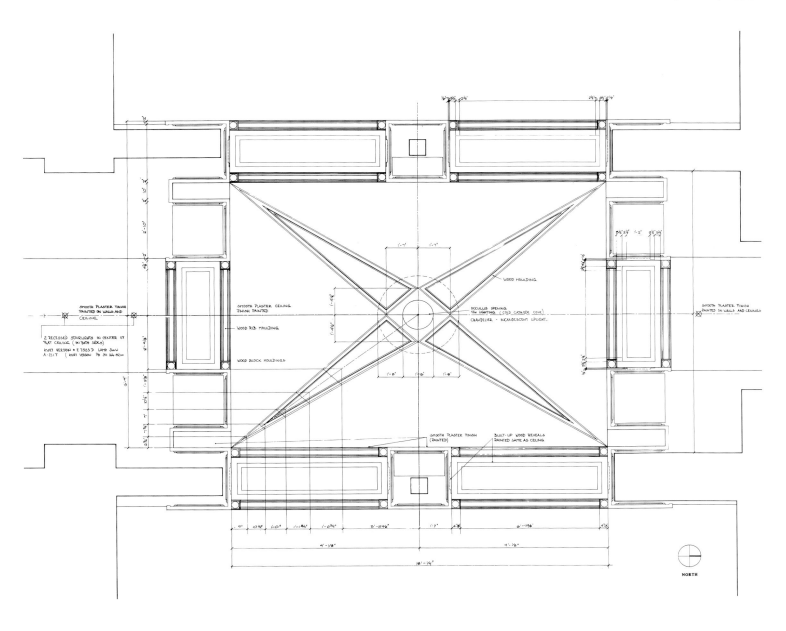

160

Charles Moore and Center Brook

Hood Museum of Art, Dartmouth, New Hampshire

First and foremost Charles Moore is a teacher and there is in his work, as there was in that of Louis Kahn, a didactic aspect that relates not only to architects, but to all those who experience it. The Hood Museum, which has come out of the Center Brook office, has been described by its director, Jacquelynn Baas, as being 'far more than a place to go and see art, it is a place where one can learn how to see art'. Moore, along with co-designer Chad Floyd, has achieved this by assiduously avoiding anonymous spaces and by creating identifiable backgrounds for a varied collection that resists quantification. As the antithesis of the universal space approach, taken by architects such as Mies van der Rohe in Berlin, or Piano and Rogers in the Pompidou Centre, where movable panels provided an anonymous backdrop, a refreshing range of different environments are provided with generic references that tie them to local forms, such as a New England mill or more general, historical associations that enhance, rather than detract from the artefacts on display. One observer has described this intentional attempt at modulated specificity as 'a three dimensional study in the power of memory to isolate, rearrange and transform the past'. The designers, it has been noted:

> have deliberately avoided the effect of art works adrift in a neutral, white continuum, preferring to furnish a variety of room shapes and degrees of luminosity congenial to different kinds of art. Several chambers distantly evoke collectors' cabinets, chapels or reliquaries.

Such an approach is tricky, because if taken too far, it can preclude certain kinds of collections, yet the Hood is proof that it can be accomplished. This direction towards variegated space, concerned primarily with human scale was not completely initiated by the Center Brook office, which true to principle, felt that it was necessary to involve the client in the design process, and the client in this case was the entire university. A series of workshops held on site narrowed the seven possible locations that had originally been considered for the museum down to an interstitial zone to the east of the Hopkins Center, designed by Wallace Harrison in 1962, next to a much loved landmark called Wilson Hall. Through this process several gated quadrangles were created, which act as open spaces to which the museum responds. The entire complex of the Hopkins Center, Wilson Hall and the museum which connects them, acts countrapunctally, encircling this series of incremental courtyards to become a symbol of the traditional campus in microcosm, and an enduring asset for Dartmouth College.

BELOW: Perspective sketch of site

Morphosis

Yuzen Vintage Car Museum, Los Angeles

While not likely to be realised, the Yuzen project is relevant as a specialised solution to a specific kind of display problem in a highly visible location. Intended for a steeply sloping site facing Sunset Boulevard, which is the vehicular nirvana of a city obsessed with the automobile, the mixed-use project that Morphosis has proposed is intended to house sixty antique cars, as well as to be used for retail and office space, restaurants, housing and parking. In keeping with the duality of commercial activity along Sunset Strip and the quieter residential neighbourhood behind it, which duplicates an unusual pattern found throughout Los Angeles, the design utilises different scales on the north and south. The Sunset Boulevard facade is animated by the museum and commercial spaces, as well as the elevator tower, which doubles as a sign. A gently sloping roof originally visualised as being covered with earth to make the building seem a continuation of the slope it sits on, pulls the streetscape scale down to residential size on the south, presenting a mound-like outline to those in the housing behind it. At another level, Morphosis has described the design as being meant:

>. . . to create a series of idiosyncratic events through a reaction to a set of systems including the city grid, a circular car circulation system and peripheral, edge-defining conditions.

To reorganise these various conditions, the Sunset Boulevard facade has been treated as a main entrance, where visitors enter the building at the middle level of the museum. From that point, access to other levels is by a two-cab elevator which reflects the priority given to cars on the street directly outside. The lower of the two cabs accommodates passengers while the upper cab, which is transparent, serves as a changeable display of cars in the collection. The cabs are connected becoming a kinetic sign for the museum.

RIGHT: Part sectional axonometric
PAGE 164 BELOW: First floor plan
PAGE 165 BELOW: Second floor plan
PAGE 166 BELOW: Longitudinal section
PAGE 167 BELOW: Cross section

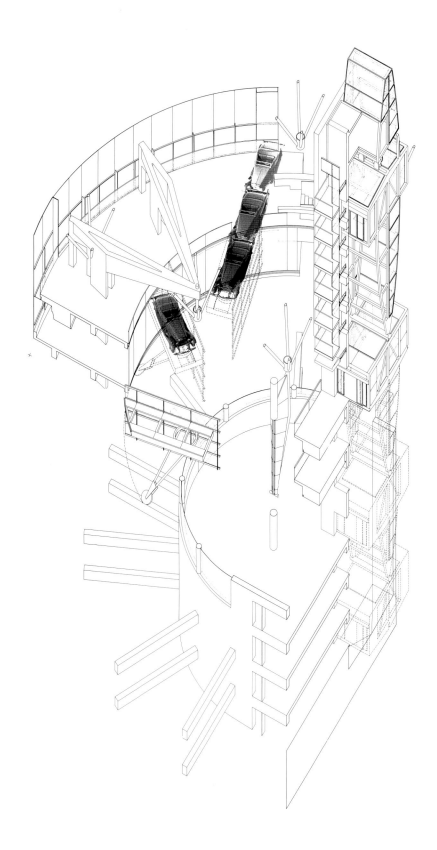

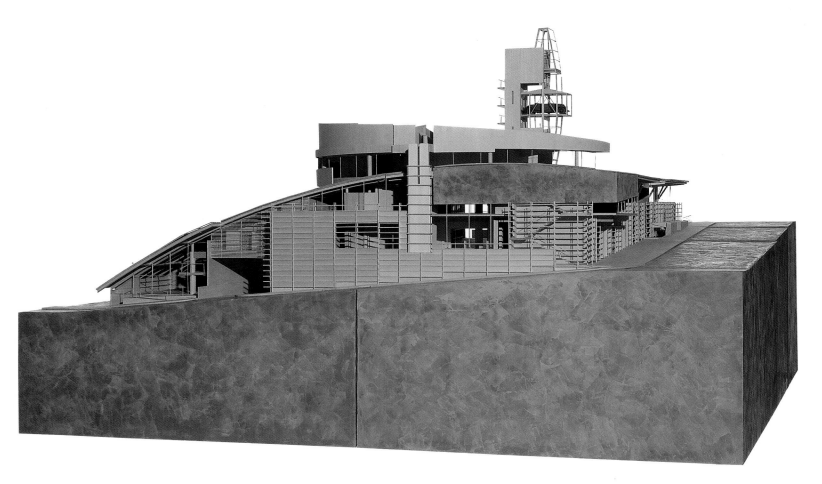

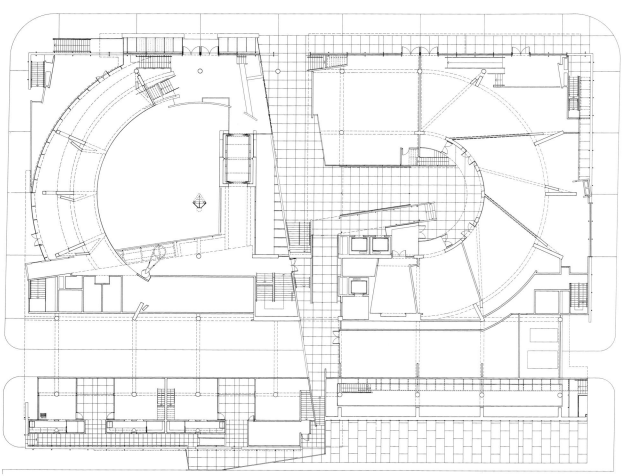

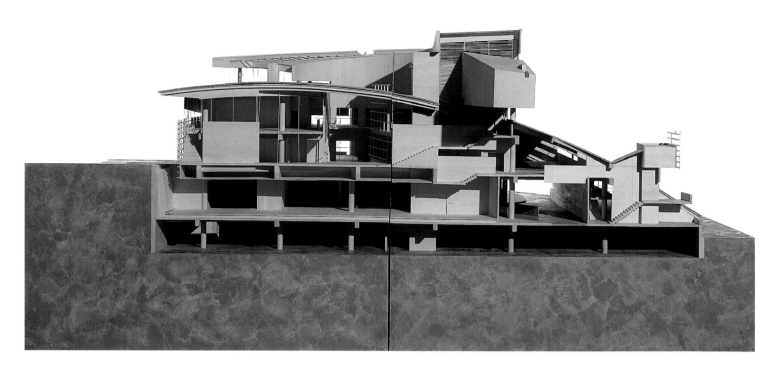

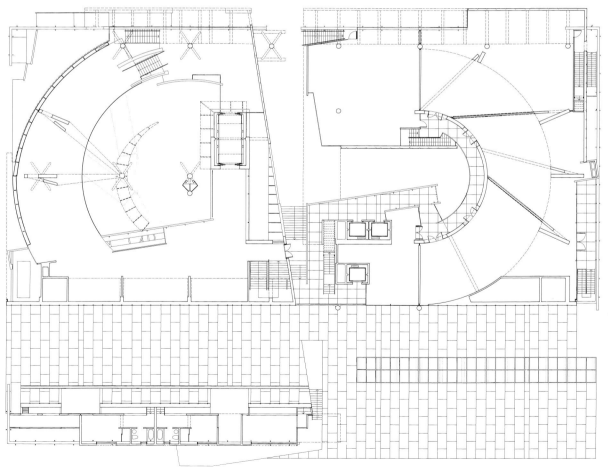

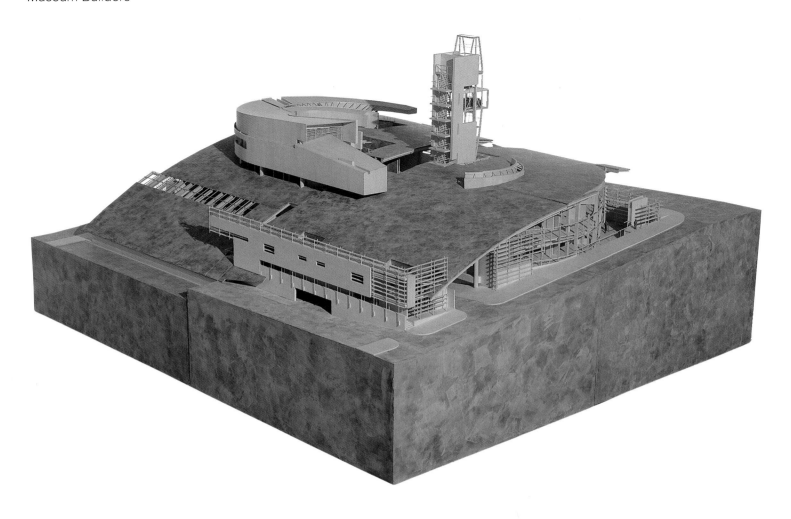

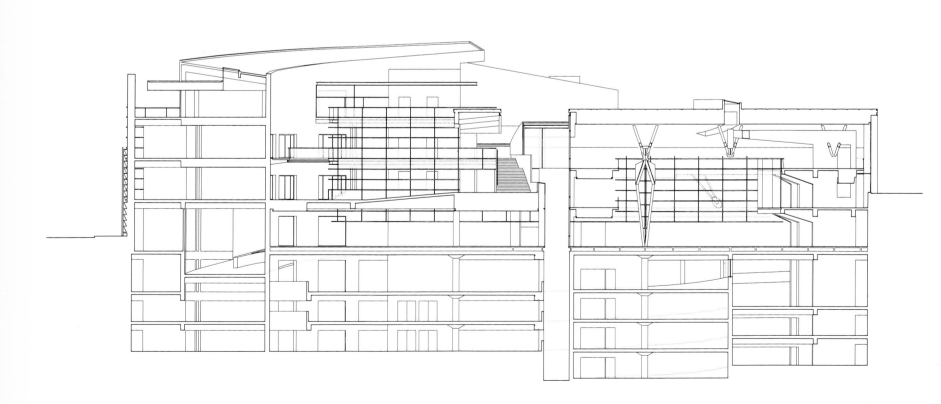

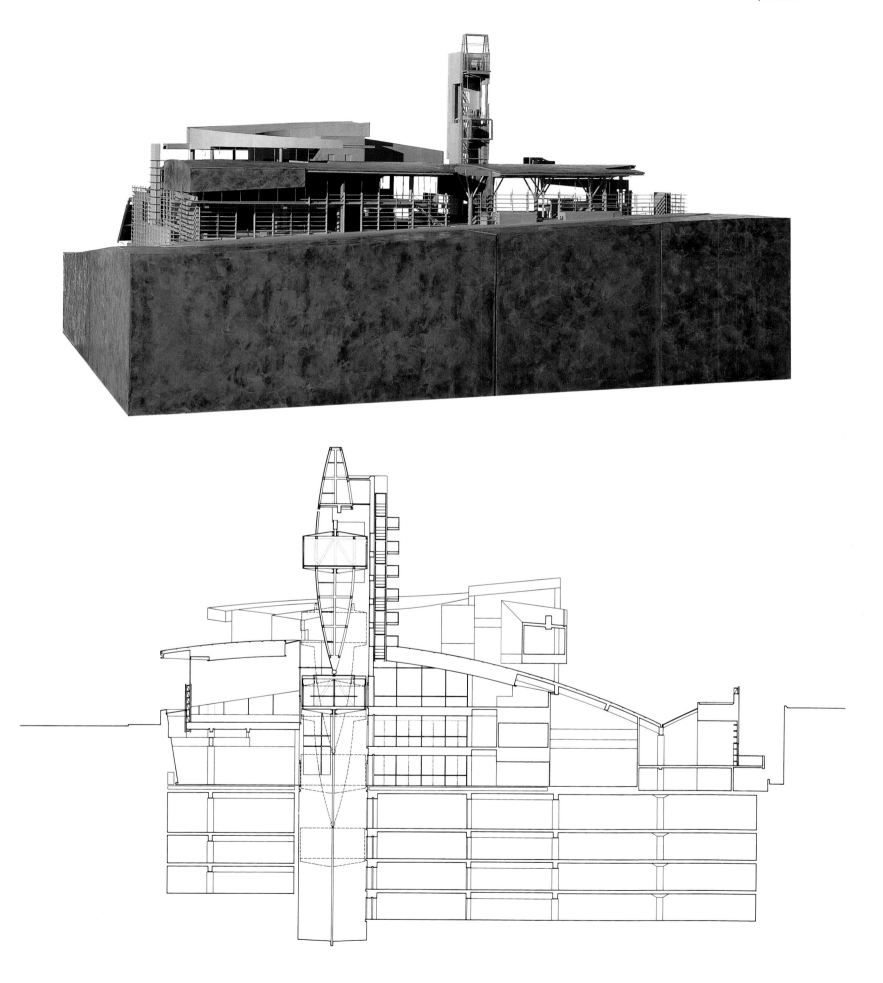

Jean Nouvel

Institut du Monde Arabe, Paris

While it may not technically meet the criteria for inclusion here, since its display of Islamic Art is only one of its several functions, this elegant new Parisian landmark fulfils a wider purpose – generally wished for but rarely achieved by many architects who design museums – of symbolising an entire culture. At a presentation given in Cairo in 1989, in acceptance of an Aga Khan Award for Architecture for this building, Jean Nouvel spoke of his intentions, and covered four main points that remain the key criteria for analysing what he has accomplished. Site constraints, as the first of these, were important because they encouraged a solution that reflects the double role of the Institute, as being both French and Arab; of representing two constituencies at the same time. The site, which is located on the Left Bank of the River Seine, at the west end of Boulevard St Germaine, is a point of transition from the river, which curves around it on one side, and a well established neighbourhood behind it giving it both a public and a private side. The second important consideration was the need to create a public identity for the Institute related to its function as a cultural repository. Using the constraints he was given to best advantage, Nouvel took the device of a central courtyard – an architectural typology found throughout the Arab world – and used it to divide the curving, public face of the building from a more secluded rectilinear element behind it that mediates between the institutional aspects of the Institute and the neighbourhood nearby. This courtyard, which is sheathed in thin alabaster sheets clipped precisely to the facade, rather than in the steel and glass used elsewhere, begins the pattern of carefully modulated spaces which Nouvel has choreographed throughout the building and indicated, in Cairo, as the third of his design criteria. These spaces, which he has characterised as 'juxtaposed' rather than 'articulated', heighten the perception of unity that Nouvel wanted to establish, and give the building a presence greater than its actual size would indicate. The choice of these subtle alabaster panels, which are translucent rather than transparent, arises

from the fourth and final criterion to be considered, namely the transformation of elements which have a cultural basis, into another context in a way that retains their original meaning, but makes them comprehensible to others. (Nouvel's now famous computerised *mashrabiyyas* are the best and most notorious example of this attempt, symbolising this 'showcase' and dialogue it represents.)

Pei, Cobb, Freed & Partners

East Wing of the National Gallery of Art, Washington DC

The design challenge presented by this museum, which has proved so popular since its completion in June 1978, lay mainly in the request by the trustees of the existing National Gallery of Art that it complement the character of this venerable Beaux Arts structure, but not be historically derivative. The programme essentially requested two different buildings with distinct functions, one to contain a museum and the other an office building. To accommodate both on a difficult site, the architects adopted a highly geometrical trapezoidal concept, which was then sliced into two complementary triangles meant to hold each building function. In plan, section and elevation the two interlocking volumes are engaged in what has been described as 'an inseparable spatial and geometric dialogue', abetted by the choice of pink Tennessee marble which mirrors the stone used in the original building.

Inside the new wing, a triangular open court is the major public space, allowing visitors to orient themselves before moving on across balconies and long span bridges to multi-level galleries – referred to as 'exhibition pods' on the plans – located in each of the three corners of the triangular structure. The court is covered by a filigree space frame made up of interlocking tetrahedrons which reiterate the underlying geometry, further animated by an enormous red mobile by Alexander Calder which throws distinctly ungeometrical shadows on the walls and floor of the main space. As Andrea Oppenheimer Dean has said:

> The relationship of the atrium and surrounding gallery rooms can be likened to a southern European village where you wander freely from the atrium-cum-town square into individual houses or shops and out again, quite a different experience from the museum as temple, which was the model for the West Building. There you proceed in straight symmetrically plotted lines along double loaded corridors from gallery to gallery.

The space synthesises the more direct appeal of the East Wing, and as Dean says thus conforms to the latest trend in which 'the museum (is a) populariser of art . . . something of an outreach programme

rather than a sanctuary'. The East Wing also contains two auditoria, including a large 440-seat hall and a smaller 100-seat theatre. Adjacent to the museum proper is a triangular study centre which contains a five-storey high reading room and six levels of library stacks. Near this space are seven floors of administrative, curatorial and academic offices, with executive offices and a board room located in a penthouse level, overlooking a roof garden below.

A landscaped plaza in front of the East Wing is integral to the complex, with a

passage below it linking the new section to the original museum. The passage is lit from above by a 'water wall', made up of a fountain on the plaza level which flows down an angled surface, falling into a pool running the length of the passage, with continuous glazing separating the two levels, another reminder of the spatial complexity that the architects have managed to balance so well.

BELOW: Overall site plan
PAGE 174 BELOW: Ground floor plan
PAGE 175 BELOW: Concourse level plan

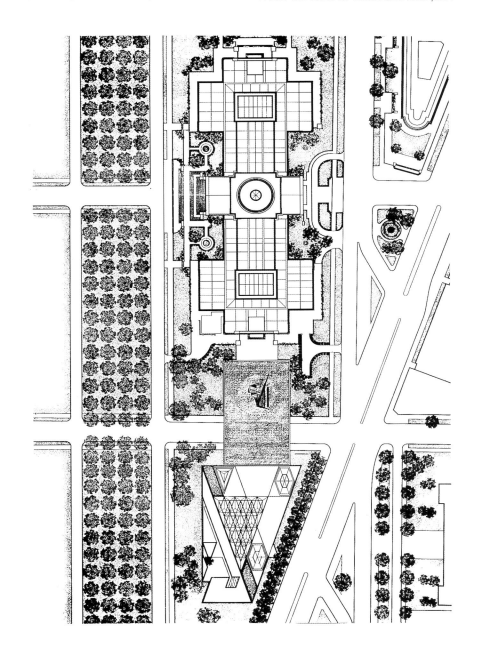

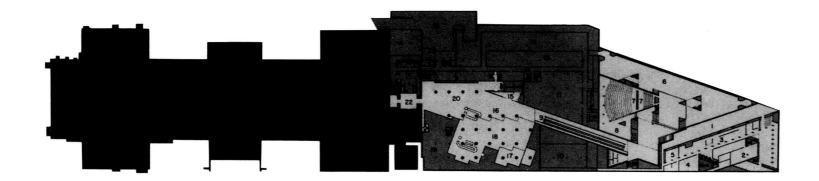

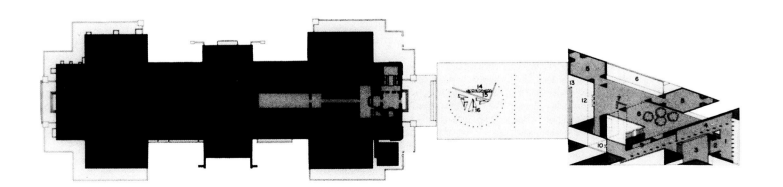

175

Pei, Cobb, Freed & Partners

The US Holocaust Memorial Museum, Washington DC

In addition to the usual challenges presented by a museum programme, here the architects had to symbolise the unspeakable in an architectural language that could be understood by everyone. Their approach, which, with the exception of the Portland Museum, is significantly different from the slick polished profiles of earlier projects, was to create a memorial, rather than just a venue for exhibits. As such only 23 per cent of the space is dedicated to the documentation of the Holocaust itself, with the majority given over to areas of commemoration and contemplation, supplemented by a library, research facility and education centre.

The building has been designed as a series of compartments, or curtains, that prepare the public for the experience within, acting as decompression chambers between the reality of the outside world and the hyper-reality of the Holocaust. Internally, the building is organised around the Hall of Witness, which is a long, three-storey ceremonial space with a conspicuous, intentional crack in its west wall, and a skewed skylight and four bridges reminiscent of those above the Warsaw Ghetto, running overhead. Such symbolism continues in the eight brick towers that surround the space, like the guard towers of the concentration camps. The four doors on the north side of the Hall echo those of the death camp ovens, and the gates that control access to the displays suggest imprisonment. The Octagonal Hall of Remembrance, which projects out as a separate entity at the 15th Street entrance, is flooded with light and lined with niches for memorial candles. It favours the southern side of the rectilinear site in order to join with an L-shaped element containing permanent exhibitions, library archives and administration that is linked to it. This element, which is treated differently in massing and materials, continues the monumentality of the Octagon Hall, and seems to embrace the brick towers, protecting them from the outside world.

This variance in formal treatment, from highly articulated, iconographic pieces joined together in an ordered network, to a monumental, scaleless wall against the street and Federal office buildings nearby, heightens the evocative character of the building, which is an anomaly among the more anonymous museums along the Washington Mall.

The layering of functional requirements, such as the circulation of the high numbers of visitors typical in the Mall museums, with the symbolic aspects that were deliberately made a part of the design agenda, has resulted in ingenious plans on every level. These plans are graphically expressive of the complexity of purpose and a remarkable departure from the calculated detachment and analytical geometry of the East Wing of the National Gallery, on Pennsylvania Avenue.

PAGE 179 FROM ABOVE: Ground floor plan; concourse plan; west elevation with Auditor's Complex to the left and the Bureau of Engraving to the right; east elevation

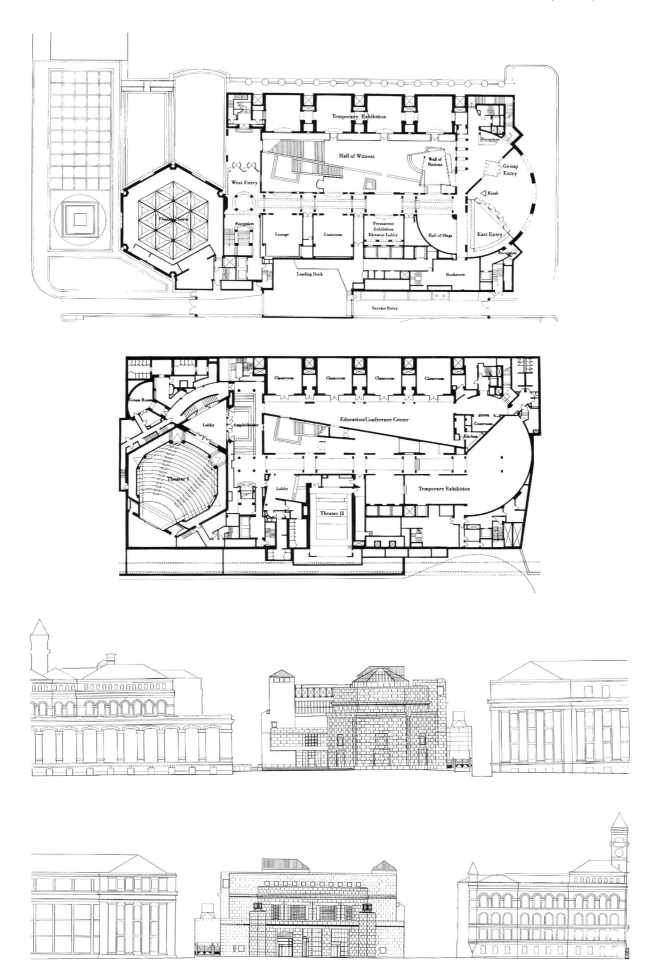

Pei, Cobb, Freed & Partners

Extension of the Louvre, Paris

With the tremendous popularity of the Louvre, one of the world's foremost museums, it was inevitable that an extension would one day be necessary. The Louvre was begun in 1202 by Philippe Auguste as a fortified castle and transformed by every French king thereafter. Having been opened to the general public at limited times by Louis XV and greatly expanded as a museum by Napoleon, this series of royal residences had never been intended to function as spaces for exhibition, and with only a fraction of the 40 per cent of support space now considered mandatory for museums, can be likened to a theatre without a back stage. The architects were commissioned to correct this historical oversight, and the challenge was to renovate and significantly expand this uniquely important national monument while enhancing its links with the city and improving the facilities necessary for public use, without compromising the integrity of the historic palace. The fact that the museum had to remain in operation during this process also added to the architect's difficulties.

The proposed solution was an incrementally phased expansion beginning with a centrally located main entrance of 500,000 square feet to provide more direct gallery access, as well as the provision of new technical and support facilities and public amenities. This is currently being augmented by a second phase, including the conversion of the former Ministry of France wing into galleries, which is expected to double the amount of exhibition space allowing the presentation of over five thousand works previously held in storage, and the first unified display of Islamic art in galleries surrounding the skylit courts of the Cour Khosabad, Puget and Marly, in addition to new parking facilities.

Until recently, public areas in the U-shaped Louvre were restricted because the Ministry of Finance occupied the Richelieu wing on the north. The relocation of this government agency has finally allowed the entire complex to function as a museum for the first time in its history, making the Grand Louvre, with 1,400,000 square feet of space, the largest museum in the world.

The main entrance is the critical part of this entire scheme, and the glass pyramid, which is the new centre of gravity in the Cour Napoleon, has also become the symbol of the museum's regeneration. On a more pragmatic level it serves as the skylight for the main reception area, which is ingeniously placed underground to be unobtrusive in the midst of such imposing historical splendour. The pyramid allows visitors to descend by escalator or spiral stairs to the Hall of Napoléon which is the new central core of the museum. This area contains tourist and staff facilities, information desks, shops, restaurants and a 450-seat auditorium, as well as two temporary exhibition galleries, storage rooms, restoration studios and the newly excavated remains of Philippe Auguste's medieval palace. An open balcony with two cafes creates an encircling mezzanine around the hall. Three wide corridors radiating out of the hall provide direct access to the art collections in the existing wings of the museum with smaller pyramidal skylights providing orientation to each of the galleries. The pyramid in the east corridor leads to a two-storey rotunda where, after 450 years, a series of limestone bas-reliefs executed for the Louvre by Jean Goujon, have finally been installed. Visitors can now avoid the frustrating and time consuming effort spent finding galleries in the past, and concentrate instead on the art they have come to see.

BELOW: Axonometric of Cour Napoléon, showing the glass pyramid and new underground reception and galleries
PAGE 182 BELOW: Ground level plan
PAGE 183 BELOW: Reception level plan

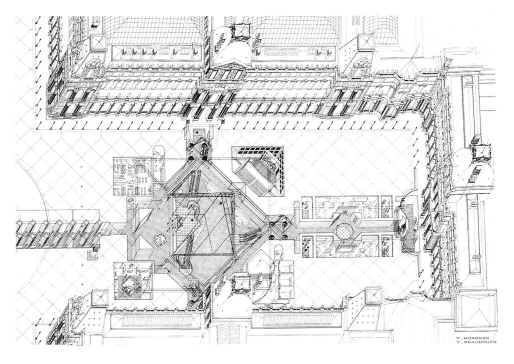

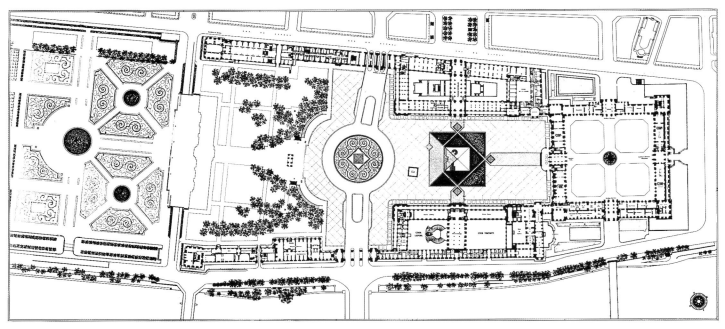

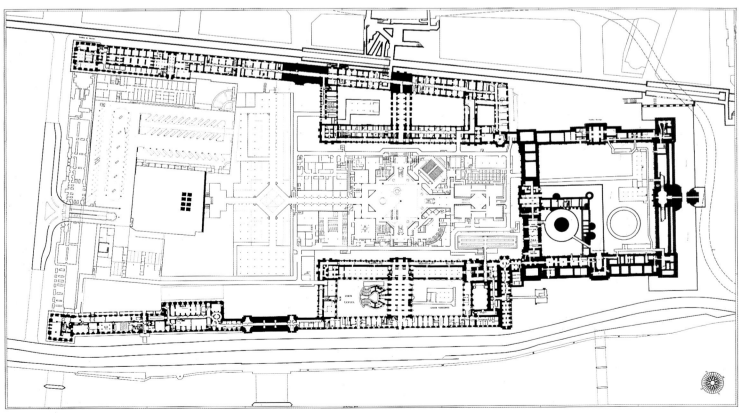

Pei, Cobb, Freed & Partners

The Charles Shipman Payson Building at Portland Museum of Art, Portland, Maine

One of the most striking features of the majority of the new museums shown here is their sympathetic consideration of context, whereas for a long time the museum existed in its own formidable, isolated monumentality. Pei, Cobb, Freed's new wing at Portland Museum of Art is a notable contribution to this trend belonging to the same genre as the Hood by Charles Moore, or Stirling and Wilford's brilliant unrealised scheme for Düsseldorf, all of which bring architectural self-effacement to new levels of efficacy. Like their solution to the difficulties posed by the Louvre, the Pei office's approach to Portland, albeit at a much more humble scale, is further proof that even those who were capable of sensational objectification – in their addition to the National Gallery in Washington DC – are now aware of localised constraints. Materials, scale and sequence of space in relationship to pre-existing conditions, are all handled in an extremely sensitive way, respecting the small New England town in which the museum is located.

In their own description of the Charles Shipman Payson wing, the architects provide an overview of their addition to Portland's traditional urban context:

The challenge presented by the new wing was largely one of integration on a constricted and awkwardly shaped downtown site. The front of the building required a strong urban statement to address a major city square; the back, by contrast, demanded a smaller-scaled response in a landscaped setting to complement the historic houses that comprised the existing museum. . . The museum is articulated with granite trim and waterstruck brick that was handmade and fired according to techniques passed down from colonial settlers. Such indigenous materials were selected to weave the building into its historic urban context, and to reaffirm the masonry traditions that have contributed so significantly to Portland's distinctive character over the past two hundred years. Technically, the outer shell is a painstakingly crafted response to the museum's rigorous requirements for climate control . . . Within the thickness of the brick envelope an innovative insulation system provides a vapour barrier that protects the museum's exhibition galleries from the moisture and extreme temperatures of Portland's northern seaport climate. [Internally the museum is organised] on a grid of primary spatial modules and interstitial zones . . . The modular system is clearly expressed on the sides and rear of the wing where the building mass, stacked like cubes in graduated rows, steps back and down to the ground . . . Such fragmentation into a series of brick boxes permits the new wing to complement the form and scale of the museum's three historic houses, themselves simple blocks of granite and brick. One enters the building through a series of simple volumes, each of which leads clearly to the next in a controlled spatial sequence . . . From the Great Hall visitors have access to all parts of the museum . . . the Great Hall, however, is much more than a mere entry space. It has been designed as a source of light, a point of orientation, and a provocative visual link to the exhibition spaces and circulation networks threaded through the museum . . . In architectural design, as in the collections displayed, the museum is dedicated to the celebration of Portland and Maine.

BELOW: Elevation of main facade

Piano and Fitzgerald

De Menil Museum, Houston, Texas

The dramatic contrast between this project's simplicity of form and the complexity of its roof accentuates the problem of lighting which is a major concern for every architect dealing with this building type and has, along with the way in which a collection is presented, historically been of prime significance in museum design.

The respective merits of top versus side lighting, which were debated in determining the configuration of galleries in the nineteenth century, were eclipsed by more specific concerns in the middle of the twentieth century, when scientific findings began to indicate the degree to which natural light damages paintings, drawings, photographs and fabrics. Findings about the detrimental effects of ultraviolet radiation, which began to appear in earnest in the early 1960s, proved that light had to be controlled. As Michael Compton has explained in *Progressive Architecture*:

> the damaging effects of light are proportionate to both intensity and time. If low levels are acceptable at times, higher levels can be permitted at others. If, however, 100 lux is felt to be a minimum below which visitors can reasonably complain and 150 the average, there is little margin for higher levels and control must be tight. In Victorian galleries the natural variation is from almost nil up to 5,000 lux plus. At the same time, variations in the humidity levels must be minimised. Accordingly systems had to be devised to shield glazing and hanging surfaces from direct sunlight, to black out galleries when not in use, and to respond to the intensity of exterior light, to keep the interiors within the limits required.

The roof of the De Menil Museum, which visually dominates the extensive elevations, is made up of gracefully curved ferrocement hoods suspended from a truss fabricated from a relatively brittle grade of cast iron, carefully specified to match the rate of expansion and contraction of the array it supports. Peter Rice of Ove Arup, who engineered the entire system, has collaborated with Renzo Piano once before, in the Piano/Rogers design for the Pompidou Centre in Paris, where a similar type of cast iron was also used. The appeal of the metallic mixture which they have devised, is that it is less dense than cast steel, has a high resistance to cracking in tension, and can be more accurately calibrated to obtain a precise configuration. While deceptively straightforward in appearance, the roof assembly, which evolved through three different configurations, was quite difficult to resolve. The result is an interior that is washed in diffused natural light, and a world class cultural institution that is the pride of Houston.

Antoine Predock

American Heritage Center and Art Museum, Laramie, Wyoming

In this enormous complex, which is one of the largest projects Antoine Predock has designed to date, the architect has demonstrated his unwavering commitment to an architecture that reflects local history and environment, which in this instance was made more difficult by the size and complexity of the programme. Using the time-honoured device of a central axis to bring order to the many functions he was required to accommodate, Predock has positioned the tepee-like Heritage Center at the head of it, with a central fireplace located in the middle of a sunken square seating area, serving to reiterate his metaphorical intent. The upper levels of this main compositional device are stepped back, opening up onto the central, public space to visually combine private office functions with the reception level below.

Using an arcing pedestrian walkway as a device with which to displace the axis, he cleverly alters its position, shifting it further north with a second, much smaller, circular rotunda serving as the second head, from which the new axis related to the museum component of the complex extends. Along this duplicated, interior spine, one large and three pairs of small galleries extend east towards a final, square space divided by spiralling partitions into additional galleries of different sizes. The outside area made available by the displacement, is connected to the gallery clusters by a series of openings between the pairs, leading out to an extended sculpture garden on the southern side of the complex, intentionally oriented to tap the sun during the short summers and long winters in Wyoming. By raising the museum up on an earth berm the architect is also able to provide the necessary service spaces directly below, using large elevators, as well as pairs of stairs along the axis, to connect the levels which are almost equal in size. In this aspect alone, Predock reveals his pragmatic ability to provide that area of a museum which most architects neglect, and the service component here is commendable, even if a trifle rigid.

RIGHT: Plan of main level

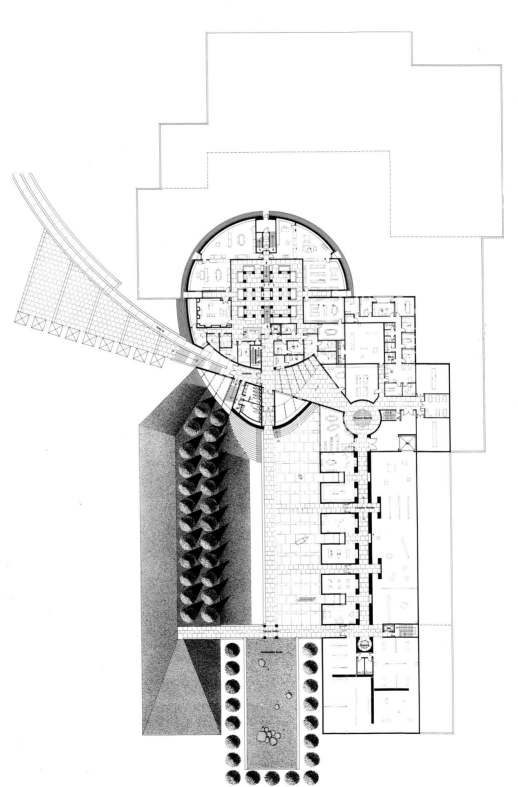

Antoine Predock

Las Vegas Library and Discovery Museum, Nevada

In 1984, the Board of Directors of both the existing Children's Museum and the Library District in Las Vegas, realising that their expansion programmes coincided in many ways, decided to collaborate in a facility that would mutually benefit both of them. The site they chose has one of the only natural Artesian wells in the high desert, which in the past made it the logical choice for a Paiute village, and also for the first community of settlers from the east that displaced them.

Predock's main concessions to this historical layering are a conical, tepee-shaped 'birthday room' in the centre of the complex, and the clustering of elements around the helical 'flagpole' of the science tower behind it, both of which recall the conflicting societies of the past. The Strip is the predominant culture in Las Vegas today, and its proximity to the site has allowed Predock to take advantage of a magnetic levitation monorail which brings visitors right to the front door of the project.

A wedge, conceptually pointing north towards the mountains in the distance, has a double purpose; it separates the library from the museums and provides 'Oasis' and 'Mountain' courtyards which are accessible to both, as well as a 'Desert' courtyard near the entrance. This completes the architectural representation of local ecology, continuing Predock's strategy of breaking down a potentially monumental structure into child-sized spaces.

The prow of this linking/dividing wedge, and the science tower next to it, are the most prominent features of an otherwise subdued complex, which seems even more modest as a result of its siting at the crest of a slope planted with regimented rows of palm trees. This area is used for parking and is connected to the main entrance by a gradual ramp. Runway lights in the top of the science tower spiral give out a red glow at night, a subliminal echo of the surreal, electric panorama of the Strip nearby. By his use of small details such as this, Predock has given his architecture additional references to its context, stressing the inside and its relationship to the children who are its primary occupants,

without neglecting the fact that the museum, like the casinos, is a sign, although of a totally different function. Comparisons between it and his Heritage Center in Laramie and Fine Arts Center at the University of Arizona show a necessary change in scale, but Predock's use of severe, referential forms, and the evolution of a regionally based language that is heuristic rather than literal is still in evidence.

BELOW: Plan of main level
PAGE 197: Cutaway isometric of site

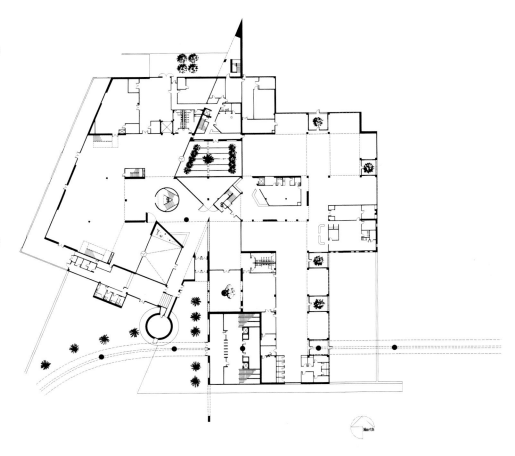

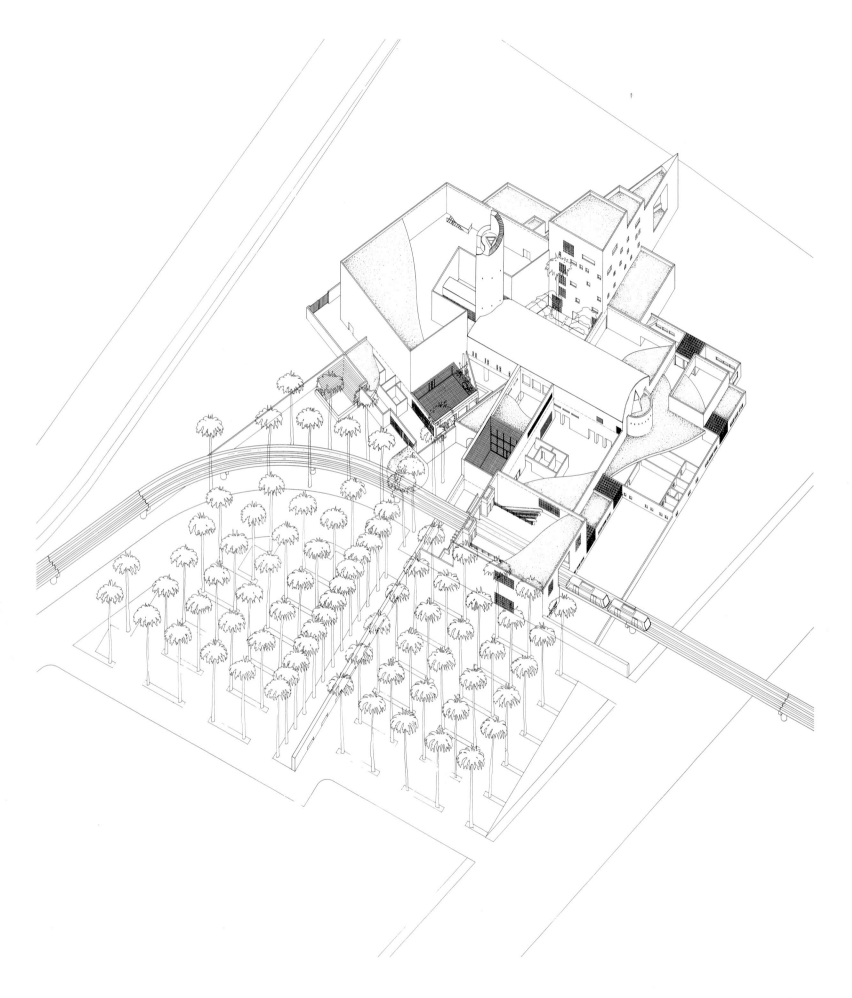

Antoine Predock

Arizona State University Fine Arts Center, Tempe, Arizona

The museum component of the enormous Fine Arts Complex houses the university's $15,000,000 art collection which consists principally of contemporary work. Rather than striving for flexibility, Predock approached the problem of the display of this permanent exhibition as a technical challenge related to the control of light and ultraviolet degradation. Steel deck with a light-weight concrete topping, as well as a single-ply membrane roof with light coloured gravel for maximum solar reflection, have been used as the primary means of achieving this protection, as have the relatively massive walls which make the museum appear like a fortress to those in the closely knit campus community surrounding it. Flying bridges, quasi-Gothic spires and metaphorical sphinxes serve to lighten this heaviness, mitigating the solidity that has been used as the environmental corollary to an inwardly focused complex. The external skin has been converted into a sculptural garden, with the architect taking maximum advantage of the impression to be gained from sharp forms outlined against a normally clear blue Arizona sky.

In contrast to the severe concrete grey exterior, gypsum board reflectors assisted by incandescent tracks mounted in light monitors selectively wash each of the galleries with controlled illumination, further particularising each of the highly individual spaces. While as minimal as the exterior walls and courts, the addition of these orchestrated patterns of light and colour transform the interior exhibition spaces into a different world, while at the same time being carefully handled so as not to overwhelm the exhibitions.

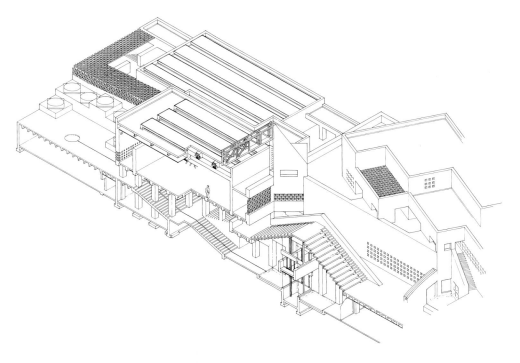

RIGHT: Cutaway isometric
PAGE 201 FROM ABOVE: Second level plan; ground level plan

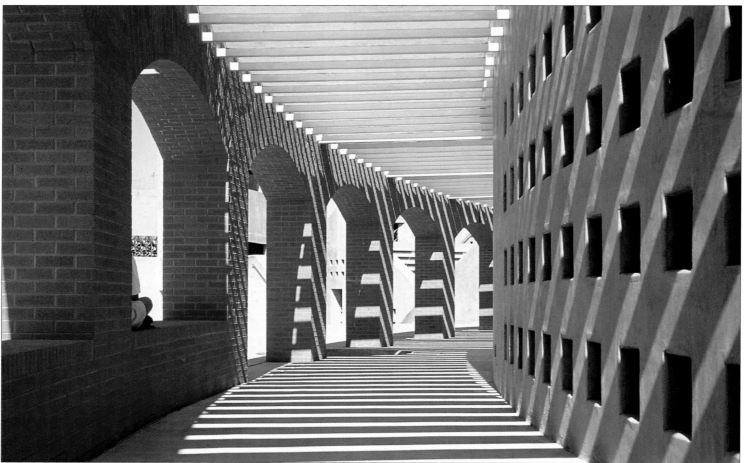

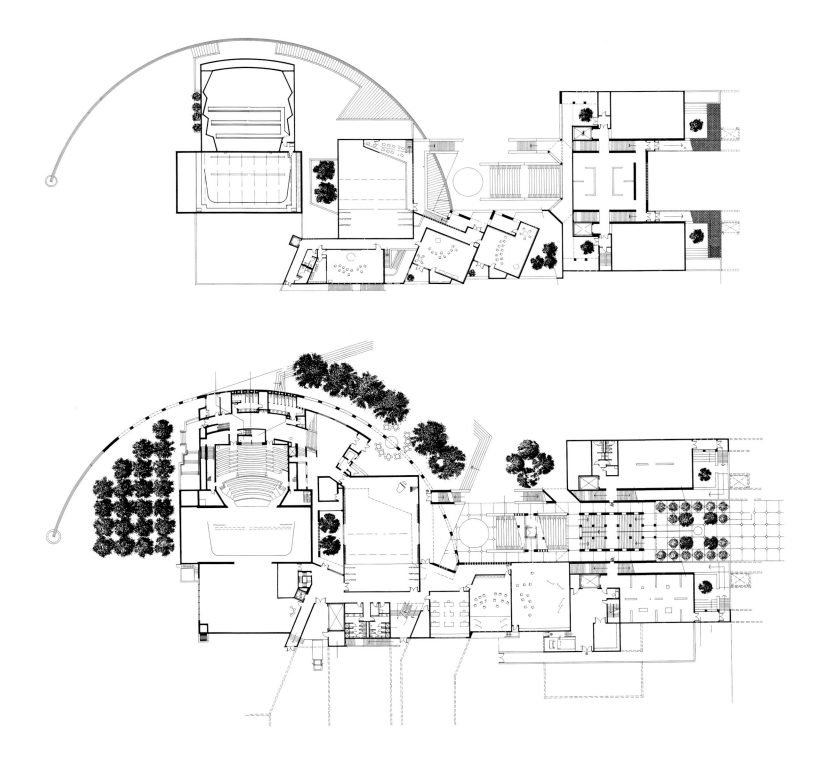

Ian Ritchie

The Ecology Gallery of the Natural History Museum, London

The essential aim of the Ecology Gallery is to inform the public of the intricacy and beauty of the planet, and the fragile balance that exists between the human and natural world. Ian Ritchie's design is centred around three requirements: the importance of a 'charismatic structure' required by the British Museum brief; the importance of complementing Waterhouse's existing building in the symmetrical planning and spatial sequence used, and of reinforcing the 'informative and witty' details decorating the 'steel armature' of this Grade 1 listed building; and finally that the exhibition is not permanent, running until 2001.

Accordingly, Ian Ritchie set out to create an exhibition that did not touch any part of the main building except the floor, sensitively responding to a pre-established linear discipline, and promoting a volumetric appreciation of the spatial qualities already inherent in the galleries. To achieve this, original details, especially those high up in the rooms, were highlighted to establish what Ritchie has called 'a visual dialogue with Waterhouse's architecture'. In doing so, the architect has also managed to cast doubt on the traditional anthropocentric view of nature by creating an awareness of the fragility of the human position in the ecological equation, and to offer exhibition designers the opportunity to create an exciting unidirectional route through the space, using the latest presentation methods. He describes his intentions here as being:

> . . . in the spirit of the original intent of Sir Richard Owen in commissioning the building, which was to bring to the general public, in a modern way, the latest understanding of the natural world. He also thought that light should be from the top, not directly overhead, but from the junction of walls and roofs. This is exactly the location we have selected for the artificial light source, which is diffused through the glass walls with decreasing intensity towards the floor, yet illuminates the column heads and ceiling through the central axis of the exhibition. We have noted from the early design drawings by Fowkes, and later by Waterhouse, that the east and west galleries were column-free, and where columns existed they were placed at the perimeter of the galleries. It appears that the late decision to add a third floor to these galleries was resolved structurally and economically by the addition of columns down the centre of the galleries, which was not the original intent for these gallery spaces.

Waterhouse used the space between the central columns and the external walls by placing large glass cabinets perpendicular to the latter. In our design approach we have restated the glass cabinet idea, but parallel to the external walls, creating large glass cabinets into which both the visitor and the exhibits are invited. This design concept thus responds both to the architecture and to the memory of Waterhouse's design, as well as accepting the current exhibition.

These concepts are supported by a spectacular, back-lit panel at the end of the gallery, which has bridges intermittently shooting in front of it, and the veiled forms of people appearing and disappearing through glass walls, all of which pull curious visitors into a symbolic dialogue with the evolution of the earth, and a deeper understanding of the degree to which natural resources have been manipulated.

BELOW: Perspectives showing space and structure

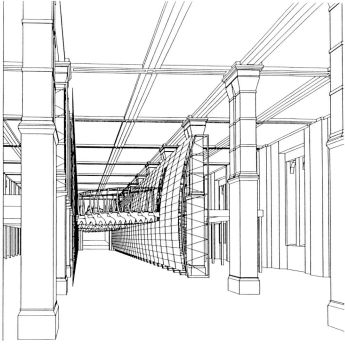

Ian Ritchie

Reina Sofia Museum of Modern Art, Madrid

The baroque building that Ritchie was asked to take on was built in the second half of the eighteenth century by Francisco Sabatini, during the reign of Charles III, and rescued from demolition only a decade ago by Antonio Fernandez Alba. Part of the building, which was originally a hospital, was converted into the Museum of the Spanish People in 1986. Through the efforts of architects Antonio Vazquez de Castro and José Luis Iniquez de Onzono the remainder became the National Art Centre, with its own permanent collection which revolves around Picasso's *Guernica*, and was inaugurated by King Juan Carlos and Queen Sofia in 1990. Ian Ritchie explains:

It transpired that the architects had discussed with several Modern Art Museum directors in Europe the essential characteristics of contemporary art galleries and their conclusion was that their intervention and architecture should be minimalist. They and the Huarte directors were familiar with our glass structures at La Villette . . . However, Huarte [the contractors] came to see us on their own initiative and it was evident that the progress of resolving and realising the vertical movement of the public was not satisfactory. It was, in Spain, incumbent upon the contractors to achieve the results and evidently they saw us as a potential International Rescue Team. In fact, the first conversations revolved around their desire to have the La Villette glass system and ours to design a tailored solution, unique to the new Centre of Modern Art.

The basic principle of the glass support devised by Ritchie is to clearly separate the external system carrying the weight of the glazing and the internal system which stiffens the glass against horizontal wind loads. The entire glass envelope of each tower is hung by stainless steel rods from the roof, and each glass panel is individually supported in order to evenly distribute differences in thermal expansion between the glazing and the steel across all of the joints between the panels. Wind loads, which were an extremely important factor in the design of these towers, are transmitted through connectors to adjoining panels and back to the main structure. Secondary vertical structural members resist wind loads between floors. The size of each glass panel is determined by wind load, economy of thickness, and the height between floors. The glazing method used by Ritchie follows a tested and pre-established procedure, but the method of suspension is more innovative, using simple components designed to allow easy monitoring of a quality and rapid manufacture in the quantities required. The story of the design of these two striking towers is best told by Ritchie himself:

. . . we investigated the idea of creating complexity from a composition and juxtaposition of individual minimal components. We also felt that the hospital building with its immense *gravitas* and its vertical fenestration, should keep its strength and character, and so the idea of working in contrast to it, thereby reinforcing the building's intrinsic character seemed totally appropriate. This should also allow the tower designs to have their own character, equally reinforced by the existing building's architecture. In essence, our concept was to create towers representing modernity (in response to the hospital's new use), suspension and transparency in contrast to *gravitas* and solidity . . . Their performance was to ensure effective movement for thousands of visitors a day, the aim being to achieve a degree of transparency that reduces visual impact from outside and allows uninterrupted views from inside, both when waiting and, more spectacularly, when riding in the lifts – a pause to make visual contact and reorient yourself with the world outside the museum. Translating these conceptual objectives in our visual research required one further proposition upon which the design of all the elements could be related. This was drawn from the existing building's surfaces and profiles, the walls, the stone window frames, with the singular exception of the circular steel window bars; and also from the intrinsic nature of manufactured materials of which the towers are made. This notion of planarity, we also felt, had a relationship to *Guernica*, which is a collage composed of black, grey and white superimposed flat cut outs.

BELOW: Sectional isometric of elevator shaft

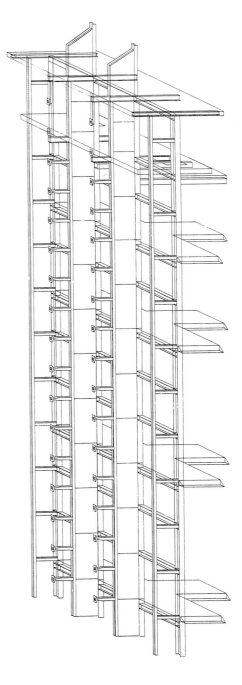

Aldo Rossi

Bonnefanten Museum, Maastricht, the Netherlands

Following the demolition of the 'Céramique' district in Maastricht, which was historically the centre of the china and porcelain industry there, the province of Limburg and the national government have selected a number of local and international architectural superstars to contribute to the redevelopment process. This will include nearly two thousand housing units, office and institute space, restaurant, retail and hotel complexes, and a 'cultural component' in which Aldo Rossi's Bonnefanten Museum is the central showpiece. As originally presented in the spring of 1991, Rossi's preliminary scheme lacked none of the bravado which has come to be expected of him, with the linear parti he is fond of this time arranged in an E-shaped configuration opening out onto the River Maas. The middle bar of the E – which begins with a monumental entry, lit by a telescoping atrium, connected by a stair that is curiously reminiscent of Stirling's Sackler to an enormous, silo-like space – is cleverly allotted as the architectonic event of the complex, leaving the outer wings available for more pragmatic designations.

Whether the circulatory association with the Sackler is deliberate or not, and early sketches indicate that the central stair was simply seen as a symbolic link between juxtaposed, inverted verticals, a further comparison between the two schemes has some justification, due to the way the galleries have been handled in each case. Rather than using the stair as a combination of staged platforms feeding into various levels of offices and exhibition space as

Stirling did, Rossi has retained the ceremonial aspect of the central block and has segregated the offices, storage and gallery functions by level; he has had much more success at arriving at an arrangement of rooms which allow flexibility of display, and yet can be lit with an ordered sequence and pattern of external fenestration.

In spite of the fact that the Céramique district covers more than 20 hectares, the space allocation for the museum was restricted to a degree that made it necessary for the architect, in his preliminary design, to request demolition of the glass factory, which has now been incorporated in his final scheme.

VAISNIERES
EN LIMOUSIN
FR.
88

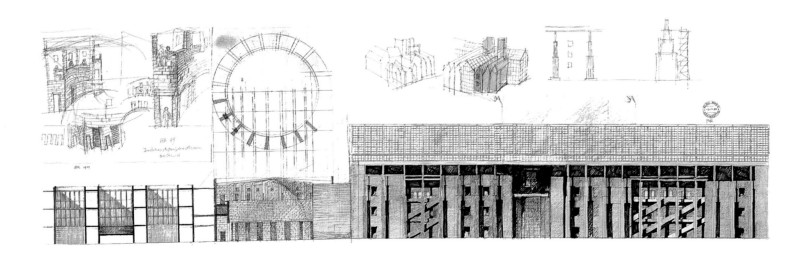

Aldo Rossi

The Museum of German History, Berlin

The setting for the museum, between the meandering curve of the River Spree, near the Moltke Bridge, and the rectilinear Republic Place, where the Reichstag was located, required a double-edged solution responding to both conditions. The purpose of the museum also demanded a theoretical stance on the question of historical reference, including Germany's position as the birthplace of Modernism. Rossi responded in a characteristically subtle way, with typologies that have universal, as well as national significance. He says of his approach:

> This is not architecture symbolic of modernity: we are convinced that architecture does not symbolise modernity or an abstract civilisation; it is the product of an era, generated by place and history. The museum does not intend to project an image of German history, since that is no longer possible today, given our dispersed capacity for synthesis. At the most, it can portray fragments of life, history and buildings, that intelligent architecture has attempted to compose.

Some of these typologies, such as the arcade that acts as a transitional element between serrated galleries and the park on the land side, are recognisable from the Gallartesse and Modena projects, and so are less specific than the circular entrance armature, and a smaller component to the left of the entry that contains a library, conference rooms, documentation services and an auditorium. Recalling Stirling's earlier use of a central drum at Stuttgart, also placed in the centre in recognition of Schinkel's Altes Museum, Rossi's rotunda differs slightly in that it is not open to the sky. It has a dome that does not protrude past the cornice line, which, perhaps coincidentally, has a distinctly Speer-like profile. In a similar way, the curtain walls between the stairwells of the library present another of the 'fragments' that Rossi mentions, recalling the *Glasarchitektur* of Sheerbart, and the Bauhaus that followed the galleries inside the protogothic.

RIGHT ABOVE AND CENTRE: Republic Place elevation; river elevation
OPPOSITE: Preliminary sketches

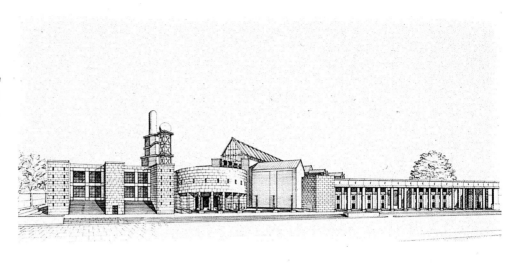

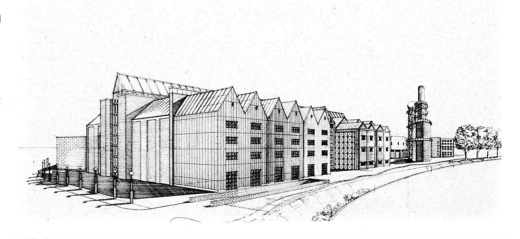

Aldo Rossi

Vassivière Contemporary Arts Centre, Limousin, France

Not likely to be initially identified as a museum, Rossi's Arts Centre, on an island in the midst of 1,000 hectares of lakes located between Limoges and Clermont-Ferrand, is an unlikely intruder in this wilderness of woods, water and rocks, but the logic behind it gradually becomes apparent. As part of a bid by local authorities to make the area one of the major tourist attractions of the Limousin region, the centre has an undeniably commercial agenda, which Rossi, with characteristic abstraction, has redirected into a more basic and timeless interface between art and nature. Not only a series of spaces for exhibition, the building is also intended to serve as a base for the artists whose work will be shown there, with their ateliers located on the ground floor of a linear, trussed, bridge-like structure. Intended to recall the horizontality of the lakes and hills surrounding it, the atelier-gallery-office-lecture hall reiterates the connection through walls of local granite, making it seem to jut out from rather than sit on the hill on which it is built, with its vertical tree-like lighthouse acting as an anchor. The hill is used to establish the level of the floors within, as in the Tate at St Ives by Evans and Shalev, but in this case the context is natural rather than architectural. It is an anomaly – on one hand an obviously unnatural intrusion into an idyllic setting and on the other a harmonious part of it, with sympathetic materials and composition – an example of the kind of tension that is part of Rossi's style. Diminutive in scale, the ensemble nonetheless holds its own in its rugged setting, defiantly pointing to the lakes on the horizon, a monastic retreat (of a religious order related to art) as much as a museum. As in Rossi's other work, it is also far more complex than an initial glance would lead one to believe, with a high level of diversity emerging from an evidently simple and deliberately rational envelope, with a tightly ordered structure. The result is a unique museum which extends the debate on the typology, and the ways in which it can and cannot change.

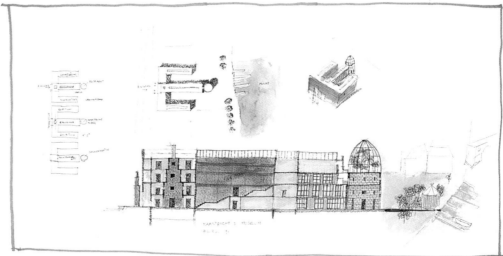

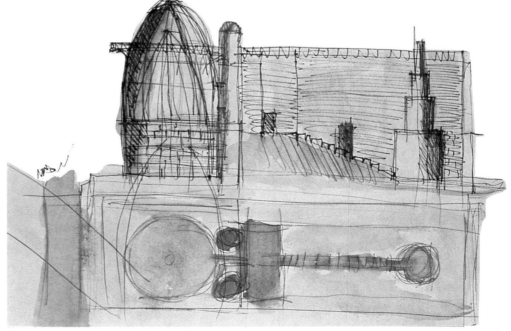

RIGHT: Preliminary and sketch plans and sections

James Stirling and Michael Wilford

The Clore Gallery at The Tate Gallery, London

The Clore Gallery was commissioned to accommodate the three hundred oils and nineteen thousand watercolours and drawings of the Turner Bequest to at last comply with the artist's wish that his finished paintings be seen together under one roof.

Significant factors in the design of the extension were concern for the surrounding landscape and sympathy for the existing architecture. With these criteria in mind Stirling Wilford designed an L-shaped building on two floors set back from the Tate Gallery frontage to connect with the existing building at a point behind its pavilioned corner, leaving its symmetry undisturbed. The extended garden in front of the gallery retains the existing plane trees and includes new lawns laid across Bulinga Street to the Lodge. Approach to the new building is along garden footpaths to a sunken terrace with seating, a pergola and pool. Indeed, James Stirling compared the new gallery to a garden building, or orangery, in its relationship to the dignified mass of the Tate itself.

The nine galleries in which the oil paintings are displayed are toplit, with external louvres to eliminate light during hours of closure. Controlled artificial lighting is provided in all those galleries housing works on paper. In addition to adequate, environmentally controlled gallery space, the architects have provided a Print Room and ancillary storage space, a paper conservation studio, a lecture theatre to seat 180 people, a public reading room and staff accommodation. Circulation between the extension and the main building is continuous and easy (the upper level in the Clore Gallery coincides with existing gallery level of the Tate) and access is normally via the original Tate building. However, separate access to the Clore, which will allow the use of other facilities at times when the galleries themselves are closed to the public, is catered for through its own distinctive entrance and entrance staircase.

One of the most distinctive features of the Clore Gallery, and something which immediately brings the Stuttgart museum to mind, is the bold use of colour and materials

with vivid green and bright red complemented externally and internally by the warm shades of Portland stone, brickwork in dark red and buff, 'London pink' granite and oak finishes.

BELOW: Sectional perspective view of entrance staircase and stairwell
PAGE 219 FROM ABOVE: Ground floor plan; first floor plan
PAGE 221 FROM ABOVE: Longitudinal section; cross section; sectional perspective of gallery level

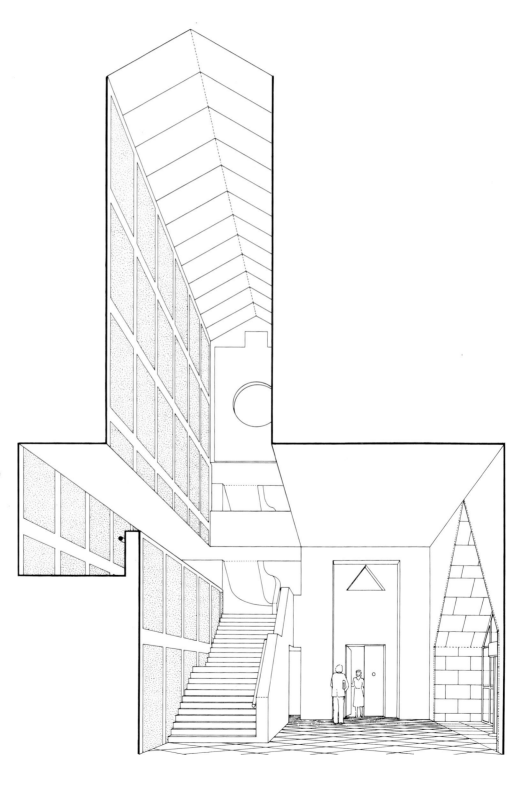

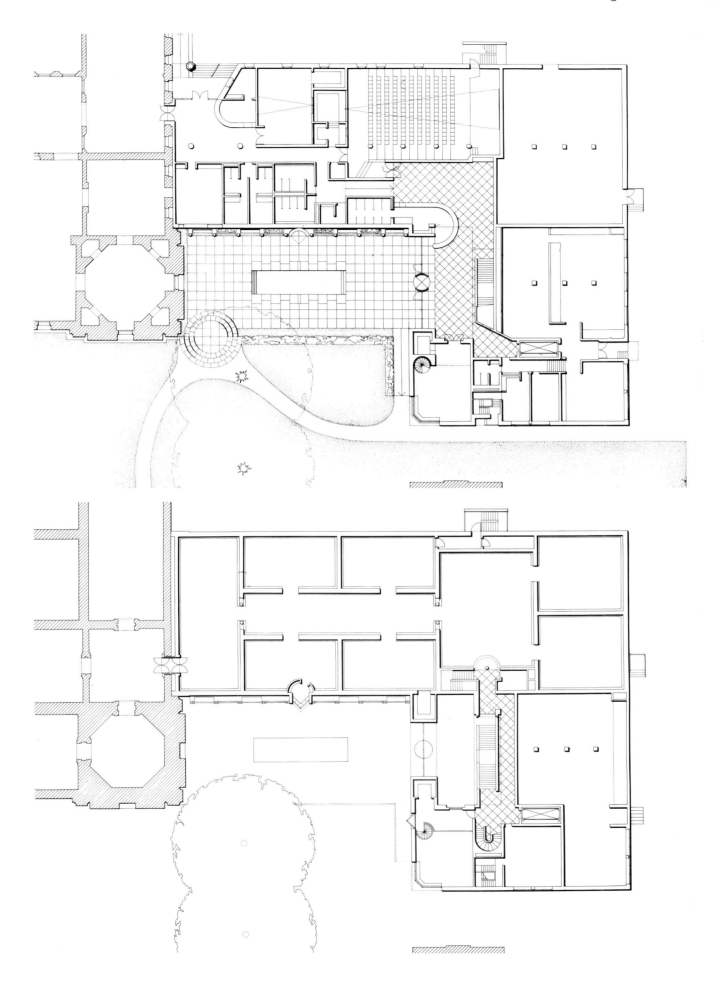

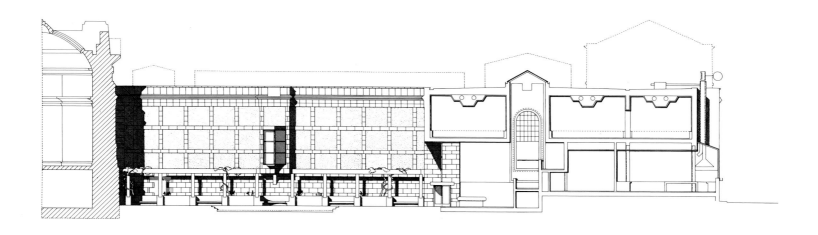

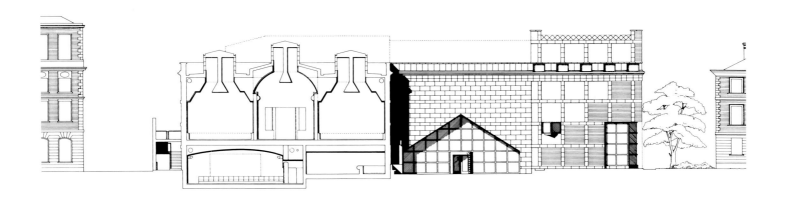

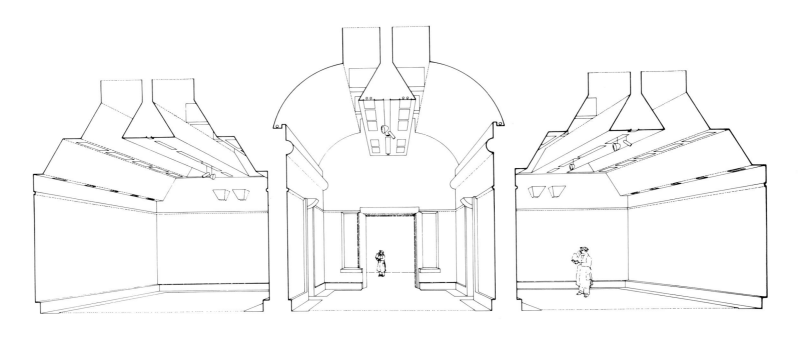

James Stirling and Michael Wilford

The Tate Gallery at Liverpool, England

Opened in 1988, Stirling Wilford's Liverpool Tate is located in the northwest corner of the mid-nineteenth-century Albert Dock, and houses the gallery's contemporary art collection. The project involved the conversion of a seven-storey warehouse which included a basement and mezzanine floor, and in plan was divided into three areas by brick spine and cross-walls. This conversion, in deference to the existing building, made alterations only where necessary.

At entry level the existing mezzanine was removed from all areas except the north end, where the minimum floor to ceiling height was adapted for administrative and curatorial offices, a reading room, videotheque and educational facilities. The dockside galleries and those along the back overlooking the River Mersey can be used independently for separate exhibitions, with the visitor returning to the entrance hall to gain access via a new central staircase and lifts to the first and second floor galleries. A double bow fronted balcony at mezzanine level overlooks the hall and accommodates a bookshop and cafe.

The major adjustment to the interior was the inclusion of a service core containing the existing stair shaft, a new central staircase, passenger lifts, goods lifts, escape staircases and vertical service ducts.

A second phase of construction will develop the Gallery in the light of six years operational experience, and create five new gallery spaces on the fouth floor, along with an auditorium and seminar rooms. Educational and information facilities will be expanded and an artist's studio introduced on the first floor.

RIGHT: Up-view isometric of entry colonnade
PAGE 224 FROM ABOVE: Ground floor plan; cutaway down-view axonometric of ground floor
PAGE 225 FROM ABOVE: First floor plan; cutaway down-view axonometric of ground and first floors
PAGE 226 BELOW: Elevation of main facade
PAGE 227 BELOW: Cross section

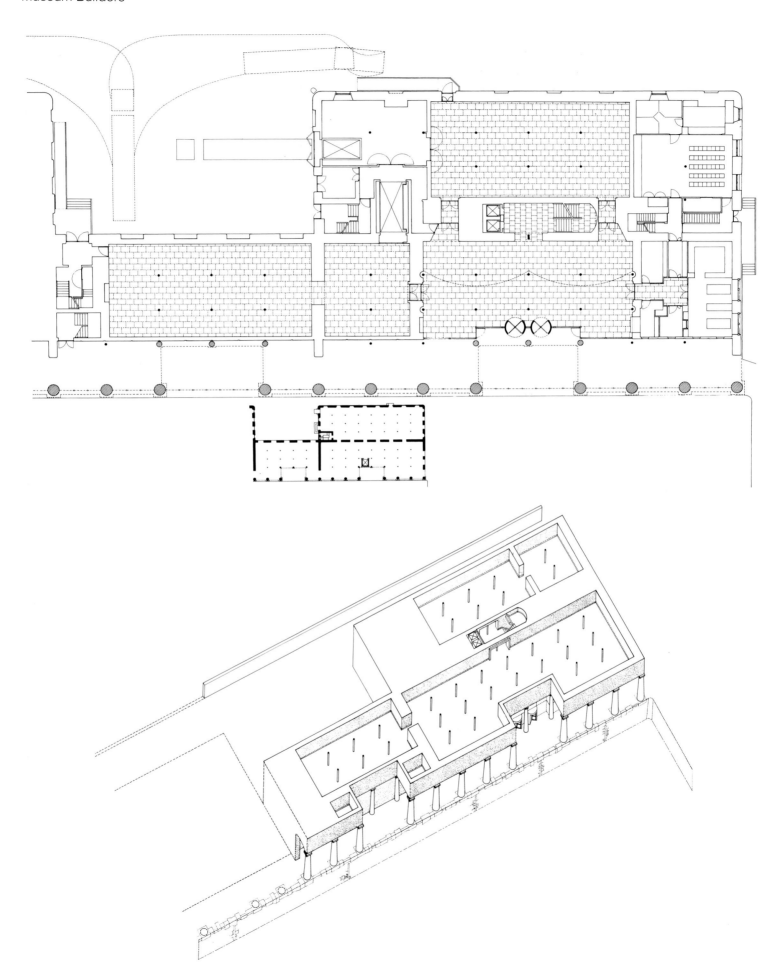

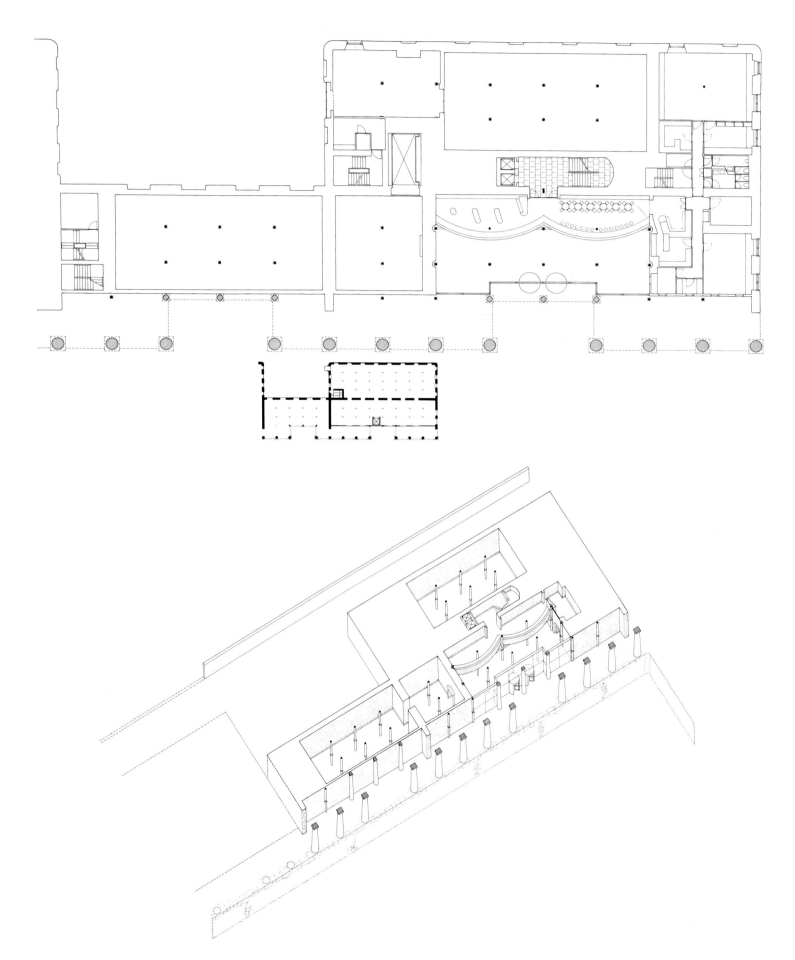

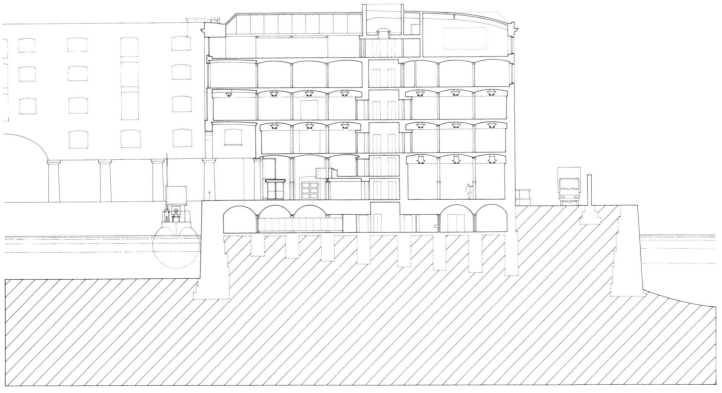

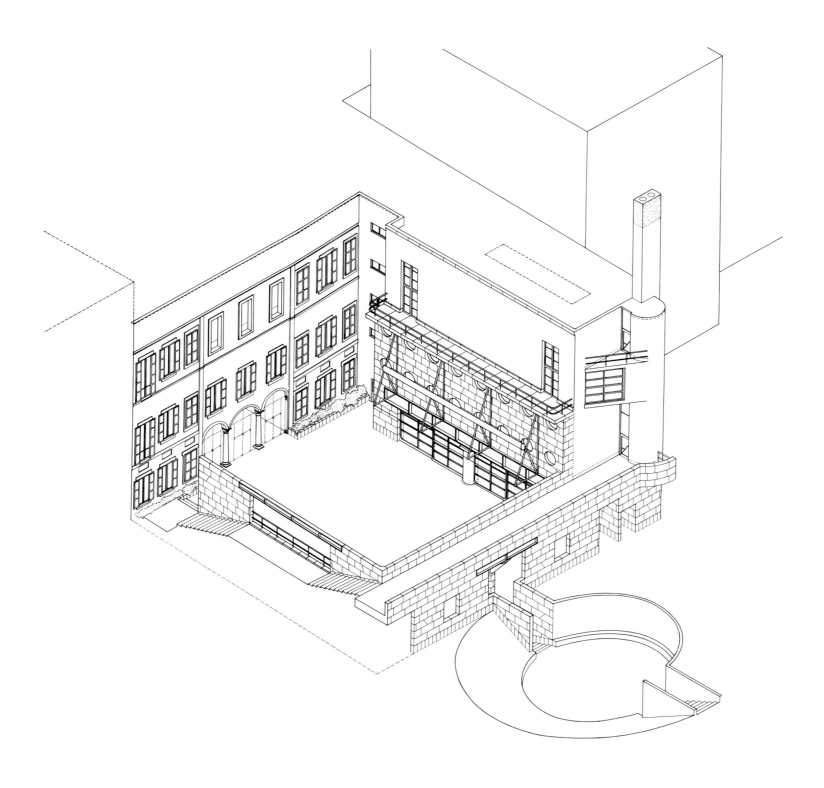

James Stirling and Michael Wilford

Palazzo Citterio Art Gallery at the Brera Museum, Milan

In 1987, a year after their completion of the Sackler Museum at Harvard University, Stirling Wilford were appointed to reorganise the Palazzo Citterio extension of the Brera Museum to create a museum of international stature. Where at Harvard they had faced severe programmatic restrictions (related to a constricted site and combination with offices) at Milan they were faced with severe restrictions arising from the conversion of the eighteenth-century Palazzo Citterio which had already suffered numerous radical transformations in its two-hundred-year history. In addition to public facilities the programme specified specialised functions including a restoration workshop, a large picture store, archive space, and a new library/reading room and catalogue. The brief also mentioned that an existing garden needed renewal.

Stirling Wilford advanced a plan that serves to amalgamate various remnants of the Palazzo with a series of new elements, which are strategically placed in areas where substantial modification has already taken place, including a new archive, library and cafeteria. A new public staircase, reminiscent of the definitive move made at the Sackler, has been placed on axis with the main courtyard, leading to the temporary exhibition gallery below ground. In addition, a core of public lifts and stairs provide access to galleries on all floors, as well as the lecture and seminar rooms in the basement. A new roof with a highly distinctive cupola has been placed over the existing open courtyard, allowing it to be used as central, orienting space, while a new garden court and open air amphitheatre have been added to retain a balance of exterior activity.

RIGHT: Perspective view of new garden court
OPPOSITE: Axonometric of new garden court with the new library/archive wing to the right
PAGE 230 FROM ABOVE: First floor plan; ground floor plan
PAGE 231 FROM ABOVE: Longitudinal section of covered courtyard facing north; longitudinal section of covered courtyard facing south
PAGE 232: Sectional perspective of covered courtyard
PAGE 233 FROM ABOVE: Cutaway axonometric showing covered and garden courts; cutaway axonometric showing first basement level and the new core of public lifts and stairs

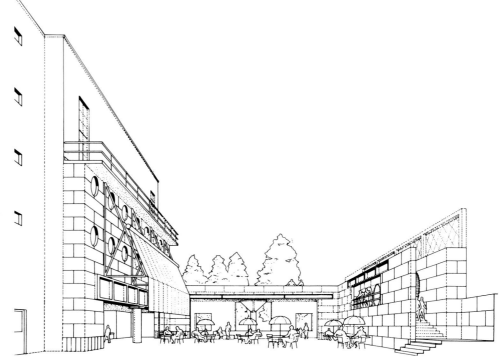

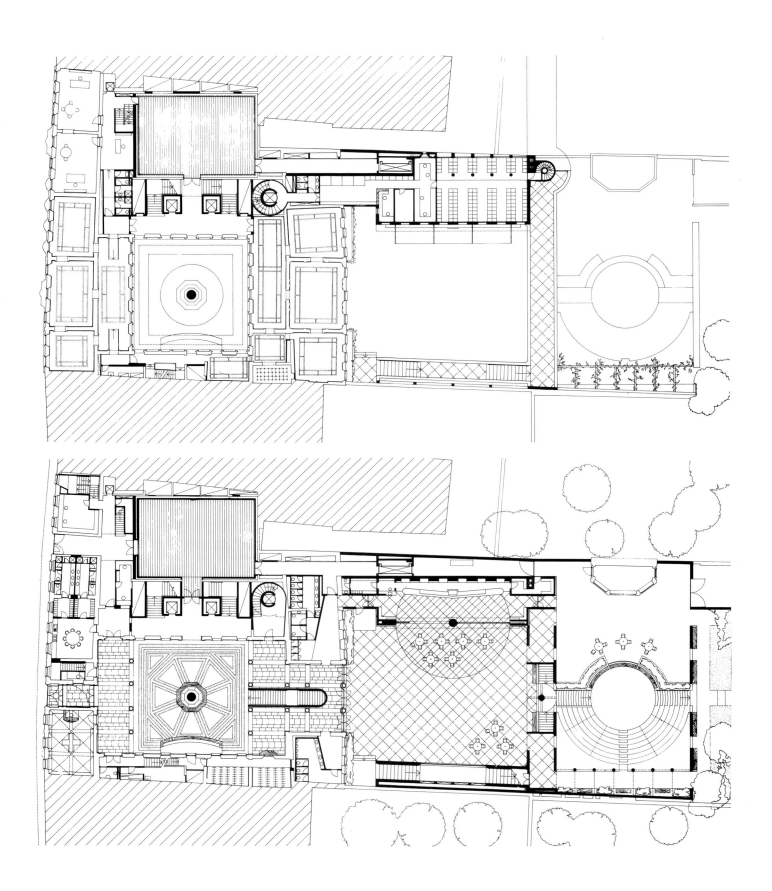

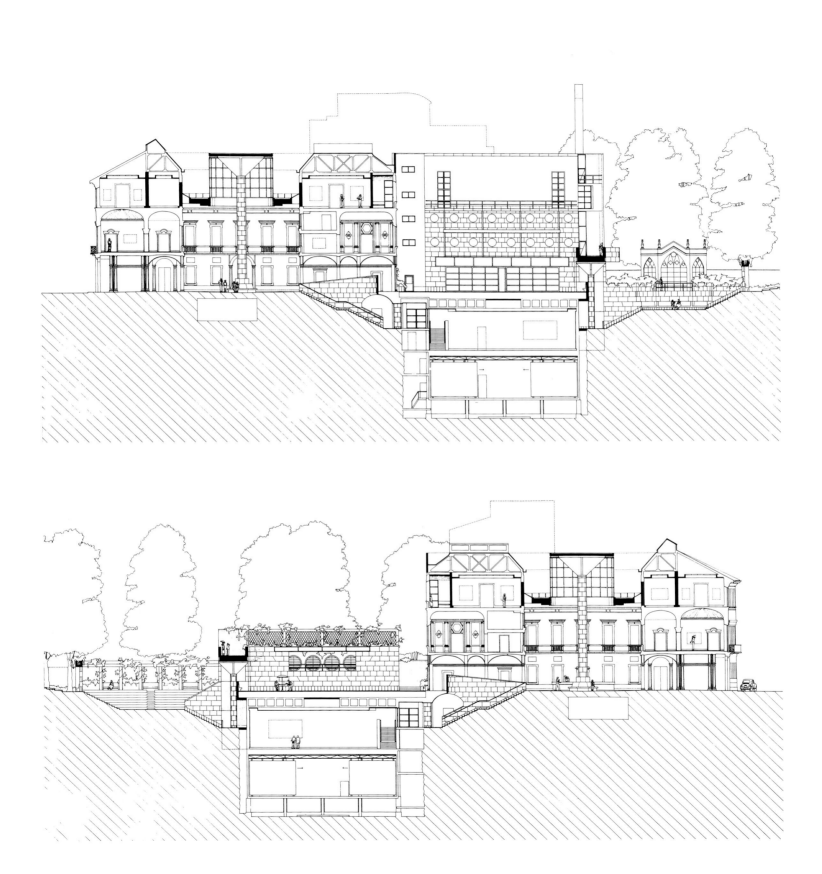

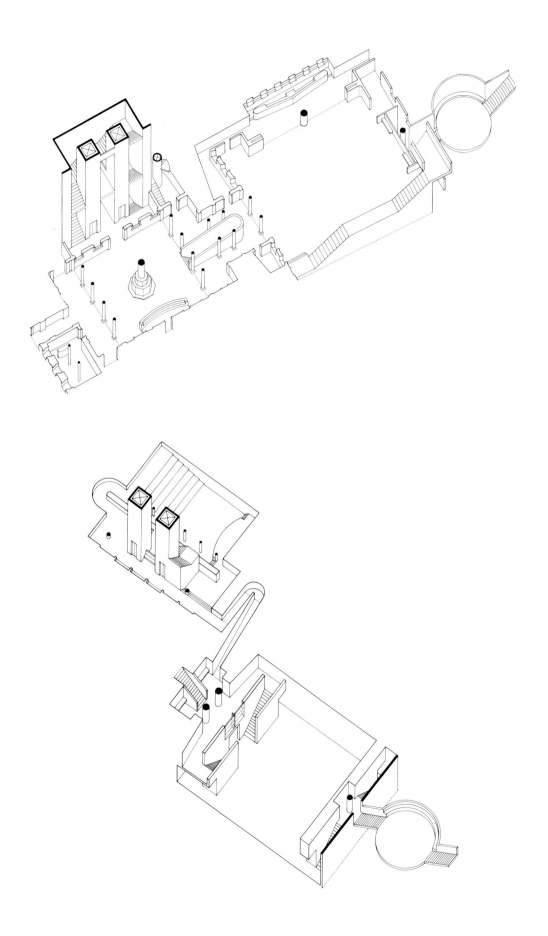

James Stirling and Michael Wilford

Neue Staatsgalerie, Stuttgart, Germany

The Neue Staatsgalerie in Stuttgart has proven to be enormously popular and is a good example of the way in which attitudes towards museums have changed. One of the main reasons for the popularity of the building is its accessibility, which allows visitors to walk up onto and through most of the exterior, horizontally organised levels that step gradually upwards from the Konrad-Adenauer-Strasse to the Urbanstrasse, creating platforms on which to see and be seen. There are indirect associations with other pieces of processional architecture, such as the Temple of Hatshepsut at Der el-Bahari or the Acropolis in Athens, as well as Stirling's intentional use of Karl Friedrich Schinkel's Altes Museum in Berlin, as a prototype. The use of an axial plan, as well as a central, circular organising space and an enfilade of rooms arranged around a rectilinear perimeter have all been carried over from the Altes Museum, but are significantly changed. In explaining his use of this prototype, Stirling has said:

> Of course it is no longer acceptable to do Classicism straight and in my building the central pantheon, instead of being the culminating space, is but a void, a room-like non-space; instead of a dome open to the sky. The plan is axial but frequently compromised; set-piece rooms conjoin with the plan and the public foot path meanders either side of the central axis – thus casually monumental.

This rotunda, which first appeared in Stirling's unbuilt but highly influential design for the Düsseldorf Museum, is indicative of an attitude towards contemporary life that is similar to that of Arata Isozaki's in his empty plaza at Tsukuba, where he comments on the Piazza del Campidoglio. As a clue to the meaning of this emptiness Isozaki has explained:

> The conventional wisdom in Japan . . . was that the central area of the city needs a monumental building with a strongly realised style of its own . . . I had the idea of approaching this tower problem in a negative way. By virtue of the centre's form and the sort of buildings that were to be grouped there, there was no possibility of doubt that this was a city

centre. A tower could not, therefore, be described as a necessity. I had the idea of making the centre of the town a void. This is a point which is very hard to get across to Europeans and Americans. I'm cast in the role of someone who's trying to steal Michelangelo's thunder, but in fact my intention was exactly the opposite: to create a hollow monument.

In spite of the similar motives of each architect, the location of this void at Tsukuba has resulted in its having become a lifeless plaza, while Stirling's 'room-like non-space' is a protective haven from the outside world that is constantly full of people who are either on the move, or are resting there and looking back through framed openings to the Stahlstich Alte Staatsgalerie next door.

Like the Altes Museum, this prototype also played an important role in the form of the new museum. With a *cour d'honneur* facing Konrad-Adenauer-Strasse, the existing building provided Stirling with additional contextual clues that make his extension seem inevitable. Through such straightforward devices as corresponding floor lines and cornice heights, down to the less obvious relationships between entrances and glass roof lights, this sense of inevitability has been reinforced at every turn, making this museum a timeless example of the re-establishment of the interrelationship between people and architecture.

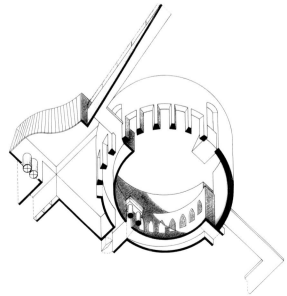

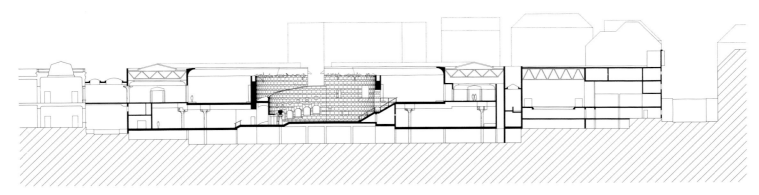

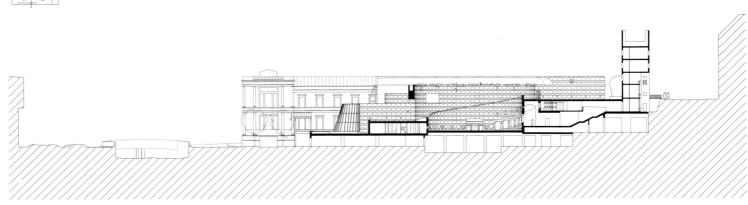

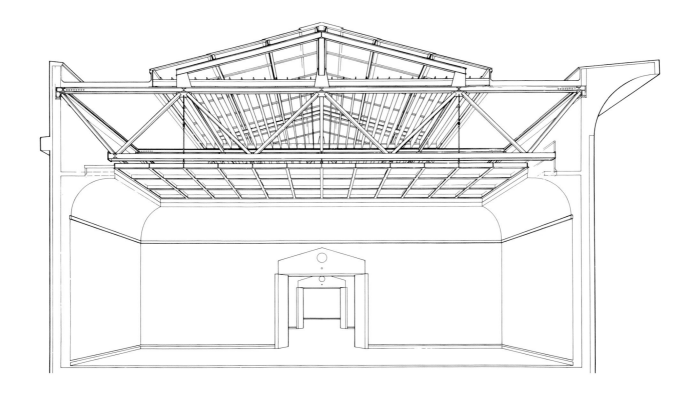

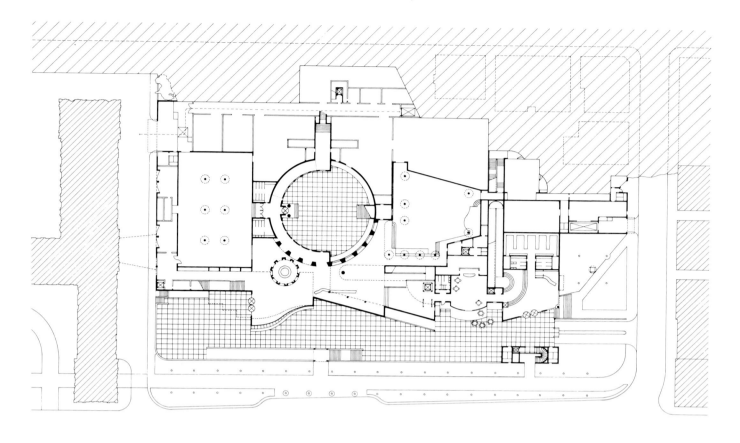

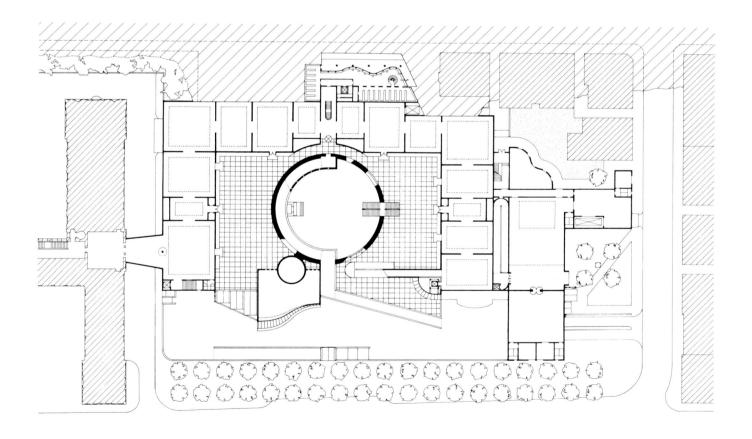

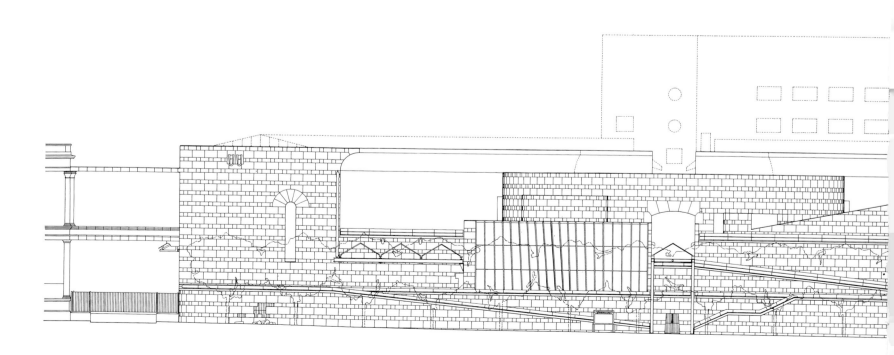

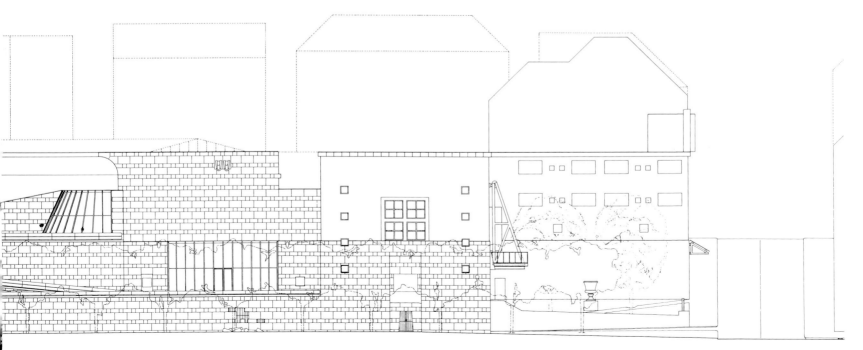

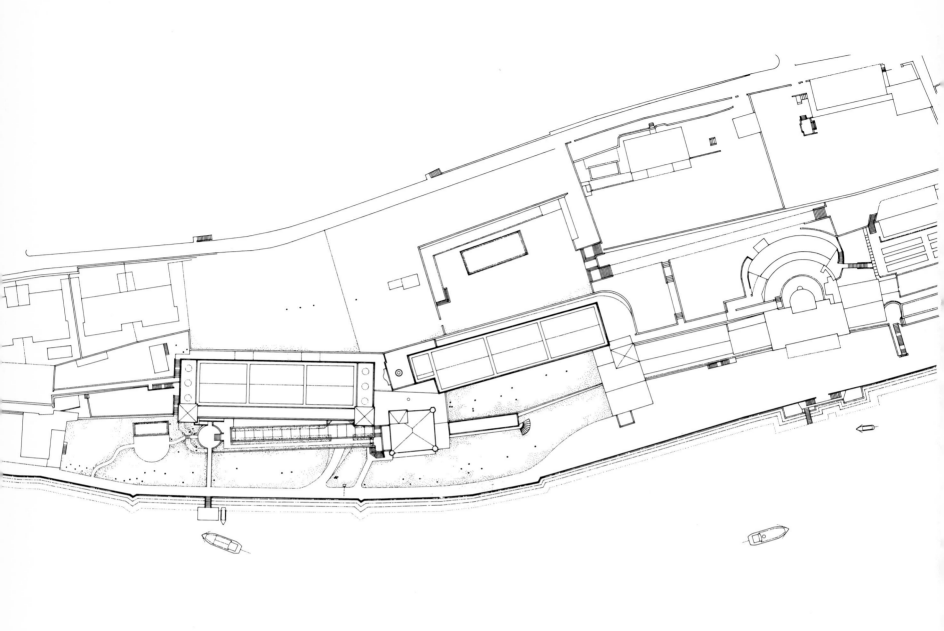

James Stirling and Michael Wilford

Thyssen Gallery, Lugano, Switzerland

Stirling Wilford's design for a new gallery on the Thyssen-Bornemisza estate consists of a three-storey building with a mezzanine. An important consideration has been the sympathetic integration of this new building into the site, which has meant respecting the scale and materials of existing buildings. Hence while the museum will have its own identity when viewed from the approach and gardens – the lakeside setting and gardens have been left largely intact, and the connection between the old and new galleries is below terrace level to avoid disruption of the Arcadian setting – it also fits in with the Romantic character of the lakeside villas, and will be finished in stucco and terracotta. The gallery is sited behind an old colonnade which will be retained to form an inviting scenic approach.

The public approach to the new and existing galleries is from the west, along the lakeside walk, or by boat to a new jetty. A ramp leads to a circular terrace from which steps and a ramp lead to the colonnade and promenade footpaths from which the new building is entered. These will also provide meeting places for visitors overlooking the lake and gardens.

The new galleries are on the main floor above the entrance and are a sequence of smaller and larger perimeter rooms around a large central area of 780 square metres which can be subdivided into combinations of rooms and spaces. This arrangement will accommodate variety in scale and grouping of pictures and allow hanging of replacement works from the collection; it will also provide for changing and special exhibitions. All rooms are 5 metres high with a 3 metre hanging zone. Access to the new galleries is from an interior arcaded galleria which overlooks the lake. The entrances to the picture galleries have protective screen walls to prevent light spilling into the exhibition areas and incorporate seats where a pause from the gallery visit can be taken. The galleries will be lit by roof lanterns above lay lights using diffusing glass, similar to the Neue Staatsgalerie, with external louvres to achieve the required 300 lux on the hanging surface.

Non-exhibition spaces are located at the entrance level and include a free space for receptions, musical events and openings. This space is designed to extend the entrance hall and includes facilities for projection and lectures with a seating capacity for over two hundred people and standing space at the rear.

The archive/library is on a mezzanine above the entrance and a private stair connects it with the entrance hall, the staff administration in the Villa Ghirlanda and the car park in the basement.

Public circulation between the new and old galleries is by means of a new monumental staircase located at the west end of the old gallery. This stair rises full height in the old building and is lit by the three arched windows in the west facade and by a new conical roof lantern. The old galleries are entered from a recessed doorway on their central axis.

OPPOSITE FROM ABOVE: Site plan; elevation of main facade
PAGE 242 FROM ABOVE: Roof level plan; third level plan
PAGE 243 FROM ABOVE: Second level plan; ground level plan

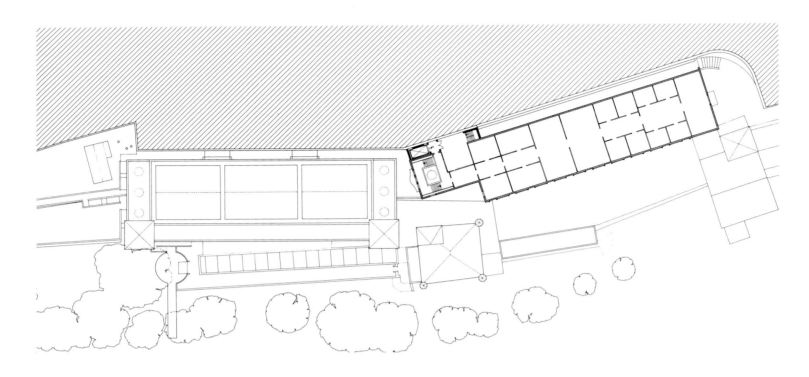

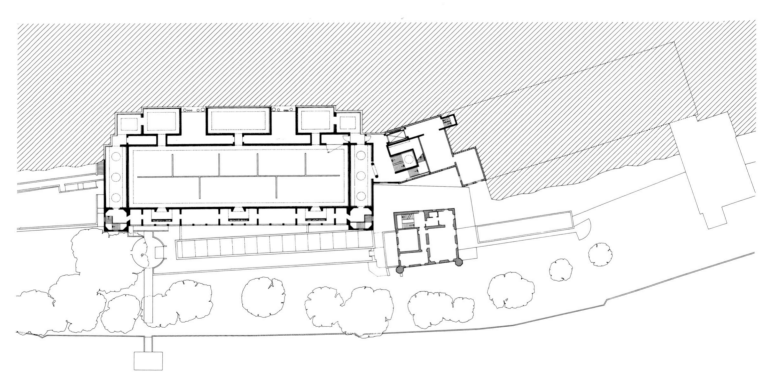

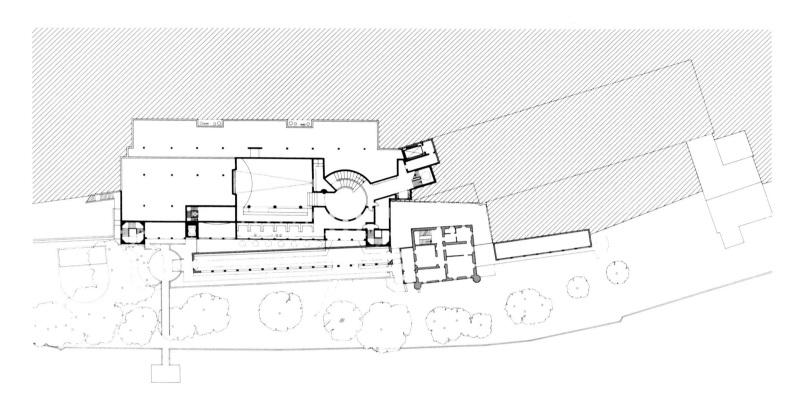

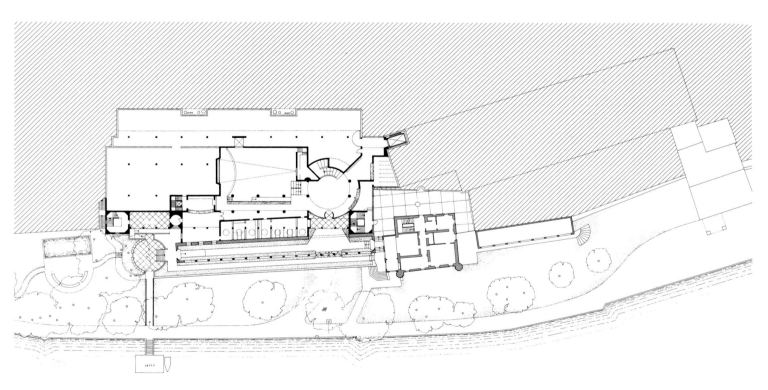

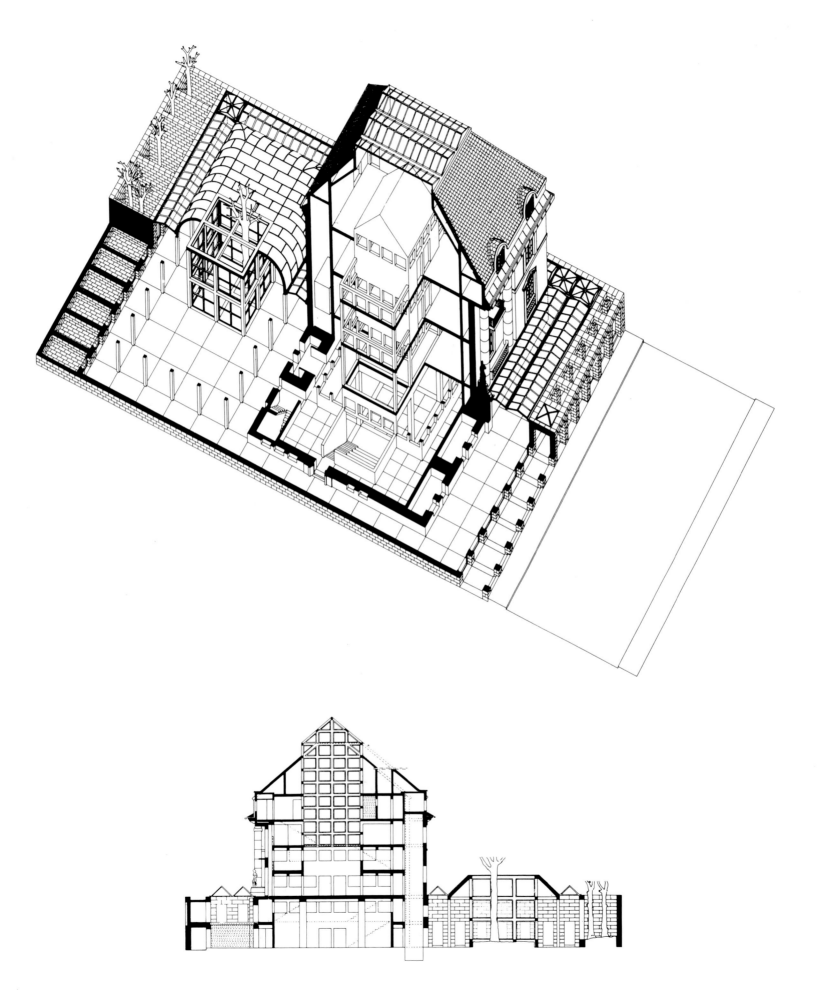

OM Ungers

The German Architecture Museum, Frankfurt

In the early 1970s, Heinrich Klotz became convinced that the sketches and drawings which accompany and record the progress of every architectural project, should be preserved and housed in a single institution in order to save them for posterity. His efforts in this direction were frustrated until 1977, when a change in Frankfurt's local government introduced a new administration that was very receptive to the idea, as part of a wider programme now known as the *Museumsufer*, which has produced thirteen museums to date. Klotz describes his role in this project by saying:

> I convinced Hilmar Hoffmann, the Minister for Science and Culture, to set up not just a single museum for architecture but several cultural institutions. Originally, the intention was to build a huge culture machine housing several museums and facilities in the middle of the city, like the Pompidou Centre in Paris. But it became clear that Frankfurt was not big enough for such a giant institution. Moreover, it was a much better idea, from an urban planning point of view, to spread the museum functions over several buildings rather than concentrating them in just one spot. The most obvious location was the row of handsome, long-unoccupied, nineteenth-century villas along the banks of the River Main. Some of these villas had already fallen into disrepair and there was a danger that some speculator might sweep them away and build highrises in their place. So the Frankfurt City Council acted quickly: the Museum for the Decorative Arts was extended to Richard Meier; the Carmelite Monastery was converted into the Museum of Pre- and Proto-History by Joseph Paul Kleihues; the Rothschild Palace became the Museum of Jewish Culture (by Ante von Kostelac); one of the villas was enlarged to serve as the German Film Museum by Helge Bofinger, while the one right next to it became the German Architecture Museum. This would never have been achieved without the rare and great fortune of having, in Frankfurt, a group of intelligent and incorruptible politicians . . . who made a seemingly

Utopian plan the keystone of Frankfurt's Cultural policy . . . [it was our intention that these museums] would reach out to people in all levels of society. And this is, in fact, what has happened.

In addition to all of the usual facilities associated with a museum such as this, such as slide and photographic archives, the library contains important historical volumes related to architecture, and the periodical section is exhaustive. A film and video section has also been added to document all of the diverse trends in the profession today. The increased interest in architectural drawings that has developed since 1980, when current works began to be considered collectors' items, meant that the value of a museum of this kind began to become more obvious, and the impressive attendance records of its early years began to increase.

OM Ungers' renovation of the historic 1901 villa that is now the basis of the museum has been sensitive, beginning with an external wall which separates the quiet, contemplative building from the nearby traffic along the Schaumainkai and Schweizer Strasse. The wall is conceived in such a way as to provide privacy, yet still affords views towards the river and a sense of space. The surprise here is Ungers' 'house within a house' that becomes a new core rising up in the middle of the existing villa, taking on a different character at each level and reinforcing the idea of layered shells, one inside the other, and what Klotz has called 'a succession of rooms'. As he says:

> Once the structure of the house is understood, it becomes clear that Ungers is making reference to the 'thematics' of architecture. This building is not an abstract container for utilitarian spaces designed only to fulfil certain given functions. Rather, it illustrates a central idea: how the four column room, or baldachin, has evolved into a house.

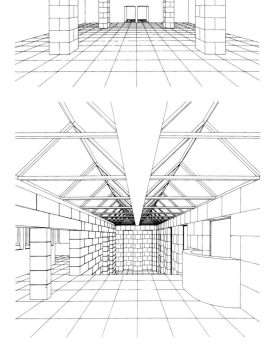

RIGHT FROM ABOVE: Sectional perspective of four column room; sectional perspective of entrance hall
OPPOSITE FROM ABOVE: Cutaway axonometric; longitudinal section

Robert Venturi and Denise Scott Brown

The Sainsbury Wing of the National Gallery, London

The circumstances surrounding the Sainsbury Wing have now entered architectural legend along with the 'Carbuncle' speech that brought it into existence. The myth continues to grow because the design of the new wing was supposedly the result of the proverbial 'back-of-the-napkin' sketch by Robert Venturi, done while he and Denise Scott Brown were on an airline, en route to Pakistan. In spite of that part of the myth, the Sainsbury Wing represents their attempt to meet a number of demanding contextual problems with sensitivity, élan and wit, and the consensus of most fair-minded critics seems to be that they have done so with mixed success.

On the exterior, visual connections with the existing east and west wings have been established by the use of techniques that are reminiscent of Venturi's unbuilt Frankfurt Museum competition scheme. In London, however, there is more verve in the tactics, with the solid Portland stone wall on the most public face of the museum treated as a screen whenever possible. Rather than carrying an entablature, as the columns on the existing Trafalgar Square elevation do, the vertical elements on this screen are reduced to flat pilasters that scurry across the wall. This paradox of solid wall as screen is further augmented by the entrances, which project up past the base of the pilasters, accentuating their thinness and mouldings which appear to be deliberately pasted on, rather than integral to the mural surface. The most obvious indication of this intention comes at the abrupt juxtaposition of this edge with the fragile glass and aluminium curtain wall facing the stair along Jubilee Walk. The message here is clearly one of 'we will play the game, but insist on not taking it too seriously'.

The ground and first floors of the Sainsbury Wing have been treated as preparatory space, meant to heighten visitors' anticipation as they move up a monumental stair, an idea also carried through in the galleries, where doorways are typically offset to maintain surprise, rather than being lined up in traditional enfilade. This approach seems to mark a return to the more conservative exhibition patterns of the past,

described well by John Millard, curator of the Laing Art Gallery in Newcastle-Upon-Tyne:

The new display in general is hidebound by unnecessary conventions. It runs the risk of intimidating rather than encouraging non-expert audiences and it certainly does not encourage the visitor to make the imaginative leap over half a millennium to the time when the paintings on display were made. It also sadly fails to give even a hint that the story of western European art from the Renaissance could be set into a wider context of other civilisations and cultures.

In his view, approach to display in the Sainsbury Wing seems to make:

an unfashionable return to the notion of a gallery as an elevated temple of the arts. Granted this extension lends a sense of occasion . . . but the building is pompously Victorian in spite of its modern look, and it fails to encourage a lively and open interest in the paintings.

Meanwhile those of an opposing position maintain that a collection as important as this requires a setting of equal gravity. It seems that the Sainsbury Wing, which was born in controversy, continues to be the centre of a professional debate of another sort, revolving around the meaning of the museum itself.

The new extension is organised on a main floor made up of sixteen galleries that contain the Early Renaissance collection of paintings from 1260 to 1510. Three ranges of rooms on this main level run the length of the building from north to south, with the walls of the central range, at 5.5 metres being the highest.

This extension reflects the National Gallery's new policy of hanging together paintings of the same period produced in different parts of Europe, and the Wing has been designed to provide the environmental control which they require. The rooms are lit from a high clerestory which provides an airy spaciousness and a monumentality unusual in modern galleries. The spectacular central sequence of tall rooms, linked by arched openings, provides a setting in which altarpieces can be displayed effectively – as they rarely can be outside the churches for which they were made. The other rooms

have an almost domestic intimacy appropriate for the smaller paintings. The plan is straightforward without the rooms being treated as a circuit. Vistas enable key paintings to be seen from afar. Altarpieces have been given plinths or consoles to suggest the altars upon which they were originally placed and some fragments have also been hung to help visitors envisage their original arrangement. The plinths and consoles are designed to harmonise with the architecture, as are the cases which contain works of art which were painted on both sides and were previously only half visible.

The chief aim of the Sainsbury Wing has been to rehouse familiar masterpieces: to show to the very best advantage what is probably the most outstanding Renaissance collection in the world, and to tell in a new way the history of Renaissance art throughout Europe.

BELOW: Main floor plan
PAGE 249: Cross section

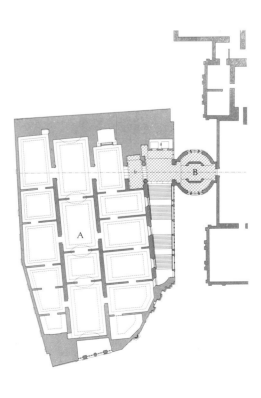

Robert Venturi and Denise Scott Brown

Seattle Art Museum, Washington

The intentional dichotomies between interior and exterior in several of Venturi's most recent museums represent a historic reversal in which there is an exquisite irony. This is seen most clearly in Seattle.

While the trend today in housing the Arts seems to be a de-institutionalisation and attainment of a balance between the popular and the monumental, the theorists most closely associated with the dismantling of architectural elitism in the 1960s are once again moving against the current. As in the Sainsbury Wing, the Seattle interiors are positively reverential in comparison to the playful attitude taken towards the outside shell, which responds in different ways to the various civic influences around it. In noting the relationship between the external wrapper and previous theories, Helen Searing has said:

> The transformation of the museum from an elite institution to a democratic one . . . propelled by market forces not less than radical changes in the practice, collecting, appreciation and evaluation of the Arts, is served by a commitment to populism that leads Venturi and Scott Brown to take an irreverent but affectionate approach. The museum is to be welcoming, hinting of pleasure as well as education and illumination. Wit and humour are writ large on the facades of their museum designs . . . They wish to bridge the gulf between those who see the museum as a rarefied temple and those who consider it a self-effacing warehouse for art.

That writing occurs quite literally in this example, in which the name of the institution becomes an alphabetical cornice extended across the top of the vertically striated middle of the building. An arcaded base which alternates between arched and pedimented bays running along the University Street and First Avenue Facades, completes the tripartite division of the major elevations, which, along with the exaggeration of the bay over the main entrance prefigures the compositional devices used in the Sainsbury Wing. Once that threshold is crossed, however, the freedom of expression that characterises the exterior is replaced by a more sombre attitude, resulting in a spatial formality that may reflect an instinctive respect for the high purpose to be served by the galleries.

In its linearity, the parti used in the Seattle Art museum is a direct descendant of the competition entry for the extension to the Villa Metzler in Frankfurt, which was not built. The long telescoping corridor that was used in that instance as an addition to the cubic eighteenth-century Villa, which was to be expanded because the collection of crafts shown in it needed more space, can be seen to have shifted to the exterior wall of Seattle.

This change, which is refined even further in the Sainsbury Wing, is important because it is a gesture towards increased accessibility, as indicated by the mirror image of the internal spine in the stairs running alongside it along the street. With a hierarchy of entrances at the bottom, middle and top of these stairs corresponding to gallery landings inside, traditional questions of openness and security appear to have been answered by this ingenious, semi-public gesture.

PAGE 253 FROM ABOVE: Longitudinal section; extended elevation; second floor plan

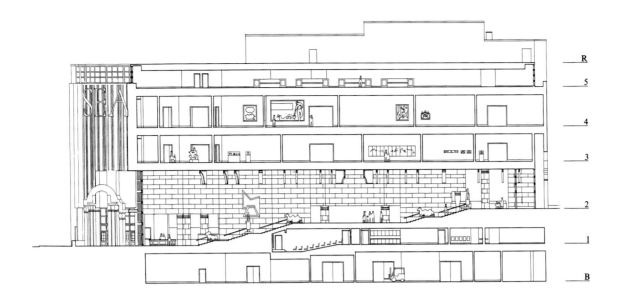

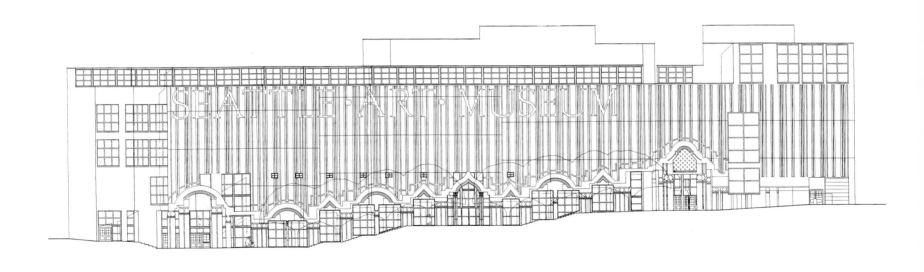

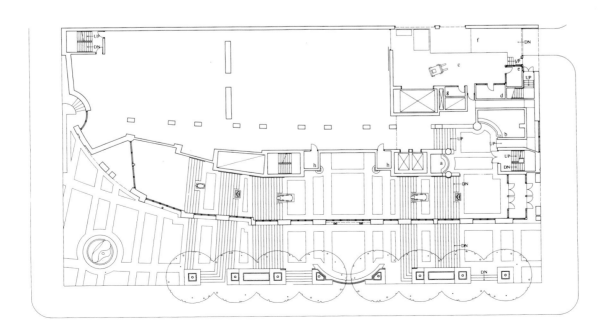

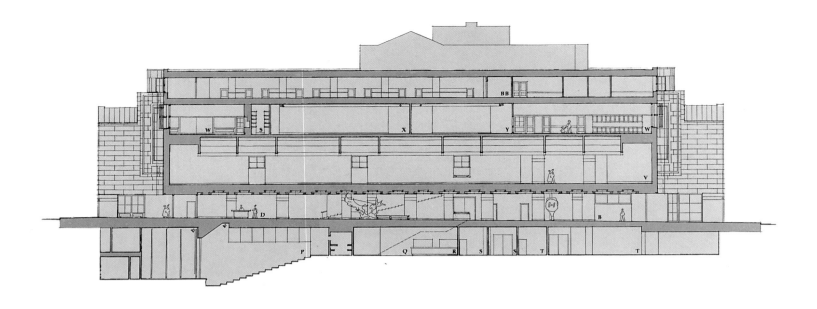

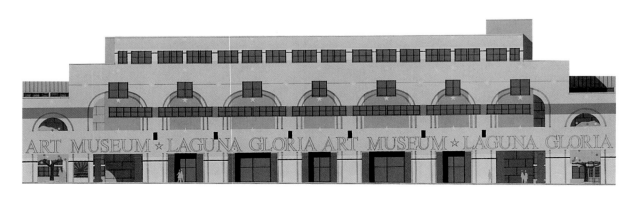

Robert Venturi and Denise Scott Brown

Laguna Gloria Museum of Art, Austin, Texas

Dedicated to the presentation of twentieth-century American art, Laguna Gloria follows a pattern in museum design now well established by the firm, which is further augmented here by the site. The main facade, running parallel to Fourth Street, faces a large public park, resulting in a long rectanglular block stretched along an east-west axis, with entrances at both corners.

As in the National Gallery and the Seattle Museum of Art, a linear band of circulation including a monumental stair is used as a means of transition between the res publica directly beyond the main boundary wall and the cultural inner sanctum at the core of the building, with the first, rather than the ground floor given over to the main galleries. Indoor/outdoor courts, partially hidden from the public park by screen walls, erode each corner: the western end is particularly compromised by the museum restaurant, which spills out into the external court to become the equivalent of a pavement cafe near the street. The central stair, rather than being simply functional, has taken on a new role in this regard, described by Sylvia Lavin:

> Although strictly speaking all the major spaces of a museum are by definition public, Venturi and Scott Brown's use of the processional stair enables the establishment of a hierarchy of degrees, of more and less public, rather than private and public. Perhaps even more important is the treatment of these stairs, which are made into independent and coherent spaces by spatial, decorative and rhythmic generosity. No longer relegated to the role of circulation devices, these stairs are places to be; they call attention and thereby give meaning to Venturi's comment that in today's museum art itself is 'remote'.

While the final content of the building may here be removed to its furthest recesses in favour of more immediately gratifying spaces, its external face, presented like a bill board to the park beyond, is treated as a populist anagram in its own right, rendered in tile and stone. Again recalling its predecessors in London and Seattle, Laguna Gloria has a wrapper that is also part of the show upstaging the work presented inside by both scale and position, like a petrified neon sign in New York's Time Square frozen in mid-sentence. Subtle visual tricks, carried over from the not-so-subtle crashing columns at the corner of the Sainsbury Wing facing Trafalgar Square, allow the eye to accelerate around the ends of this particular study in perceptual imagery, as one more instance of Venturi and Scott Brown's exploration of the semiotic potential that architecture can fulfil.

OPPOSITE FROM ABOVE: Longitudinal section; perspective view showing the park and Fourth Street facade; Fourth Street elevation.

Robert Venturi and Denise Scott Brown

Franklin Court, Philadelphia

More formally known as the Benjamin Franklin Memorial Park, the Franklin Court scheme is a model of delicate intervention in a sensitive pre-existing urban context, as well as of the reinterpretation of a client brief in a positive way. When asked by the United States Park Service to restore both the printing shop and house of this famous Philadelphian, the architects were concerned that nothing except the foundations of the original structure had survived, which would have meant a speculative restoration at best. Since both buildings involved were built according to instructions that Franklin had sent in numerous letters to his wife while he was serving as the American Ambassador to France, detailed descriptions of vital features, such as the number of storeys and fireplaces in the house, did exist. These descriptions prompted a counter proposal by the architects that the house be ghosted out in steel frame to convey an impression of its presence rather than attempting a problematic physical representation which could not be authenticated. In addition, the architects proposed an underground museum as an alternative to the one which the Park Service had asked them to provide at ground level to house important examples of Franklin's inventions, as well as paintings of both him and his wife, and memorabilia such as clothing, glasses, hats and shoes. This solution not only retained the original setting that had existed around the two buildings as described by Franklin, but also gave the open steel frames additional impact because of the elimination of visual clutter. The entrance to the underground museum is incorporated into a long arcade that runs along a recess in the garden wall, becoming a perfectly believable continuation of the partially real and partially fantastic setting that has been created here.

Seen through the long passageway that connects Market Street with this interior courtyard (and which passes under the conventionally restored Post Office established by Franklin, the first in the United States), the open steel frames have an eerie quality and are actually far more memorable than an inaccurate reproduction because

they allow visitors to fill in the details of each building in their own imagination, based on the clues that the architects present. The museum which they have designed, because it lacks natural light, serves as a striking counterpoint to the tableaux outlined above it. By resisting the temptation to follow the original brief, Venturi and Scott Brown have managed to provide a much more appropriate memorial to this remarkable man.

BELOW FROM ABOVE: Plan of the main exhibition level underground; section of the garden and main exhibition level

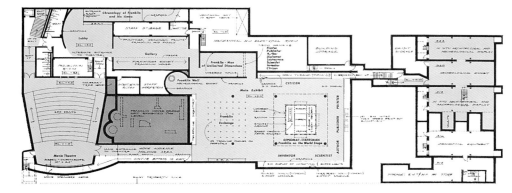

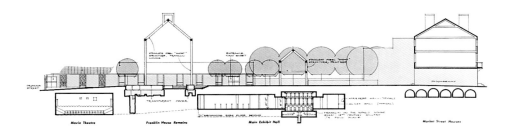

SELECT BIBLIOGRAPHY

Gae Aulenti: Museum of Catalan Art

Miguel Conde, 'Barcelona: Controversy over the Catalan Art Museum', *Art International*, vol 12 (Autumn 1990), p28

Gae Aulenti: Gare d'Orsay

Gae Aulenti, 'ACT Architecture', *GA Document*, vol 19 (1988), pp94-113

Gae Aulenti, Jean Jenger, Michael Laclotte, *Gae Aulenti e il Musée d'Orsay*, Milano: Electa: Distribuzione per l'Italia, Messaggerie Libri

Gae Aulenti, 'Musée d'Orsay', *A+U*, vol 201 (June 1987), pp19-34

Gae Aulenti, 'Tendencious Interview with a Visitor of Musée d'Orsay', *A+U*, vol 201 (June 1987), pp35-46

Carlo Bertelli, Jean-Claude Garcias, 'Gae Aulenti: l'architettura interna del museo', *Domus*, vol 679 (January 1987), pp24-29

Gilberto Botti, 'Gae Aulenti: Architecture and Museography', *Lotus International*, vol 53 (1987), pp56-85

Kenneth Brozen, 'The Renaissance of a French Railroad Station', *Interiors* (New York), vol 146 (May 1987), pp344-47

Peter Buchanan, 'Museum of the Nineteenth Century: Gare d' Orsay', *The Architectural Review*, vol 180 (December 1986), pp344-47

Tita Carloni, 'Musée d'Orsay und Grand Louvre', *Du*, vol 12 (December 1988), pp50-57

Raoul Ergman, Henri Mercillon, 'Orsay', *Connaissance des Arts*, vol 418 (December 1986), pp57-99

Charles K Gandee, 'Musée d'Orsay, Paris, France', *Architectural Record*, vol 175 (March 1987), pp128-39

Thomas Hoving, 'Pompiers and Circumstance', *Connoisseur*, vol 217 (September 1987), p27

Sylvia Lavin, *Interiors* (New York), vol 48 (September 1988), p21

Patricia Mainardi, 'Postmodern History at Musée d'Orsay', *October* (Cambridge, Massachusetts), vol 41 (Summer 1987), pp30-52

Thomas Matthews, 'The Controversial Musée d'Orsay', *Progressive Architecture*, vol 68 (February 1987), pp35-36

Linda Nochlin, Robert Rosenblum, 'The Musée d'Orsay; a Symposium', *Art in America*, vol 76 (January 1988), pp84-107

'Musée d'Orsay, Paris', *L'Architecture d'Aujourd'hui* , vol 248 (December 1986), pplxxii-25

'Orsay en Bonne Voie', *Connaissance des Arts*, vol 399 (May 1985), p14

Günter Behnisch: The German Postal Museum

Behnisch & Partners: Bauten 1952-1992, Winnenden: Wilhelm Nusser GMBH & Co (1992)

'Gunter Behnisch: the German Postal Museum, Frankfurt', *Architectural Design* (London), vol 60, no 1/2 (1991), pp22-29

Luigi Biscogli, 'Museo delle Poste sullo Schauminski a Francoforte', *L'Architettura*, vol 36 (Autumn 1990), pp110-22

Peter Blundell-Jones, Post on the Main', *The Architectural Review*, vol 187 (June 1990), pp38-47

Julius Poesner, 'Deutsches Postmuseum', *Domus*, vol 722 (December 1990), pp29-37

'Post Museum', *GA Document*, vol 31 (1991), pp44-53

Mario Botta: Watari-Um

Mario Botta, *Mario Botta: Watari-Um Project in Tokyo 1985-1990*, Watari-Um (Tokyo), 1990

Coop Himmelblau: East Wing of the Groningen Museum of Art

Ken Powell and others, 'New Museums', *AD Profile 94*, *Architectural Design*, vol 61, no 11/12 (1991)

Mark Wigley and others, 'Deconstruction 3', *AD Profile 87*, *Architectural Design*, vol 60, no 9/10 (1990)

Jol Meijer, Ernie Tee (ed), *What a Wonderful World!: Music Videos in Architecture* (1990)

Peter Eisenman: The Wexner Center for the Visual Arts

Robert Benson, 'Eisenman's Architectural Challenge', *New Art Examiner*, vol 17 (Summer 1990) p27-30

Peter Eisenman, 'The OSU Center for Visual Arts, Columbus, *Architectural Design* (London), vol 55, no 1/2 (1985), pp44-55

Peter Eisenman and Richard Trott, introduction by Philip Johnson, essays by Kurt W Forster, Charles Jencks and RE Somol, *Wexner Center for the Visual Arts*, Academy Editions (London), St Martin's Press (New York), 1989

Diane Ghirardo, 'The Grid and the Grain', *The Architectural Review*, vol 187 (June 1990), pp79-86

'In Progress: Wexner Center for the Visual Arts', *A+U*, vol 208 (January 1988), pp11-14

Andreas C Papadakis (ed), *Wexner Center for the Visual Arts*, Academy Editions (London), St Martin's Press (New York), 1989

Evans and Shalev: The Tate Gallery at St Ives

'Go ahead for St Ives "Tate of the West"', *Architects Journal*, vol 193, no 14 (3 April 1991), p13

'St Ives Tate goes on site', *Building Design*, no 1039 (14 June 1991), p7

'The Tate by the Sea', *World Architecture*, no 13 (1991), pp62-65

'Artistic Judgement', *Architects' Journal*, vol 197, no 2 (13 January 1993), p10

Elspeth Moncrieff, 'The St Ives Tate', *Apollo*, vol 137, no 373 (March 1993), pp178-80

Building Design, no 1129 (18 June 1993), p2

Alan Groves and others, 'A Gallery Rooted in Context', *Architects Journal*, vol 197, no 25 (23 June 1993), pp25-39

Clare Melhuish, 'Cold Embrace of a Windswept Tradition', *Building Design*, no 1130, (25 June 1993), p2

Colin Davies and others, 'Recreation' (Special issue), *Architectural Review*, vol 194, no 1157 (July 1993), pp4-9, 17-71

David Jenkins and Louise Rogers, 'Picture Gallery', RIBA Journal, vol 100, no 7 (July 1993), pp33-39

David Dunster, 'Primitive Sophistication', Architectural Design, no 40 (July 1993), pp34-36/39-40

Maurice Davies 'Every Town Should have One', Museums Journal, vol 93, no 9, (September 1993), pp27-28

Nick Jones, 'Bricks and Blocks', Building Design, no 1143 (24 September 1993), pp24-25/27

Helen Webster and Peter Howard, 'Visioni di St Ives', Spazio e Societa, vol 17, no 65 (January/March 1994), pp104-11

Norman Foster: Carré d'Art

The Architectural Review (1985)

Architecture Intérieure (March/April 1985)

Building Design (9 November 1984)

Connaissance des Arts (January 1985)

Gustavo Gill (ed), Norman Foster, Quaderns Monogratis, Col-legi d-Arquitectes de Catalunya (1989)

L'Architecture d'Aujourd'hui (December 1984)

Techniques et Architecture (December 1984-January 1985)

Norman Foster: The Sackler Galleries at the Royal Academy of Arts

Lynda Murdin, 'Controversy at Burlington House', Museums Journal, vol 89 (September 1989), p19

Norman Foster: The Crescent Gallery of the Sainsbury Centre

Tony Warner, 'The Crescent Wing Extension to the Sainsbury Centre for the Visual Arts (Norwich, England)', Arts Review (London), vol 43 (12 July 1991), pp368-69

Richard Wilcock, 'Frontis (Crescent Wing, Sainsbury Centre for the Visual Arts, University of East Anglia, Norwich)', RIBA Journal, vol 98 (July 1991), pp6-7

Frank Gehry: Frederick R Weisman Art and Teaching Museum

'University of Minnesota Art Museum', Progressive Architecture, vol 73 (January 1992), pp74-75

Frank Gehry: Vitra International Furniture and Design Museum

Hugh Alderesy-Williams, 'Cathedral for a Chair', ID (New York), vol 37 (May/June 1990), p18

Oliver Boissere, Martin Filler (translation by Michael Robinson), The Vitra Design Museum: Frank Gehry, Architect, Rizzoli International Publishers (New York), 1990

'Design museum a Weil am Rhein, Germania', L'Architettura, vol 36 (April 1990), pp290-91

Brigitte Fitoussi, 'Vitra Design Museum', L'Architecture d'Aujourd'hui, vol 267 (February 1990), pp168-72

Frank Gehry, Alexander von Vegesack, 'The Vitra Design Museum', Architectural Design (London), vol 60, no 9/10 (1990), pp20-31

Barbara Gerosa, 'Se la sedia va al museo', L'Architettura, vol 36 (January 1990), pp66-67

Françoise Jaunin, Théme et variations sur un chaise, L'Oeil (Lausanne), vol 431 (July 1991), pp66-69

Herbert Lechner, 'The Vitra Chair Museum', Graphis, vol 46 (January/February 1990), pp86-97

Rowan Moore, 'Frank Gehry, Vitra Design Museum', The Architectural Review, vol 189 (January 1991), p12

'Museumtime: the Vitra Design, Weil am Rhein', Abitare, vol 288 (September 1990), pp248-55

Andrea Nulli, Vitra Design Museum, Weil am Rhein', Domus, vol 713 (February 1990), pp58-65

Mayer Rus, 'In Weil am Rhein, Frank Gehry Designs an Audacious Setting for Vitra's Design Collection', International Design (New York), vol 61 (October 1990), pp192-97

Pilar Viladas 'Cranked, Curled and Cantilevered', Progressive Architecture, vol 71 (May 1990), pp94-99

'Vitra International, Furniture Manufacturing Facility and Design Museums', GA Document, vol 27 (1990), pp66-85

'Vitra International, Furniture Manufacturing Facility and Design Museum, Weil am Rhein, West Germany', A+U, vol 239, pp7-70

David Webster, 'Vitra Design Museum', Crafts (London), vol 104 (May/June 1990), p48

Klaus Dieter-Weiss, 'Kunst al Bau', Werk, Bauen + Wohnen, vol 77/44 (March 1990), p48

Michael Graves: Emory University Museum of Art and Archaeology

Allen Freeman, 'Moods of Mauve and Indigo: Emory University's Carlos Hall (Atlanta)', Architecture, vol 76 (May 1987), pp160-62

Loring Leifer, 'In Support of the Arts: the Emory University Renovation by Michael Graves wins Praise', Interiors (New York), vol 145 (June 1986), pp178-81

'Michael C Carlos Hall, Emory University Museum of Art and Archaeology (Atlanta)', Abitare, vol 76 (September 1986), pp372-73

'Michael Graves – Michael C Carlos Hall (Museum of Art and Archaeology, Emory University, Atlanta)', GA Document, vol 14 (1985), pp30-35

Pilar Viladas, 'Full Circle', Progressive Architecture, vol 66 (September 1985), pp127-34

Bonna P Wescot, Monique Seefried, 'Emory University Museum of Art and Archaeology reopens', Archaeology, vol 38 (May/June 1985), pp60-63

Michael Graves: Newark Museum

Alison Eckhardt Ledes, 'A New Newark Museum', Antiques, vol 136 (November 1989), p27-29

Roger K Lewis, 'Surprising Intimacy Pervades the new Newark Museum', Museum News, vol 69 (March/April 1990), p27-29

'Newark Museum', Architectural Design (London), vol 54, no 3/4 (1984), p60

Peter C Papademtriou, 'Four not-so-easy Pieces', Progressive Architecture, vol 71 (March 1990), pp88-95

Angela MH Schuster, 'The Pride of Newark', Archaeology, vol 43 (September/October 1990), pp58-61

Gwathmey Siegel: Extension of the Guggenheim Museum

'The Guggenheim Museum Addition', A+U, vol 223 (April 1989), 124-27

Lynn Nesmith, 'Proposed Guggenheim Addition debated at Municipal Hearing', Architecture, vol 75 (August 1986), pp10-12

Lynn Nesmith, 'Gwathmey Siegel's Guggenheim Addition draws Mixed Reactions', Architecture, vol 74 (December 1985), p11

Hans Hollein: The Guggenheim Museum in Salzburg

Dietmar Steimer, 'Un museo a Salisburgo di Hans Hollein', *Casabella*, vol 54 (March 1990), pp18-22

Arata Isozaki: Museum of Contemporary Art

Marc Angelil, Sarah Graham, 'Architectur fur eine establierte Avantgard', *Werk, Bauen + Wohnen*, vol 74/41 (April 1987), pp4-8

'Arata Isozaki a Los Angeles: un piccolo iceberg, *L'Architettura*, vol 33 (July 1987), pp526-27

Viola Drath, 'LA's New MOCA: Showy Space, Shakey Start', *New Art Examiner*, vol 14 (May 1987), pp33-35

Patricia Falling, 'Los Angeles gets a New Temple of Art', *Art News*, vol 85 (November 1986), pp88-94

Christopher Flacke, 'Isozaki's MOCA', *The New Criterion*, vol 5 (April 1987), pp46-50

Kenneth Frampton, 'MOCA, Museum of Contemporary Art, Los Angeles', *Domus*, vol 677 (November 1986), pp36-49

Ziva Freiman, 'Isozaki Revisited at MOCA', *Progressive Architecture*, vol 72 (May 1991), pp28-29

Arata Isozaki, 'The Museum of Contemporary Art, Los Angeles', *The Japan Architect*, vol 62 (February 1987), pp14-23

'LA – Museum of Contemporary Art', *Abitare*, vol 247 (September 1986), p380-81

'The Los Angeles Museum of Contemporary Art: What's in a Name?', *Architectural Record*, vol 175 (May 1987), p83

Phil Patton, 'Isozaki: Japan's Best Architect gives Los Angeles a Great Museum', *Connoisseur*, vol 216 (November 1986),pp118-25

Mildred F Schmertz, 'MOCA and More: the Future of California Plaza at Bunker Hill', *Architectural Record*, vol 175 (May 1987), p82

Pilar Viladas, 'MOCA moves in', *Progressive Architecture*, vol 67 (November 1986), pp83-95

Kisho Kurokawa: Wakayama Prefectural Museum

Kisho Kurokawa, *Kisho Kurokawa: From Metabolism to Symbiosis*, Academy Editions (London), 1992

Kisho Kurokawa: Musée de Louvain-la-Neuve

Michael de Visscher, 'Le Musée du dialogue a Louvain-la-Neuve', *A plus*, No 111 (1991), pp60-63

Hirashi Watanabe and others, *GA Document*, no 33 (1992)

'Louvain Museum, Belgium', *Formes et Structures*, no 3 (1992), pp83-84

Kisho Kurokawa: New Wing of the Vincent Van Gogh Museum

'Japanese go Dutch for Van Gogh Wing', *Architects Journal*, vol 194, no 15 (9 October 1991), p11

Hans van Dijk, 'Interview with Kisho Kurokawa', *Archis*, no 12 (December 1991), pp31-34

'Extension of the Vincent Van Gogh Museum in Amsterdam', *Formes et Structures*, no 3 (1992), pp83-84

'Amsterdam', *Architecture Today*, no 37 (April 1993), p10

Kisho Kurokawa, *Kisho Kurokawa: From Metabolism to Symbiosis*, Academy Editions (London), 1992

Kisho Kurokawa: Honjin Memorial Museum of Art

Silvano Stucci, 'Tradition within the Contemporary: Three works by Kisho Kurokawa, *Industria delle Costrozioni*, vol 25, no 233 (March 1991), pp4-25

'Honjin Memorial Museum', *Formes et Structures*, no 3 (1992), pp79-82

Kisho Kurokawa, *Kisho Kurokawa: From Metabolism to Symbiosis*, Academy Editions (London), 1992

Kisho Kurokawa: Hiroshima City Museum of Contemporary Art

Kisho Kurokawa and others, 'Kisho Kurokawa', *The Japan Architect*, vol 63, no 8 (376), (August 1988), pp8-43

Charles Jencks and others, 'Kisho Kurokawa', *SD*, no 297 (6), (June 1989), pp4-176

Deyan Sudjic and others, 'I Grandi Spazi', *Arca*, no 30 (September 1989), pp1-87

Kisho Kurokawa, 'Works of Kisho Kurokawa', *The Japan Architect*, vol 64, no 8 (388), (August 1989), pp6-48

'Musée d'Art contemporain, Hiroshima', *Architecture d'Aujourd'hui*, no 264, (September 1989), pp76-79

Kazukiyo Matsuba, 'Japan '90', *GA Document*, no 25 (1990)

'Postmodern Age 1989', *The Japan Architect*, vol 65, no 8 (400) supplement (August 1990)

'Musée d'Art Contemporain de la ville d'Hiroshima', *Formes et Structures*, no 4, (1990), pp25-28

Charles Jencks and others, 'Post-modernism on Trial', *Architectural Design*, vol 60, no11/12 (1990)

Silvano Stucci, 'Tradition within the Contemporary: Three works by Kisho Kurokawa', *Industria delle Costrozione*, vol 25, no 233 (March 1991), pp4-25

Luis Fernandy-Guliano and others, Star Museums, *A+U Monografias*, no 18 (1989), pp2-80

Kisho Kurokawa, *Kisho Kurokawa: From Metabolism to Symbiosis*, Academy Editions (London), 1992

Kisho Kurokawa: Nagoya City Art Museum

Stanley Abercrombie, 'Nagoya Museum', *Interior Design* (New York), vol 59 (April 1988), pp242-43

Stanley Abercrombie, 'Nagoya Museum', *Interior Design* (New York), vol 60 (June 1988), pp246-53

Françoise Daulte, 'Le Musée Municipale des Beaux-Arts de Nagoya', *L'Oeil* (Lausanne), vol 414-15 (January/February 1990), pp64-69

Philip Jodidio, 'Le Musée Municipal d'Art Moderne de Nagoya', *Connaissance des Arts*, vol 433 (March 1988), pp108-13

Kisho Kurokawa, 'Nagoya Municipal Museum of Modern Art,1987', *Architectural Design* (London), vol 58, no 5/6 (1988), pp40-43

'Museo Municipale d'Arte Moderna di Nagoya, Giappone', *L'Architettura*, vol 34 (May 1988), pp364-65

Gabriele Vorreiter, 'Nagoya MOMA', *The Architectural Review*, vol 184 (September 1988), pp40-49

Aldo Benedetti, Nagoya City Museum of Modern Art, *Industria delle Costruzione*, vol 24, no 222, April 1990, pp6-18

Kisho Kurokawa 1978-89, Kajima Institute, 1989

Josep M Montaner, *New Museums*, Architecture Design and Technology Press, 1990

Kisho Kurokawa: Saitama Prefectural Museum of Art

Francoise Chaslin (intro), Kisho Kurokawa, *Kisho Kurokawa: The Architecture of Symbiosis*, Rizzoli International Publications (New York), 1987

Kisho Kurokawa, *Kisho Kurokawa: From Metabolism to Symbiosis*, Academy Editions (London), 1992

Kisho Kurokawa 1978-89, Kajima Institute, 1989

Fumihiko Maki: Yerba Buena Gardens Visual Arts Center

Fumihiko Maki, 'Yerba Buena Gardens Visual Arts Center', *The Japan Architect*, vol 65 (August/September 1990), pp72-77

Richard Meier: Museum of Contemporary Art

'Museum of Contemporary Art', *Progressive Architecture*, vol 72 (January 1991), pp94-95

'Richard Meier to Design Museum of Contemporary Art, Barcelona, Spain', *A+U*, vol 220 (January 1989), p7

Richard Meier: The Getty Center

Daralice Donkervoet, 'Plans for the Getty Center unveiled', *Progressive Architecture*, vol 68 (July 1987), p85

The Getty Center, Harold Williams . . . (et al), J Paul Getty Trust (Los Angeles), 1991

'Gargantua et grangousier (Project du Getty Center, LA; Nouvel hotel de ville et bibliotheque, The Hague)', *L'Architecture d'Aujourd'hui*, vol 254 (December 1987), p69

'The Getty Trust and the Process of Patronage', *The Harvard Architectural Review*, vol 6 (1987), pp122-31

'J Paul Getty Center a Los Angeles di Richard Meier', *Casabella*, vol 54 (April 1990), pp32-33

'Meier Architect for Getty Complex', *Art in America*, vol 72 (December 1984), p200

'Meier wins (Commission for the Getty Trust Complex in LA)', *Architects' Journal*, vol 180 (7 November 1984), p41

John Pastier, 'J Paul Getty Museum unveils Preliminary Scheme by Meier', *Architecture*, vol 76 (July 1987), p18

Richard Meier: Arp Museum

Richard Meier Building for Art, Birkhauser Verlag Basel (Germany), 1990

Richard Meier: Des Moines Art Center Addition

'Ampliamento del Des Moines Art Center', *L'Architettura*, vol 32 (February 1986), pp126-27

Andrea Oppenheimer Dean, 'Eliel Saarinen, then Pei, then Meier', *Architecture*, vol 74 (October 1985), pp32-41

Vittorio Magnago Lampugnani, 'Des Moines Art Center Addition, Iowa', *Domus*, vol 671 (April 1986), pp36-43

Richard Meier, 'Des Moines Art Center Addition', *Architectural Design* (London), vol 55, no 1/2 (1985), pp64-69

Richard Meier: High Museum of Art

'The High Museum of Art, Atlanta, Georgia', *Architectural Design* (London), vol 54, no 11/12 (1984), pp36-39

Gary Indiana, 'Points South (Three New Art Museums: Dallas, Atlanta, Miami)', *Art in America*, vol 72 (December 1984), pp126-30

Richard Meier Building for Art, Birkhauser Verlag Basel (Germany), 1990

Richard Meier, 'Ein kunstmuseum als Kunst der Museumarchitectur (High Museum of Art, Atlanta, Georgia)', *Werk, Bauen + Wohnen*, vol 39 (April 1984), pp4-10

'Selearchitettura; Richard Meier irradia Atlanta (High Museum of Art)', *L'Architettura*, vol 30 (June 1984), pp456-58

Richard Meier: Museum for the Decorative Arts

'Architectur: ein in juwel fur Frankfurt', *Der Spiegel*, (20 July 1981), pp132-34

Peter Cannon-Brooks, 'Frankfurt and Atlanta: Richard Meier as a Designer of Museums', *International Journal of Museum Management and Curatorship*, vol 5 (March 1986), pp39-64

Peter Cook, 'Meier handwerk', *The Architectural Review*, vol 178 (November 1985), pp48-57

Peter Cook, 'White Magic', *Interiors* (New York), vol 144 (July 1985), pp202-05

Yukio Futagawa (ed), 'Winning Scheme, Museum for the Decorative Arts Competition', *Global Document*, vol 2 (1981), pp66-67

Fulvio Irace, 'Radiant museum: Museum for Kunsthandwerk, Frankfurt', *Domus*, vol 662 (June 1985), pp2-11

Philip Jodidio, 'Quand les cathedrales etaient blanches', *Connaissance des Arts*, vol 401/402 (July/August 1985), pp20-31

Vittorio Magnago Lampugnani (ed), *Museum Architecture*, Prestel, 1990

Richard Meier, 'A Personal Manifesto', *Architectural Design* (London), vol 55, no 1/2 (1985), pp56-69

Richard Meier, 'Ein kunstmuseum als kunst de museumarchitec-tur', *Werk, Bauen + Wohnen*, vol 71/38 (December 1984), pp36-41

Richard Meier, Norbert Huse, *Museum fur Kunsthandwerk, Frankfurt am Main*, Wilhelm Ernst and Sohn (Berlin), 1985

Peter Murray, 'Frankfurt's Carbuncle', *RIBA Journal*, vol 92 (June 1985), pp45-47

Richard Meier, *Building for Art*, Berkhauser Verlag Basel (Germany), 1990

'Richard Meier a Francoforte', *L'Architettura*, vol 31 (October 1985), pp710-12

Suzanne Stephens, 'Frame by Frame (Museum for the Decorative Arts)', *Progressive Architecture*, vol 66 (June 1985), pp710-12

Mirko Zardini, Kenneth Frampton, 'Il Museo di Arti applicate a Francoforte', *Casabella*, vol 49 (July/August 1985), pp4-17

Archimede de Zublo, 'L'architecture est toujours de l'urbanisme (le Musee d'Art Decoratif de Francoforte-sur-le Main', *L'Architecture d'Aujourd'hui*, vol 244 (August 1986), ppv-vii

Richard Meier: Museum of Ethnology

Museum of Ethnology, Frankfurt, Germany', *GA Document*, vol 36 (1993), pp60-63

Rafael Moneo: Museum of Roman Art

Peter Buchanan, 'Moneo Romano Merida', *The Architectural Review*, vol 178 (November 1985), pp38-47

Francesco Dalta, 'Roman Brickwork: the Museum of Roman Art of Merisia by Raphael Moneo', *Lotus International*, vol 46 (1985), pp22-35

Paolo Fumageli, 'Ein museum als ausstellungsgegenstand das Museum fur Romisch Kunst in Merisia, 1984, (Spain)', *Werk, Bauen + Wohnen*, vol 71/38 (December 1984), pp18-23,

'The Idea of Lasting (interview)', *Perspecta*, vol 24 (1987), pp146-57

Enrico Morteo, 'L'interno del Museo Arte Romano a Merisia (Spain)', *Domus*, vol 690 (1988), pp52-61

Charles Moore and Center Brook: Hood Museum of Art

Daralice Donkervoet Boles, 'Dartmouth's Hood Museum: a Modest Triumph for Moore', *Progressive Architecture*, vol 67 (January 1986), p30

Douglas Brenner, 'Hood Museum of Art, Dartmouth College, Hanover, New Hampshire', *Architectural Record*, vol 174 (February 1986), pp108-09

Robert Campbell, 'An Architecture of Verve and Invention: the Hood Museum at Dartmouth', *Architecture*, vol 75 (January 1986), pp32-39

'Hood Museum of Art – Dartmouth College (Hanover, New Hampshire)', *Abitare*, vol 247 (September 1986), pp378-79

Kate Norman, Charles Guilano, 'Good neighbours (Williams College Museum of Art and the Hood Museum of Art)', *Art News*, vol 86 (January 1987), pp51-52

Morphosis: Yuzen Vintage Car Museum

Catherine Slessor, 'Mercurial Motor Show', *The Architectural Review*, vol 191 (September 1992), pp48-50

'Yuzen Vintage Car Museum', *Progressive Architecture*, vol 73 (January 1992), pp57-59

Jean Nouvel: Institut du Monde Arabe

'Arab World Institute', *Mimar*, vol 33 (December 1989), p33

Tita Carloni, 'Institut du Monde Arabe', *Du*, vol 12 (December 1988), pp38-45

Charlotte Ellis, 'Self-effacing IMA', Architectural Review, vol 185 (January 1989), pp24-29

'Institut du Monde Arabe', *L'Architecture d'Aujourd'hui*, vol 255 (February 1988), pp1-22

'Institut du Monde Arabe, Paris', *The Architectural Review*, vol 186 (November 1989), pp104-05

Stephani Williams, 'Museum Review: L'Institut du Monde Arabe, Paris', *Apollo* (London), vol 130 (September 1989), pp189-91

James Steele (ed), *Architecture for Islamic Societies Today*, Academy Editions (London), 1994

Pei, Cobb, Freed & Partners: East Wing of the National Gallery

Carter J Brown, 'The designing of the National Gallery of Art's East Building', *Studies in the History of Art*, vol 30 (1991), pp278-95

Pierre Daix, 'Deux des nouveaux musées', *Gazette des Beaux-Arts*, vol 6/104 (September 1984), pp1-3

Andrea Oppenheimer Dean, 'The National East: an Evaluation', *Architecture*, vol 73 (December 1984), pp74-79

Wendy Staebler, 'IM Pei and Partners create Kinetic Art at the National Gallery', *Interiors* (New York), vol 146 (September 1986), pp36-37

Pei, Cobb, Freed & Partners: The US Holocaust Memorial Museum

Marc W Angelil, Sarah Graham, 'Historische Referenzen als Collage', *Werk, Bauen + Wohnen*, vol 72/39 (January/February 1985), p74

Benjamin Forgey, 'A Powerful Testament', *Art News*, vol 92 (April 1993), p40

'Memorial to Atrocity', *Progressive Architecture*, vol 74 (February 1993), pp60-73

Ferdinand Protzman, 'Declining a Gift', *Art News*, vol 92 (Summer 1993), p74

Michael Sorkin, 'The Holocaust Museum: Between Beauty and Horror', *Progressive Architecture*, vol 74 (February 1993), p74

'US Holocaust Museum challenges Literal Architectural Interpretations of History', *Architectural Record*, vol 181 (May 1993), p27

Pei, Cobb, Freed & Partners: Extension of the Louvre

Sabine Cotte, 'IM Pei, l'architecte des musées (interview)', *La Revue sur Louvre et des Museés de France*, vol 39, no 2 (1989), p13-15

Charlotte Ellis, 'Pei off centre (proposed pyramid for the Louvre)', *The Architectural Review*, vol 177 (June 1985), p4

Philip Jodidio, 'Le Louvre selon, IM Pei (interview)', *Connaissance des Arts*, vol 444 (February 1989), pp82-87

Sylvia Lavin, 'Three museum renovations startlingly opposed to each other can be explained only by differences in existing conditions (Paris)', *Interiors* (New York), vol 148 (September 1988), p21

Jean Lebrat, Yahn Weymouth, Rene Provost, Philip Jodidio, 'L'avenir du Louvre', *Connaissance des Arts*, vol 461-62 (July/August 1990), pp50-67

Pei, Cobb, Freed & Partners: The Charles Shipman Payson Building

Darl Rastorfer, 'Brickwork at the Portland Museum of Art, Portland, Maine', *Architectural Record*, vol 172 (June 1984), pp162-65

Marc W Angelil, Sarah Graham, 'Historische Referenzen als Collage', *Werk, Bauen + Wohnen*, vol 72/39 (January/February 1985), p74

Piano and Fitzgerald: De Menil Museum

Colin Amery, 'The Golden Touch of Renzo Piano', *RIBA Journal*, vol 96 (May 1989), pp43-47

Jonathan Glancey, 'A Homely Gallery', *Architect (RIBA)*, vol 94 (September 1987), pp24-27

Renzo Piano, 'Renzo Piano', *The Harvard Architectural Review*, vol 7 (1989), pp76-81

Antoine Predock: American Heritage Center and Art Museum

'American Heritage Center and Art Museum', *Progressive Architecture*, vol 71 (January 1990), pp96-98

'Antoine Predock: University of Wyoming American Heritage Center and Art Museum', *A+U*, vol 218 (November 1988), pp124-25

Antoine Predock: Las Vegas Library and Discovery Museum

'Antoine Predock: Las Vegas Library and Children's Museum, Las Vegas', *A+U*, vol 218 (November 1988), p126

'Architectural Mirage in Las Vegas', *L'Architettura*, vol 37 (June 1991), pp548-49

'Las Vegas Library/Discovery Museum', *GA Document*, vol 30 (1991), pp108-17

'Las Vegas Library and Discovery Museum, Nevada', *Progressive Architecture*, vol 68 (July 1987), p35

Antoine Predock: Arizona State University Fine Arts Center

'Antoine Predock: Fine Arts Complex for Arizona State University', *A+U*, vol 218 (November 1988), p123

'Arizona State University Fine Arts Complex Architectural Competition', *Architectural Record*, vol 174 (March 1986), p63

Ian Ritchie: The Ecology Gallery of the Natural History Museum

'Ecology Gallery', *L'Architecture d'Aujourd'hui*, vol 276 (Spring 1991), pp92-93

Ian Ritchie: Reina Sofia Museum of Modern Art

John Baldessari, *Ni por esas=Not even so*, Ministerio de Cultura, Direccion General de Bellas Artes y Archivos, Centro, Nacional di Exposicionses, Madrid, Spain

Kim Bradley, 'Reina Sofia Expansion Plans', *Art in America*, vol 78 (February 1990), p33

Victoria Combalia, 'A New Reign in Spain', *Art News*, vol 88 (January 1989), p58

Jose Maria Puig de la Bella casa, 'Quand l'art modern rajeunit les monuments: Madrid, d'hôpital en centre d'art', *Connaissance des Arts*, vol 436 (June 1988), pp88-95

Aldo Rossi: Bonnefanten Museum

Hank Engel, 'The Bonnefanten Museum: a Moment in the Career of Aldo Rossi, a Landmark for Maastricht', *Kunst & Museumjournal*, vol 3 no 3 (1991), pp1-6

Aldo Rossi, 'Une architecture pour les musées', *L'Architecture d'Aujourd'hui* , vol 263 (June 1989), pp184-87

Aldo Rossi: The Museum of German History

Mary C Pepchinski, 'Berlin Win for Aldo Rossi', *Progressive Architecture*, vol 69 (August 1988), p25

Aldo Rossi, 'German Historical Museum, Berlin', *Architectural Design* (London), vol 58 no 11/12 (1988), pp92-93

Aldo Rossi: Vassivière Contemporary Arts Centre

Didier Laroque, 'Aldo Rossi: un centre d'art en Limosin', *L'Architecture d'Aujourd'hui*, vol 258 (September 1988), pp72-73

James Stirling and Michael Wilford: The Clore Gallery at the Tate Gallery

'Clore Gallery', *A+U*, vol 204 (September 1987), pp11-46

The Clore Gallery: an Illustrated Account of the New Building for the Turner Collection: architects, James Stirling, Michael Wilford and Associates, Tate Gallery (London),1987

'The Clore Gallery for the Turner Collection', *Architectural Design* (London), vol 57, no 1/2 (1987), pp26-30

Francesco Dal Co, 'Among Stirling's Museums: the Clore Gallery by Stirling, Wilford and Associates, *Lotus International*, vol 55 (1987), pp6-35

Evening Standard (22 January 1980)

K Gosling, *The Times* (UK), (22 January 1980)

K Gosling, *The Times* (UK), (7 May 1980)

Robin Hamlyn, Peter Wilson, 'The Clore Gallery', *International Journal of Museum Management and Curatorship*, vol 6 (March 1987), pp19-62

'James Stirling, Michael Wilford and Associates', *GA Document*, vol 19 (1988), pp72-89

Charles Jencks, 'Interview: the Clore Gallery', *A+U*, vol 204 (September 1987), pp38-45

John McEwen, 'Museums Expand: The Clore, National Gallery', *Art in America*, vol 75 (July 1987), pp31-32

D Searle, *Building Design* (9 May 1980)

'Tate and Clore', *Architecture Review*, vol 181 (June 1987), pp38-50

Ian Boyd Whyte, 'The Clore Gallery, London', *Domus*, vol 685 (July/August 1987), pp44-51

James Stirling and Michael Wilford: The Tate Gallery at Liverpool

Christopher Kerr, 'Tate Gallery Liverpool', *Apollo* (London), vol 127 (April 1988), pp264-66

Brian Hatton, 'Contextualism run Rampant: Stirling's Tate', *Progressive Architecture*, vol 68 (May 1987), pp43-44

Jose Manser, 'British Design: James Stirling designs a Colorful Addition to the Classical Tate Gallery', *Interiors* (New York), vol 146 (March 1987), pp134-41

James Frazer Stirling, 'James Stirling, Michael Wilford and Associates', *Architectural Design* (London), vol 60, no 5/6 (1990), pp6-112

James Stirling and Michael Wilford: Palazzo Citterio Gallery at the Brera Museum

James Stirling, 'Ristrutturiazone e ampliamento di Palazzo Citterio, Milano', *Domus*, vol 724 (February 1991), pp29-39

James Stirling + Michael Wilford, Architectural Monographs, Academy Editions (London), 1993

James Stirling and Michael Wilford: Neue Staatsgalerie

Gunild Berg, Rolf-Gunter Dienst, 'Die Neue Staatsgalerie in Stuttgart', *Das Kunstwerk*, vol 37 (June 1984), pp45-51

Maria Botero, 'The New State Gallery in Stuttgart', *Abitare*, vol 239 (November 1985), pp80-84

'Democratic Movement', *Architecture Review*, vol 176 (December 1984), pp18-47

Barbara Dierterich, 'Inauguracion de la Nueva Galeria Estatal de Stuttgart', *Goya*, vol 183 (November/December 1984), pp186-87

Charlotte Ellis, 'Stuttgart, after the Hoopla', *Architecture*, vol 78 (December 1989), pp47-49

Martin Filler, 'Neue Staatsgalerie and Chamber Theatre, Stuttgart', *Architectural Record*, vol 172 (September 1984), pp140-49

Irmela Franze, 'Staatsgalerie Stuttgart', *Pantheon*, vol 42 (July/September 1984), pp298-301

Rene Furer, 'Klassizistische tendenzen heute: transmoderne aneignungen', *Werk, Bauen + Wohnen*, vol 73/40 (June 1986), pp38-41

Douglas A Greenaway, 'Museum without a Facade centered on a Massive Drum', *Architecture*, vol 74 (September 1985), pp94-101

Jean-Marc Ibos, Dominique Lyon, 'Les travaux d-Hercule: le nouveau Musée de Stuttgart de James Stirling et Michael Wilford', *L'Architecture d'Aujourd'hui* , vol 235 (October 1984), ppvii-xv

Charles Jencks, 'The Casual, the Shocking and the Well Ordered Acropolis', *Architectural Design* (London), vol 54, no 3/4 (1984), pp48-55

Jurgen Joedicke, 'Erste Eindrucke', *Werk, Bauen + Wohnen*, vol 71/38 (May 1984), pp10-12

Peter Lemos, 'A Populist Palace of Art', *Art News*, vol 84 (February 1985), pp125-26

'Nouveau musée signe Stirling', *Connaissance des Arts*, vol 388 (June 1984), p27

Giacomo Polin, 'Stirling a Stoccarda, l'attitudine del camallonte', *Casabella*, vol 48 (June 1984), pp38-41

James Frazer Stirling, 'Die neue Staatsgalerie, Stuttgart', *Domus*, vol 651 (June 1984), pp38-41

'Stirling in Stuttgart', *Progressive Architecture*, vol 65 (October 1984), pp67-85

'Stirling work', *Architects' Journal*, vol 180 (17 October 1984), pp48-49

Giles Waterfield, 'James Stirling's masterpiece? The Neue Staatsgalerie, Stuttgart', *Apollo* (London), vol 126 (July 1987), pp41-43

Frank Werner, 'The New Acropolis of Stuttgart', *Lotus International*, vol 43 (1984), pp22-47

James Stirling and Michael Wilford: Thyssen Gallery

Francesco dal Co and Thomas Muirhead, *I musei di James Stirling Michael Wilford Associates*, Electa (Milan), 1990

Donatello Smetana, 'Stirling wins Lugano Contest', *Progressive Architecture*, ol 68, no 3, March 1987, p34

New Gallery for the Thyssen-Bornemisza Collection, Villa Favorita, Lugano, *Composicion arcquitectonica art and architecture*, no 2, February 1989, pp45-66

Francesco dal Co, Recent Works of James Stirling and Michael Wilford, *A+U Supplement*, May 1990, pp4-267

'Competition for the Enlargement of the Thyssen-Bornemisza Collection', *Domus*, no 678, December 1986, pp72-80

OM Ungers: The German Architecture Museum

Colin Amery, 'Frankfurt First (New Museum of Architecture)', *Architects' Journal*, vol 180 (8 August 1984), pp34-38

Barry Berdoll, 'Deutsches Architekturmuseum, Frankfurt, West Germany', *Architecture Record*, vol 172 (August 1984), pp104-117

Peter Jost Blake, 'DAM! (Deutsches Architekturmuseum, Frankfurt am Main)', *Interior Design* (New York), vol 55 (September 1984), pp320-21

Andrea Oppenheimer Dean, 'Old and New melded in a Museum for Architecture Itself (Deutsches Architekturmuseum, Frankfurt am Main)', *Architecture*, vol 74 (September 1985), pp102-07

Volker Fischer, 'The German Museum of Architecture', *International Journal of Museum Management and Curatorship*, vol 5 (March 1986), pp19-26

Philip Jodidio, 'L'architecture au musée', *Connaissance des Arts*, vol 395 (January 1985), pp30-37

Heinrich Klotz, 'The German Museum for Architecture in Frankfurt am Main: the Project by OM Ungers and the Function of the Museum', *Lotus International*, vol 43 (1984), pp6-21

Vittorio Magnago Lampugnani, 'Ungers' boxes: Architecture Museum, Frankfurt', *Architecture Review*, vol 176 (August 1984), pp30-38

'Museum of Architecture at Frankfurt', *Architectural Design* (London), vol 54, no 11/12 (1984), pp84-85

Walter Arno Noebel, 'A Francoforte sul Meno, Realizzato il museo de

architettura di OM Ungers', *Casabella*, vol 48 (July/August 1984), pp28-29

OM Ungers, 'Deutsches Architekturmuseum, 1984 (Frankfurt am Main)', *Werk, Bauen + Wohnen*, vol 71/38 (39) (December 1984), pp44-45

OM Ungers, 'La maison dans la mansion: Musée allemand de l'architecture, Frankfurt-sur-le-Main', *L'Architecture d'Aujourd'hui*, vol 233 (June 1984), pp10-13

Robert Venturi and Denise Scott Brown: Sainsbury Wing of the National Gallery

'Editorial: the Sainsbury Wing at the National Gallery', *Apollo* (London), vol 134 (July 1991), pp3-6

William Feaver, 'Sainsbury Wing', *Art News*, vol 90 (September 1991), p146

Graham Hughes, David Brown, 'The Sainsbury Wing', *Arts Review* (London), vol 43 (9/23 August 1991), pp422-23

Karen D Stein, 'The Sainsbury Wing: an Extension to the National Gallery in London', *Architecture Record*, vol 175 (May 1987), p65

Robert Venturi and Denise Scott Brown: Laguna Gloria Museum of Art

'Laguna Gloria Art Museum', *Lotus International*, vol 50 (1986), pp102-05

Sylvia Lavin, 'Venturi, Rauch and Scott Brown discuss the Plan for Three New Museum Projects', *Interiors* (New York), vol 147 (November 1987), pp131-37

'Musée d'art Laguna Gloria', *L'Architecture d'Aujourd'hui*, vol 273 (February 1991), pp97-98

Robert Venturi and Denise Scott Brown: Franklin Court

'Exponent', *National Park Service Quarterly*, vol 1, no 1 (October 1974), p2

Y Futagawa (ed), *GA Document*, special issue 1970-80, (1980), pp220-01

T Hine, 'Franklin Shrine to centre on Abstract "Ghost house"', *The Philadelphia Inquirer*, (19 July 1974), pp1-D, 3-D

T Hine, 'Shrine for Now, a Park Forever', *The Philadelphia Inquirer*, (18 April 1976) pp1, 8-B

C Knight II, 'Park Service opens Franklin Court', *Preservation News*, (August 1976), pp1-6

S Stephens, 'Franklin Court', *Progressive Architecture*, April 1976, pp69-70

'Venturi and Rauch: pour Franklin Court une acte poétique', *Architecture Intérieure* (December 1977/January 1978), pp72-73

Robert Venturi, 'Inszenierung der Erinhereng (drei beispiele von Venturi, Rauch und Scott Brown', *Werk, Bauen + Wohnen*, vol 39 (April 1984), pp28-33

Venturi, Rauch and Scott Brown', *A+U*, extra edition (December 1981), pp82-86

Stanislaus von Moos, *Venturi, Rauch and Scott Brown: Buildings and Projects*, Rizzoli International Publications (New York), 1987